Advance Praise for *What's My Type?*

"This ... re a One,
a Six ... nation
in th ... ."
—D... *...ing*
Men...

"Fro...
Ted ... n.
The ... patterns
to d...
—D...

"I foun... ...d helpful
spiritual ... transform our bro-
kenness ... is a significant contri-
bution to perso...al growth. It also give ...lues to empowering relationships."
—Douglas W. S..., Ph.D., ...ector of the Sa...aritan Center
for Counseling ... ...Colorado

"Self-discovery ... *Type?* is one of
those rare resou... ...the E...neagram, in
clear, readable, ...hors, anecdotes,
and illustrations ... ...r who may
discover more a...
—Dolores Curr...

"The most outs... ...ion of the
Enneagram writ... *Type?* is a
detailed step-by ... ...ortant journey
of one's life. Bec... ...orever change
the reader's life ...or the better.

"As presented in this wonderful book, the Enneagram is eminently broader
and deeper than other personality 'theories and indicators,' and is therefore of
greater value to those seeking to know the real person who lies inside each of
us, what motivates us, and how to b... ...t we can.

"An added bonus is the marvelou... ...the
Enneagram's teaching has on others ... ...of
my suggested reading list for friend... ...asso-
ciates—because I want the best for... ...
—Betsy C. McGee, president, The McGee C... ...orporate
Relations, University of Denver

"Increasing numbers of North Americans are looking for help with the inner side of being human. In *What's My Type?* Kathleen Hurley and Ted Dobson offer their fresh interpretation of the Enneagram and demonstrate that this ancient body of wisdom is one of the best guides available for the inner journey."
—Ronald S. Fellows, president and co-founder of the Applewood Centre, a Canadian-based growth center

"We have never seen a typology that wasn't helpful in understanding the complexity of human personality. The Enneagram, as elucidated by Kathy Hurley and Ted Dobson does much more.

"It presents in clear, available, non-jargon language not only self-understanding but a direction for growth and development. They invite you to look at the 'bad news' first, but then point the way out.

"The book is a delightful combination of a serious delineation of the grace available to us and practical pointers for how to claim the freedom and wholeness which that grace offers."
—Jean Dalby Clift and Wallace B. Clift, authors of *The Hero Journey in Dreams*

WHAT'S MY TYPE?

What's My Type?

*Use the Enneagram System
of Nine Personality Types to
Discover Your Best Self*

Kathleen V. Hurley
Theodore E. Dobson

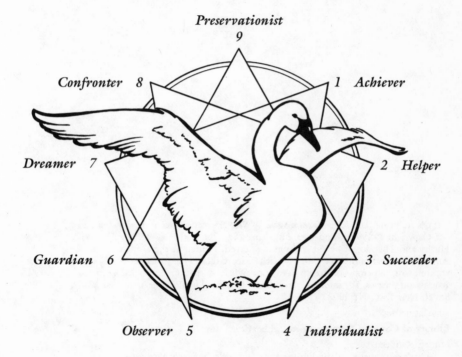

Preservationist
9

Confronter 8

1 Achiever

Dreamer 7

2 Helper

Guardian 6

3 Succeeder

Observer 5

4 Individualist

HarperSanFrancisco
A Division of HarperCollinsPublishers

155.26
HUR
5/92

FIRST EDITION

Library of Congress Cataloging-in-Publication Data

Hurley, Kathleen V.
    What's my type? : use the Enneagram system of nine personality types to discover your best self / Kathleen V. Hurley, Theodore E. Dobson.
        p.   cm.
Includes bibliographical references.
ISBN 0-06-250421-5
1. Enneagram. I. Dobson, Theodore Elliott. II. Title.
BF698.3.H87 1992
155.2'6–dc20   91–55279
                                                                                    CIP

92   93   94   95   96   HAD   10   9   8   7   6   5   4   3   2   1

Dedication

From Kathy:
To my children
Mike, Casey, Erin, and Mark
who have loved and encouraged me, laughed and dreamed with me,
and who now celebrate with me

From Ted:
To Brandon
my little friend
whose laughter, love, and vulnerability in the midst of suffering
transform my world and teach me the true meaning of life

And from Kathy and Ted:
To all who have participated in our
Enneagram seminars
You have been our faithful teachers,
communicating to us the wisdom of life

To be able to learn is to to be young, and whoever keeps the joy of learning fresh is forever young.

—John G. Bennett

CONTENTS

Awakening the Sleuth

Revealing Human Potential

INTRODUCTION

We have to remember the principle that certain desires and certain pleasures are willed for us by God. We cannot live in the truth if we automatically suspect all desires and all pleasures. It is humility to accept our humanity, pride to reject it.

Baron Friedrich Von Hugel, in one of his letters, writes of W. G. Ward ("Ideal Ward") as an "eager, one-sided, great, unintentionally unjust soul" who on his deathbed saw the mischief of his life—he had consistently demanded that all others be like himself!

This is the root of inhumanity! —THOMAS MERTON

I n all of creation there is nothing more puzzling, more fascinating, more mystifying, or more sacred than the human person!

Human beings have crossed and explored every frontier on earth, defied gravity through flight, walked on the moon, explored space, and reached for the stars. Nearly every doctor's office displays a poster showing the miracle of a human being, with all the muscles, nerves, organs, blood vessels, and everything else contained in the body clearly defined—and in color.

Yet with all the knowledge accumulated by the greatest minds over the centuries, we have not been able to unravel the mystery of people—those we love, work with, and relate with every day.

Brilliant people who daily solve complex problems with apparent ease are completely baffled by the behavior of their co-workers, family, and friends. Musicians, poets, artists, and story tellers among us have poured out their hearts trying to communicate with, understand, and connect with other human beings. Many among us struggle in unspoken agony for countless days, hours, months, and years for the understanding needed to save a relationship, a job, a child.

Who are these people around me? What do they want or need from me? Why do they do or say those things? How can I understand them? How can I understand myself? Why do I long for and work for something with all my heart and then, in a momentary flash, do the very thing that will destroy my chances of getting it?

Some years ago, after having worked in the area of personal growth and spirituality for a combined total of over thirty years, we were introduced to a secret wisdom known as the Enneagram. It was purported to be over four thousand years old and intertwined in the bases of many of the world's major religions. It was said of the Enneagram that it not only held solutions to the questions we have just raised, it also answered the even more significant questions lying dormant within the depths of the unconscious mind.

Since our initial contact with this wisdom, our years have been filled with study, research, personal inner work, and teaching of the Enneagram to thousands of people throughout North America—and now the book *What's My Type?*

Indeed, we have found the Enneagram's wisdom to be the most valuable single tool available to deal with the everyday life issues that people face. The Enneagram goes beyond the level of describing characteristics and preferences that other personality typing systems reach. It pierces through to the level of *motivation: why we do the things we do.* Although the Enneagram does not provide easy answers, it does explain the mysterious pieces of the puzzle of human nature. The uniqueness of each individual emerges from the intricacies of each person's life story—the fabric of experience, with its triumphs, failures, and wounds—and in the continuing unfolding of life.

Appropriately, the Enneagram is often described as a journey. Those courageous people who embark on this inner journey—and their numbers are increasing at an amazingly rapid rate as we approach the twenty-first century—will meet themselves in unexpected disguises of both strength and weakness. They will awaken their own inner sleuth, who will find the clues and search through the maze leading to the discovery of their true personality—the priceless treasure buried under the debris of survival.

The journey will wind through the peaks and valleys of spirituality and relationship. On the journey, almost imperceptibly, the traveler will grow strong with the knowledge of what is worth fighting for in life and what is as inconsequential as fool's gold.

This is not a journey for the fainthearted. This journey is for those of us who are willing to look honestly at ourselves and others, discovering, recovering, and respecting the treasure of being human.

The Enneagram is an unfolding system of knowledge. It is our task as authors to sift through this ancient wisdom and present to you the pieces that have been hidden in the sands of time. It is your task to sort and study each fragile and beautiful piece—gently fitting each one into its proper place.

The only puzzle we can ever assemble—the only mystery we can ever hope to solve—is our own. Yet in the process of working with the pieces of our own lives, we will also learn to appreciate, understand, and communicate with every other person, no matter how different from ourselves.

We begin at the beginning—reaching back in time to speak of the mysterious origins of the Enneagram and to trace the often obscure journey of this secret wisdom into the present moment.

The Mysterious Origins of the Enneagram

The Enneagram is a system of spiritual psychology that directs us toward a personal understanding deeper than we have ever known before. It seems to have ancient origins, going back perhaps even 4,500 years. Its source is in the Middle East—where so many spiritual philosophies and traditions find their beginnings and even today converge.[1]

Many people in the East and the West have contributed to this body of knowledge throughout the millennia as well as in recent years. Today the Enneagram is portrayed as a circle surrounded by nine numbers, one for each of nine personality patterns it describes. Lines connect the numbers in a way that at first may seem haphazard but upon closer scrutiny follows a clear pattern.[2] The diagram entitled "The Enneagram" on page 18 shows each of these personality patterns with its number and its primary name. The names given to each pattern are our own; others use different names in teaching the Enneagram, so it is common to refer to each pattern by its number as well as a name.

There are also signs that the Enneagram has influenced most of the world's great religions, many of which have flourished in the Middle East. One of these religions is Christianity, the tradition of thought and faith that has shaped Western civilization for centuries; there are indications that several of the New Testament writers were familiar with and used the Enneagram. Echoes of it can be found in other religious traditions as well.

One source of the Enneagram seems to be a brotherhood of ancient wisdom seekers whom some identify with the Magi. Philosophers, theologians, astrologers, psychologists, and mathematicians of the ancient world, they began a search for truth long before the advent of the major philosophical or religious systems of the modern world. Their study established the unity between mathematics and philosophy. Awareness of this unity has continued throughout the ages and is seen today in modern physics and chemistry. The investigations of these wisdom seekers predate and have contributed to the great books of the world's religions.

After the founding of Islam, the tradition seems to have fallen into the hands of one school of Sufis, the mystics of the Moslem faith, who then became the caretakers of this secret wisdom. They are to be credited with preserving the tradition of the Enneagram, attaching the Arabic numerals to each of the personality patterns, and developing the mathematics that underlie the system as it is known today.[3]

In many ways, Sufis of the Middle East could be compared to the Benedictine monks of Christianity. They live in communities and devote themselves to the spiritual life. People come to Sufi masters for enlightenment, knowledge of the spiritual life, and spiritual direction.

It was in the teaching of personal enlightenment as well as in their own spiritual development that the Sufis used the Enneagram. A Sufi master would

1. John G. Bennett, *Enneagram Studies* (York Beach, ME: Samuel Weiser, 1983), pp. 1–3. Bennett, a noted teacher of the Enneagram in the West, mentions both the ancient brotherhood of wisdom seekers, whom we have named Magi (with some scientific foundation and for literary clarity), and Pythagoras as contributors to this knowledge.
2. In *Enneagram Studies*, Bennett also points out that the significance of the Enneagram is in the mathematical discovery in the fifteenth century of recurring decimals: $1/3 = .33333$; $2/3 = .66666$; $3/3 = .99999$; and $1/7 = .142857142857$, *all the other numerals in exactly the sequence in which the Enneagram connects them*.
3. For example, see Kathleen Speeth and Ira Friedlander, *Gurdjieff, Seeker of the Truth* (New York: Harper Colophon Books, 1980).

explain to a student only the part of the Enneagram that pertained to that person, however; the complete knowledge was never given to students but was reserved for and shared only among the masters. Among them it was an oral tradition, following the Sufi proverb that says teaching can happen only when time, place, and brotherhood are appropriate.[4]

Another source of the Enneagram seems to have been Pythagoras. Little is known of this master theoretician of the ancient world except what is revealed through Plato, his chief disciple. Born in the sixth century B.C.E. on the Greek island of Samos, he left home at an early age and wandered the known world, traveling as far as India. While in Persia Pythagoras studied with Zoroaster, that land's foremost religious reformer and wise man. He then went home by way of Judea, where he touched the wisdom that came to be known as the Kabbalah, the Jewish mystical revelation of God and the universe. Eventually Pythagoras settled in southern Italy, where he founded his school of esoteric knowledge and personal transformation.

Considered the father of mathematics, Pythagoras developed deep insights into the universe through numbers. He believed, consistent with the philosophy of modern physics, that "all things are numbers." In making the distinction between numbers and figures, he revealed his true nature as a philosopher: figures were the basis of measuring things on the physical plane, whereas numbers had a more qualitative and nonmaterial reality. Pythagoreanism established, therefore, the relationship between numbers and philosophy; his system used the numbers one through nine to explain the universe.

The Enneagram's Path to the West

The most extensive documentation for the Enneagram in the West lies in the work of George I. Gurdjieff (1869 [77?]–1949) and his followers.[5] Son of a Greek father and an Armenian mother, Gurdjieff was born in a little town in Armenia.

Armenia in the late nineteenth century was a place where people of Eastern Orthodox, Roman Catholic, Moslem, Hindu, Jewish, Buddhist, and other religious traditions lived side by side. Gurdjieff's social milieu thus presented to him many different points of view.

His father—a remarkable man in his own right—had a great influence on him as well, bringing forth in him, by Gurdjieff's own account, poetic images and high ideals through their conversations on many philosophical topics and through the principles he raised him by. His father was a master of poems and folk traditions from Russian, Greek, Sumerian, and other sources and, at various stages in his life, a wealthy sheepherder, a businessman, and a carpenter.

---

4. Speeth and Friedlander, *Gurdjieff,* p. 116.
5. In *The Enneagram: A Journey of Self-discovery,* Patrick O'Leary, S.J., Maria Beesing, O.P., and Robert Nogosek, C.S.C., say that "Oscar Ichazo is credited with bringing the Sufi Enneagram to public attention first in Chile and then in the United States" ([Denville, NJ: Dimension Books, 1984], p. 1). They describe this knowledge as passing from an unnamed source to Ichazo and coming with him from Chile to California. There it was passed on to Claudio Naranjo, from him to Robert Ochs, S.J., and finally to O'Leary. Don Richard Riso describes a similar transmission of the knowledge and also mentions Gurdjieff as another source for it in *Personality Types: Using the Enneagram for Self-discovery* (Boston: Houghton Mifflin, 1987), pp. 11–22.

Though a genius, Gurdjieff was a careful student and studied simultaneously for the medical profession and the Russian Orthodox priesthood. However, when he did not find in either discipline the answers to the questions he was asking about life—why most of us never awaken to the real purpose of life, and how we can become free—he began a long historical, anthropological, and spiritual quest.

In his later teaching and writing Gurdjieff was unclear, possibly on purpose, about the origins of the Enneagram, but a chronology for his contact with it can be assembled. For many years he traveled throughout the Middle East to Egypt, Jerusalem, Crete, and Turkey, and through the Gobi desert, and to Tibet and India, and finally in 1905 to the monastery where he learned the tradition from which the Enneagram originates.

This monastery seems to have been related to an ancient wisdom society called the Sarmoun Brotherhood. (*Sarmoun* is the Sanskrit word for bees; they used it to describe themselves because they saw their work as analogous to that of bees who gather nectar to make honey and then preserve it.) The members of the Sarmoun Brotherhood claimed to have inherited their knowledge from the wisdom seekers of ancient times whom many identify with the Magi.

Gurdjieff took this wisdom first to Moscow and Saint Petersburg, where he attracted a small group of students and colleagues, including Pietr Ouspensky. Before the revolution of 1919 he led this group through western Asia and Europe, finally settling in Paris. There in 1923 he set up an institute to continue and develop his teaching and attracted, among others, John G. Bennett and Maurice Nicoll to his work.[6]

In the 1920s and 1930s Gurdjieff wrote and traveled to various European cities and to America, where he also taught groups of people in several locales. During the Second World War he did very little work and became something of a recluse, rarely leaving his apartment in Paris. Not long after the war, in 1949, he died of injuries sustained in an automobile accident.

Though for a long time he did not practice the Russian Orthodox faith he learned as a child, Gurdjieff said he was teaching esoteric Christianity. It is said of Gurdjieff that he believed he was imparting an ancient wisdom by which humanity could be set free from that which drives it to destruction.[7]

The Nine Prime Addictions of the Enneagram

One approach to the Enneagram finds its starting point in an idea that comes from Christian antiquity, the list of the seven capital sins—pride, greed, lust, anger, gluttony, envy, and sloth—plus two more, fear and deceit.[8] The word

---

6. It is from the writings of these men that the Enneagram is known and studied today. See especially John G. Bennett's *Transformation* (Charles Town, WV: Claymont Communications, 1978), and *Enneagram Studies* (York Beach, ME: Samuel Weiser, 1983); see also Maurice Nicoll's *Psychological Commentaries on the Works of Gurdjieff and Ouspensky* (Boston and London: Shambhala, 1985), 5 vols.

7. In their book, *Gurdjieff, Seeker of the Truth,* Speeth and Friedlander report these facts of Gurdjieff's life.

capital comes from Latin and means "head." Capital sins are the head sins, or the prime spiritual and psychological addictions, the sources from which grow dysfunctional motivation and behavior.

The word *sin* creates its own difficulties for many modern people, however. For the purposes of this book, sin is defined as alienation from self and from the Self (the God image within). This alienation inevitably leads to personal fragmentation and to separation from others through unconscious dysfunctional and destructive behavior.

In the Enneagram these behaviors are seen as addictions to a particular way of perceiving life. The word *addiction* is not used lightly here. *Webster's Ninth New Collegiate Dictionary* defines addiction as devoting or surrendering oneself to something "habitually or obsessively." One's Enneagram number describes an obsessive way of approaching life–focusing in on one aspect of reality while discarding the rest. This addiction is so psychologically blinding that it causes a distortion in perspective–reality appears as illusion and so we are not compelled to deal with it; illusion masquerades as reality and entices us into collusion with it.

Thus do the nine prime addictions described by the Enneagram work upon the human spirit. These drives within the human personality cause distortion that prevents us from seeing or acknowledging the truth about our lives. Each of these nine fixations of attention is so addictive that every person can have only one prime addiction at the root of his or her personality.

Thus, although people can identify with several or many of the faults and gifts that the Enneagram describes, only one personality pattern is deeply rooted in any human soul. The capital sins of the other patterns may cause difficulties in a person's life, but they are not the genesis of the pain that person creates for self and others.

These prime addictions have led each of us to embrace illusion, thus stunting our growth. Conversely, when we can identify our prime addiction and choose to act against it, like a plant freed from the strangulating effects of unchecked weeds, we encounter new life in dramatic ways. As we acknowledge our limitations and embrace our weaknesses, we are experiencing the grace of spiritual awakening and consciousness.

Throughout the ages, teachers of wisdom traditions, both religious and philosophical, have posited the need for some energy outside human nature to initiate and assist a person's struggle against addiction. Among the first teachers of the Enneagram in the West, George I. Gurdjieff and John G. Bennett were utterly convinced of the blindness of humanity to its own destructive behavior. They taught about an energy from God that would awaken humans from addictive life as from a dream and begin to lead them into reality. This energy–not a part of human nature but definitely available through surrender to higher laws and principles and to God, the Higher Power–has been commonly referred to in many cultures as grace.

---

8. O'Leary, Beesing, and Nogosek describe the nine patterns of the Enneagram using the seven capital sins plus two in *The Enneagram,* p. 127.

Contrary to the secular assumptions of the modern era—that human nature contains within itself all it needs to achieve its potential—the notion of *grace* is neither outdated nor arcane: it is common to cultures throughout the world. If this notion seems childish to certain intellectual circles in the West, they only have the traditions of Western Christianity to blame for their mechanized understanding of this ancient universal concept. If Christianity is failing to transmit the wisdom of the ages in the West, that does not invalidate the wisdom itself.

Gerald May reports that not only does grace occupy a central place in Western Christianity,

> but in fact [it] has its counterparts in all religions. The Torah of Judaism is suffused with cries for God's loving salvation. Islam finds its very heart in Allah's mercy. Even for Buddhists and Hindus, with all their emphasis on personal practice and effort, there could be no liberation without the grace of the Divine. Tibetan Buddhists, for example, pray for "gift waves" from deities and gurus. A Tibetan Buddhist hymn pleads simply, "Please bestow your compassionate grace upon us." In the Bhagavad Gita, the Hindu God proclaims, "United with me you shall overcome all difficulties, by my grace. Fear no longer, for I will save you from sin and from bondage." And in the twentieth century, Mohandas Gandhi was very clear: "Without devotion and the consequent grace of God, humanity's endeavor is vain."[9]

The Enneagram reveals humanity's need for grace as it demonstrates the addictive nature of human behavior. Our attachment to psychological and spiritual addiction is relentless because, unassisted by grace, it is blind. To give in to one's prime addiction not only appears to be the most natural way to respond to a person or situation, it also appears to be the only logical or correct choice.

The experience of failure is often the direct result of our acting from a motivation fueled by a psychological and spiritual addiction. Failure can either cause us to intensify the prime addiction through anger, denial, withdrawal from life, and blaming others, self, or God or prompt us to accept grace and weed out the destructive elements in life that led to this experience, thus opening the possibility of new and exciting growth.

Recognition of your prime addiction is essentially a spiritual awakening. The persistent inner voice of consciousness has refused to be silenced by the boisterous demands of the ego. What had been identified as sacred—the ego-fashioned belief system—is revealed as profane in the light of heightened consciousness, which, once awakened, takes hold and modifies the problems caused by deeply rooted dysfunctional motivation. The choice to pursue the inner voice releases a spiritual longing that accompanies us as seekers in our discovery of the richness of life.

With all the benefits that accompany personal growth, one may wonder why anyone would not choose this exciting path. Often the answer is simple: changing our conscious values can cause our egos to scream out in pain, even though the promise that change brings is freedom, new life, and fulfillment. Identifying your prime addiction can be difficult, embarrassing, and painful; however, it is the beginning of a process that can unearth the irresistible treasure of a new and more fulfilling life.

---

9. Gerald G. May, M.D., *Addiction and Grace* (San Francisco: Harper & Row, 1988), pp. 16–17.

Choosing Illusion over Reality

The Enneagram does not describe personality types by simply portraying characteristics, tendencies, and preferences. Rather, its goal is to unveil *motivation*. It invites us to look deeply into self and touch that core that can only be identified as spiritual. It holds up to the human soul a stark mirror of reality, allowing those of us who dare to look into it the opportunity to acknowledge the distorted ways we have perceived ourselves, others, God, and the world. As the insight and intuition of a great portrait artist can reveal the breadth and depth of a subject's character, so too does the secret wisdom of the Enneagram delve beneath the appearance created by personality and reveal the essence or spirit of a person.

Some people think that *spirit* and *spiritual* are words that name something unknowable, unreal, or illusory. This is not the approach of the Enneagram or of this book. In the language of the Enneagram, the essence or spirit of a person is the true self. Jesus of Nazareth said, "Anyone who tries to preserve life will lose it; anyone who loses it will keep it safe" (Luke 17:33). His insight was that we live on two levels, one of appearances and the other of reality. We must detach ourselves from the first to discover the second.

The level of appearances is the untrustworthy aspect of a person, what modern psychology identifies as the ego infected by egocentricity. Ego often operates out of illusion and leads a person into unreality. The Enneagram treats the spirit as the preeminent aspect of a person, but one that must come to be known, experienced, and liberated. This goal is accomplished as the illusions of the ego are unmasked and discarded.

In studying the Enneagram, a person's essence or spirit is at first revealed by examining personality tendencies and characteristics. However, as students of the Enneagram we must not allow ourselves to be caught up in these observations, for they will distract us from the Enneagram's deeper intent.

The true focus of the Enneagram is to present the basic spiritual issues of human life: the ways people hurt themselves and others, the path of transformation, the possibilities for unleashing spiritual potential, the capacity to become a fully mature person, and the principles of constructive relationship with other people. Thus, the Enneagram is not so much about the way we are perceived by others as it is about the way we perceive ourselves, others, God, and the universe.

Although through the Enneagram we first identify ourselves in negative terms, the Enneagram's perspective is that every one of us begins life as an expression of the Divine. At the core of every person is a Divine Image, a strength signifying that each person is created whole and free. This whole and free person is born into a selfish world in which destructive attitudes control us from childhood on, leading us down the blind alleys of life. As Fritz Kunkel has written, human beings come into a world controlled by egocentricity and become egocentric to cope with life. Soon egocentricity takes control. In a hopeful but desperate search for love, we bend and twist our human souls and in the process lose our integrity.[10]

Egocentricity so blinds us to the realities of life that freedom to respond is soon replaced by mechanical reactions. In manipulating reality to meet our own

---

10. John A. Sanford, ed., *Fritz Kunkel: Selected Writings* (New York: Paulist Press, 1984), pp. 66–86.

needs, we hold hostage our own individual and communal freedom, thus preventing ourselves from experiencing the fullness of life.

The Enneagram describes the choices people make to live in illusion rather than in reality—on the level of ego rather than spirit. Attitudes that are objectively destructive are subjectively seen as helpful. Attitudes that are objectively helpful are subjectively evaluated as inferior. By organizing these pretenses around egocentricity, people conclude that they are lovable and acceptable only when they choose to give in to their prime addiction. The Enneagram reveals how prime addiction and dysfunction always masquerade as good; the notion of what makes people good, of what is important or real in life, is turned upside down and inside out.

Thus although much of our initial work with the Enneagram is spent in identifying self-defeating attitudes and behaviors, the underlying purpose is to discover that these compulsive attributes are but distorted gifts. In taking an honest look at ourselves, we find the raw material of goodness and creativity that, freed from distortion and compulsion, will propel us into a future of dreams fulfilled.

Becoming a Work of Art

The secret wisdom of the Enneagram is revealed in its extraordinary accuracy in describing human nature, thus forcing each individual who studies it seriously to know him- or herself thoroughly. Through self-knowledge each person is then able to relate freely with self, others, the universe, and God.

As you work with the Enneagram in the following pages you will experience a wisdom that is, in a certain sense, endless. It is an evolving knowledge that begins with an awakening—to the truth of human nature and to the true potential human beings possess and to the ways people get caught in an ever-narrowing labyrinth that compresses and distorts their true selves. This awakening process is the invitation to embark on the journey of genuine personal growth.

If you accept the invitation and follow the path, this mysterious journey will lead to transformation, regardless of your pattern in the Enneagram. Those who continue to pursue this journey become seekers of wisdom who see and understand the importance of the inner work to which human beings are called during their earthly lives.

There are many different approaches to the Enneagram available today through books, workshops, and institutes. We present an approach that is our own, coming from our own research, observations, philosophy, theology, and insights. Though we are familiar with the work of others, we have used our own perceptions as the main guide for this work.

This book is an introduction to the secret wisdom of the Enneagram, but the true potential of the Enneagram is revealed in the living of it. There is a principle in the Work—the name Gurdjieff gave to the ideas that support the Enneagram—that says, "Books are like maps, but there is also the necessity of travelling."

The Enneagram's potential is the ability to guide us in practicing the art of awakening and transformation—to help us choose the wisdom and grace that can set us free. Freed from the entanglements of our own egocentricity, we will no longer see other people as puzzles to be solved but works of art to be appreciated.

What Type Am I?

The Nine Prime Addictions

CHAPTER ONE

One's own self is well hidden from one's own self: of all mines of treasure, one's own is the last to be unearthed.
—FRIEDRICH NIETZSCHE

C hildren's stories that begin with "Once upon a time . . ." embody some of life's deepest wisdom. For children, fairy tales become the secret passageway that leads to the magical world of vivid imagination, excitement, and a life lived happily ever after. Children delight in hearing these stories over and over because in their mind's eye they always discover something new.

Adults, however, easily forget the ever-changing world of imagination in order to get down to the serious business of living. As grown-ups we tend to believe that we know what life is all about, and we deal with day-to-day existence as the only reality. Thus we seldom consider the possibility that fairy tales could reveal a greater, more creative reality. Indeed, children's stories were brought forth by the minds and hearts of adults who had learned many of life's lessons, often under difficult circumstances. Their stories, whether about people or animals, tell of the struggles, joys, pain, and healing that is available to all children—no matter how old they are.

The animals talk; the children are wise; the flowers whisper warnings; the winds of the heavens come gently to caress or to blast the land with the fury of an angry avenger. Throughout the story everything in the heavens and on earth, good or evil, works together intentionally or unintentionally to lead the hero or heroine into greater freedom, beauty, and goodness.

These stories of happy endings, so filled with hope and promise, are completely plausible to the wide-eyed child. As adults, unfortunately, we all too often exchange the childlike freedom to believe for the chains of cynicism. In the adult world this is called maturity.

Is it? Is maturity increased with cynicism?

Perhaps these fairy tales were written by adults for adults, to open adult eyes to a realm of reality that is hidden to one who has been beaten down by life's difficulties. Because adults can no longer hear, understand, or believe, they read them to their children—whose understanding is complete! But once in a while, in a magical, mystical, sacred moment, the cynical adult touches the wide-eyed, believing child who still lives within. Then the wry smile expands into a grin and the eyes shine with hope rekindled.

The true self. It was in one such moment that Hans Christian Andersen's fairy tale "The Ugly Duckling" became our paradigm for the remarkable wisdom that has lain hidden for centuries in the Enneagram. "The Ugly Duckling" is a story of rejection and confusion caused by a lost or misplaced identity.

After enduring many struggles—and at a critical moment being assisted by a power greater than himself—the duckling undergoes a transformation into the most beautiful of all the water fowl. Emerging in his new identity as a swan, he finds dignity and also discovers a reason for all his trials. He is no longer misplaced and confused—he is an exquisite creature universally admired.

This is the story that the Enneagram also tells. *What's My Type?* will unveil to careful readers the mysterious reasons for their unhappiness and pain. It will provide a light through the shadowy maze of self-destruction and open a new and mystically shimmering world of creativity and transformation.

As the duckling's search for true identity began he believed that he was unquestionably ugly because everyone told him so. After all, he was different from the others. Ridiculed, scorned, and rejected, the lonely duckling went from place to place trying to find others like himself—others he could fit in with, others who would love him. Isn't this what we all search for?

The story told by the Enneagram begins similarly. Within all of us is a self-definition that is reinforced by the world in which we live. It becomes an identity we believe to be true and complete. Then, like the ugly duckling who was mystified and hurt when he was not accepted, we protect ourselves in whatever way we can, hoping that someday we will find a home. We search for someone who will recognize, respect, and love us.

The wisdom of the Enneagram says that this puzzle of confusion and misunderstanding is an inner mystery that can be unraveled only by a closer examination of ourselves, and especially of our own motives. This investigation will not turn up what we expect, however. Though most people perceive themselves to be simple and their motives clear, closer scrutiny of the evidence will bring to light clues to hidden patterns.

The Enneagram reveals that the underlying reason for our unhappiness is cleverly disguised in our basic motivation, which is *patterned* in one of nine different ways. This *motivational pattern*—often unconscious to the person who bears it—causes us to limit our perspective to a predetermined set of issues and responses. Living in this mechanical way, we can experience nothing but the frustration of the ugly duckling who longed to be loved but could not fit in.

By describing the nine patterns of unconscious motivation, the Enneagram begins to unravel the mystery of unhappiness. Every person has one and only one of these motivational patterns. Using the blurred lens of his or her individual pattern, each of us sets out to investigate self, others, God, and the world.

In the beginning the Enneagram reveals the addictive and dysfunctional motivations in each pattern. Initially, this approach may seem unduly negative; however, we soon come to know that the darkness of unconsciousness is quickly consumed in the brilliance of truth. In this light, our eyes slowly adjust to see our surroundings in new ways. Our minds are alerted to discern the difference between real and imagined enemies.

Sharpening the mind. Some time ago we heard the story of a forensic anthropologist whose task it was to research and describe ancient Egyptian society, and so on. In her office she keeps a two- or three-thousand-piece jigsaw puzzle that she works on for at least one hour every day—but she lays out the puzzle pieces upside down so that she can't see the picture they create.

Why does she do this? She believes that in every aspect of life people define truth through their prejudices, preconceived ideas, and personal experiences. They thus make automatic judgments based on how they see the picture they are looking at and what they expect it to become. Losing objectivity, they come to conclusions that have nothing to do with the truth. They force the puzzle pieces into spaces they were never intended for and, by pretending they fit, distort the entire picture.

The anthropologist's purpose is to teach herself to keep an open mind, to sharpen her vision, to eliminate prejudice, and to remain detached from the outcome so that truth will prevail.

In a sense, the Enneagram is like the process of working a jigsaw puzzle with the picture facing down. It describes without judging, it opens the mind to new ways of thinking, it expands the heart to new possibilities for relating, and it reveals how we can live in a different way. Both the responsibility and the choice of the individual are respected.

Deepening perception. The core of each Enneagram pattern is a psychological addiction to a point of view called a prime addiction: *prime* because these inappropriate reactions are root causes for the pain and confusion that we experience; *addiction* because the Enneagram reveals that our responses to most situations are unfree, unthinking, and inappropriate.

The nine prime psychological addictions described by the Enneagram graphically reveal the secrets of human nature, especially its problems. Our own thoughts, feelings, and actions become clear. Our perceptions of others alter uncannily and deepen. Relationships that have been mystifying suddenly open to the light of truth, and situations that seemed too complicated to understand become simple.

The Enneagram reveals that every person carries within both ecstasy and struggle. The struggle is caused by psychological addictions and illusions that obscure reality and lead to internal paralysis and to habits of inappropriate reaction. We feel the ecstasy whenever we glimpse the marvelous potential hidden within each of our compulsive qualities, for addictions are but strengths that are overused and thus misused!

Like the ugly duckling, we learn to protect ourselves from feeling pain and confusion. In fact, in its youth the duckling avoided so much as looking into the water for fear of having to confront its own ugly reflection.

"The Ugly Duckling" begins like a mystery story. How did the good, respectable Mrs. Duck come to have a great, oversized egg in her nest? The plot thickened when the egg finally cracked and out tumbled a monstrously ugly duckling! No one who visited could figure out what he was or how he got there. Poor Mrs. Duck!

As in any great mystery story, what seems to be is not what is. Although the duckling was destined to go through a painful search and to feel rejection, loneliness, and, in the end, surrender, everything worked together for his ultimate good. The happy ending was his transformation into the most beautiful of all the swans.

Transformation is not a painless process, but its pain is creative and healing. Each of us has a choice between, on the one hand, the painful destruction of self and others that is the inevitable result of unconscious living or, on the other, the healing pain of conscious awareness that demands growth, struggle, and the surrender of egocentricity.

The purpose of learning the secret wisdom of the Enneagram, therefore, is not to eliminate or destroy your personality. No, it is to transform it: to neutralize compulsions, which are simply distorted strengths, so as to release your fullest potential and beauty.

Hidden aspects of self. The Enneagram portrays the nine prime addictions in terms of the motivations that underlie each person's thinking, feeling, and behaving. As we each awaken to the Enneagram's challenge and recognize the prime psychological addiction that drives our lives, we begin to understand how predictable our reactions are, how limited our freedom is. With eyes opened we begin to see that all of us are caught in a trap of failure, and it is unconsciousness of self that is ensnaring us. Our new awareness leads us to self-observation and to perceiving the challenges for growth more clearly.

Maturity demands self-awareness–knowledge of one's motivations and intentions. These perceptions then become signposts in the search for something far more positive: the lost secrets of one's Divine Image. This Divine Image at the core of each of us is an imprinted attribute that we either repress, distort, or reflect to the world in a uniquely personal way. Restrained by our self-protective egocentricity, this sacred gift is hidden beneath layers of strength that, through overuse, have become twisted and distorted. These misused, warped strengths have become our prime addiction.

Once we identify our Enneagram number, we have in hand a dazzling prism through which God can be reflected through our lives into the world. With self-observation comes the needed vision and motivation to choose transformation, thus revealing the hidden Divine Image. By catching glimpses of our own inner truth reflected in the waters of self-awareness, we begin to perceive the brilliance of a new identity–our true self, our best self.

Discovering Your Own Enneagram Pattern

The goal of this chapter is twofold: to describe each pattern clearly so that you can understand and recognize it and to help you discover your own Enneagram pattern.

Knowledge of all the patterns is essential for understanding the Enneagram and unearthing its wisdom. Recognition of your Enneagram number is the first step in the process of neutralizing your own prime addiction. For those of us who have the wisdom and self-discipline to seize these sacred moments of opportunity, the process of transformation will begin to trickle like pure water through the bedrock of psychological addiction, unleashing the flow of creativity and human potential.

Having one pattern. It is important to remember that each person has *one,* and only one, Enneagram number. Your Enneagram number identifies the driving prime psychological addiction that controls your life. By definition, then, one person cannot have—nor, if you value your sanity, would you want to have— more than one prime psychological addiction.

Even though the Enneagram teaches that every person has only one pattern, as people learn the Enneagram many feel they can identify with several different numbers. The result is confusion: "If I am only one number, which one is it, and how can I tell?" If this quandary is to be sorted out, we must beware of getting caught on the level of personality characteristics and qualities and instead keep our attention on the deeper level of *hidden motivation.*

In the descriptions of the patterns, each number is delineated by certain qualities, characteristics, and typical behaviors, but we must not let these prevent us from delving beneath the surface to discover the *motivating force* of the pattern. Similar behavior patterns in various people do not necessarily have the same motivation at their base.

Remember: What appears to be is not what necessarily is. It is *the deeper level of motivation* for which you must search. Once you have identified a motive, you can follow a logical trail toward the pearl of great price, the treasure to be searched for and unearthed by discovering your Enneagram pattern—your best self! Revealing motivation—especially unconscious motivation—is the purpose of the Enneagram.

Some people remark that it is limiting to insist that each of us has only one Enneagram number. Indeed, the opposite is true. Your Enneagram pattern is not something you *have,* but who you *are.* Thus discovering your Enneagram pattern is a liberating experience, pregnant with possibilities for a future dynamically imbued with meaning and purpose. For in revealing secret self-defeating motivations, the Enneagram gives you the power to overcome them and to change your life. In following the process through toward transformation, you begin to release the strengths that have been distorted into compulsions.

Furthermore, if it were possible to have more than one pattern, you would be prevented from reading your own prime motivation clearly. It is by identifying this motivating pattern that you discover the hidden lake of self-knowledge where you can wash clean the problems of life and be revitalized.

How to recognize your pattern. You can't choose your Enneagram number; rather, you *recognize* your own pattern through your personal response to the descriptions. There are some principles, however, that may help you.

First, you may find it helpful not only to refer to your life as it is today but also to remember how you lived and what you valued before reaching your mid-twenties. Normal human development dictates that we explore our prime addiction in all its limitations during childhood and adolescence.

Another kind of reflection that may be helpful is to become aware of how you react under stress. In difficult situations it is often your basic and most trusted defense systems that operate automatically. Your prime psychological addiction is basic to those defense mechanisms.

A third possible aid to discovering your Enneagram number is to seek the observation of a friend. However, because freedom from personal responsibility affords a friend the luxury of objective honesty, you would be well advised to be prepared to hear the truth or to ask only the most tactful of people for such assistance.

In all these approaches, an attitude of objective self-observation will be most helpful. Neither self-justification nor self-condemnation creates the freedom to experience and accept the truth. Objectively examining the clues allows the detective to see beyond seemingly unrelated data and emerge with the right solution.

You might well wonder why it may be difficult to discover your Enneagram number. The answer is that most of us live with an inner image of ourselves as we wish we were and so do not recognize ourselves as we really are. Moreover, the Enneagram describes psychological addiction, limitation, dysfunctional behavior, and sin. We often choose to remain unconscious of the clearest expressions of these elements of selfishness and weakness. As denial takes over, we aren't able to see ourselves as we are.

Do you remember the classic scene in every mystery story? Leaping from the chair, the detective exclaims, "Of course! It was right in front of my nose all along!" It is in such an "Aha!" moment that the Enneagram detective becomes aware of what is hidden—of what, in this case, is unconscious.

Unconsciousness of one's true self is what the psychologist Carl Jung referred to as the seedbed of sin. For many of us today, unconsciousness has become a free pass that excuses us from the hard work of growth and allows us to proceed through life in a sleepwalking state. Living in this undemanding way, we evade the truth about our authentic selves. However, by abdicating responsibility for personal actions and choices, we become our own adversary and worst enemy in life.

With these observations in mind, we can proceed to a full description of the nine patterns of the Enneagram. Each description will be in five parts: first, *questions* to assist you in ascertaining the central motivation of each pattern; the *personal perspective* typical of the people of the pattern; descriptions of how people in the pattern *orient themselves to the world* and how they *live with family and friends;* and finally some *positive qualities* of the pattern.

The positive qualities are evidenced in a person's life to the degree to which that person is allowing negative, patterned qualities to be neutralized. As we wake up, become conscious, and accept life's invitations to grow, we embrace the transformation process and begin clearing away the obstacles that have prevented us from discovering the buried treasure hidden within.

These positive qualities also reveal that *the negative qualities that often dominate in the description of each compulsion are but distortions of the person's strengths.* A strength overused becomes misused. This is the basic positive thrust of the Enneagram: by exploring the compulsive qualities of each pattern we can begin to view the underlying strength and beauty of every human being.

A note on the questions that begin each description: Though quizzes are the bane of every student, once people leave school they seem to enjoy taking a quick quiz to discover a new or interesting aspect of their personalities. These questions are not to be seen as such a quiz. Discovering your unconscious motivation takes careful self-reflection, and there is no way of avoiding that effort. The questions are another tool to help you understand the essence of each pattern more deeply.

As you read each description, remember that all the negative qualities of each number are but distortions of that pattern's strengths and positive qualities.

THE ENNEAGRAM

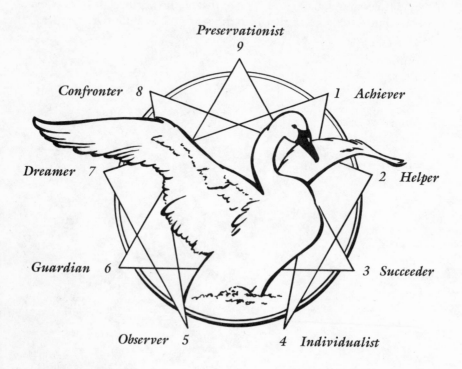

Copyright © 1990 Theodore E. Dobson and Kathleen V. Hurley

One: The Achiever

To be angry is to revenge the faults of others upon ourselves. —ALEXANDER POPE

Questions

1. Do you continually think about ways you could have done something better or ways you might have responded to a person or a situation more to your advantage?
2. Is there a voice in your mind that criticizes everything you do and many things other people do?
3. Have you frequently had to sacrifice your desires or opportunities because people close to you are more verbal or more aggressive about their needs, or because they have needs that seem to take priority?
4. Do you make "To Do" lists for yourself and for others?

5. When you are working on a project, do interruptions break your concentration on the details and trigger a "slow burn" of anger?
6. Do you think you try hard at everything in life and often wish you could be more laid back or easygoing?
7. Do you feel revulsion toward people who are always needy or looking for a "free ride" in life and silently criticize them for not taking charge of their own lives?
8. When planning to make a purchase, do you ignore the person who tries to give you a sales pitch and look for someone who will give you the information you need and let you make up your own mind?
9. Do you consistently find yourself redoing tasks because others failed to do them right the first time?

Personal perspective. Achievers focus their energy—which they experience preeminently as the drive to improve the situations in which they find themselves —on themselves and on their own concerns. They experience life as a cacophony that they are incapable of bringing into harmony. Feeling inept at sorting out the discord of society, they work hard to bring order into their personal space while shutting out the noise of the world.

Like the intensive care unit of a hospital, their interior life is controlled, watchful, and sterile. But just as every new crisis case causes change and upheaval in the ward, so every unexpected situation puts Achievers in turmoil. Only the most vigilant can sort out and maintain the proper balance between personal and relational needs, between priorities of work and relaxation.

Achievers feel caught in, and so they want to avoid, imperfection. Their dysfunctional motivation leads to a striving to feel perfect. Their basic life issue is order, and their prime psychological addiction is anger.

Orientation to the world. Achievers possess a well-developed instinctual energy—a spontaneous, often impulsive, and short-lived inner power. This energy is a contained force that becomes sharply defined as they focus it on specific projects or tasks that will affect their lives and the lives of those with whom they are directly connected. Although these self-starters are active people, perpetually in motion, they have difficulty maintaining a consistent, moderate energy flow as they work hard to improve one thing at a time.

Because they have difficulty just lettings things be, they impulsively start new projects, but as soon as the day is over, or if they become emotionally disconnected from the project before it is fininshed, they have a hard time getting back to it again. Continually having several projects at various stages of completion creates in them a persistent feeling of dissatisfaction, frustration, guilt, and anger.

Constant efforts. For Achievers, nothing is as it should be, and they are energized only when putting forth the effort to make the necessary corrections. They react against evil, chaos, and error, attempting to set things right. Although they use the energy from their anger in an attempt to achieve, they rarely attain the inner satisfaction that comes from hitting the mark. Theirs is a raw energy that drives them each day to attempt to improve existing conditions.

Negative feelings toward self. Achievers feel both great anger and a compelling drive to be good. They fear that expressing their anger will lead to their being disliked or disapproved of. The tension that this fear creates causes them to take out their anger on themselves first. They resent themselves for not measuring up to their own standards. Judging themselves inadequate, they are prone to depression and lack of self-esteem.

Although they perceive the world as overdemanding, they are too rigid to consider modifying their high ethical standards. Therefore, even though they know that others are aware of their judgmental attitudes, they are unable to find a moral way of resolving their dilemma.

Attitudes of this kind lead them easily toward condemning themselves and even toward being overscrupulous. These are people who are filled with contradictions that propel them to swing from overcautious behavior to displays of sudden rashness. Their impulsiveness will inevitably lead them into periods of intense worry, commonly interspersed with bouts of profound self-pity.

Need for perfection. Perfection becomes an obsession for Achievers. But it is not anyone else's idea of perfection they seek, only their own. Within their own mental framework, they value being exact, precise, and meticulous about detail. Their approach to life is structured and can become rigid. Rigidity causes them to become highly attached to their important projects. They are oversensitive to any criticism that might suggest incompetence. Reactions to criticism can range from total withdrawal to a severe loss of self-control.

As a way of protecting themselves from any criticism, their own or others', having the right information becomes especially important when they take on a new responsibility. Because of their need to do things the right way they search out expert advice from impersonal sources—"how to" books that span the broad spectrum from raising a puppy to management techniques.

Structured approach to life. Achievers prefer short-term projects so that results will be quick and tangible. Loners who organize their projects in their minds, they feel angrily frustrated when circumstances or other people prevent them from accomplishing these projects in the way they think they should.

In certain highly valued areas of their lives, neatness and order will be top priority. Less important areas may be in constant disarray. Extreme awareness of both their own energy level and the effort required to do their high-priority jobs right forces them to choose where they will expend their energy.

Because others rarely seem to share their standards or do their portion of the work, Achievers often feel so overwhelmed that they turn negative and are tempted—many times successfully—to give up before they begin. The consequent frustration causes them to attempt, with great determination, to impose their high standards on people and situations in their little part of the world.

Intensity. For Achievers, there is a right way and a wrong way to do everything. They constantly and unswervingly work against their enemy, the clock, whose steady ticking reminds them that there is never enough time to do everything that needs to be done. Needless interruptions or insignificant chitchat will irritate them because it breaks their concentration; therefore, they are happiest when working uninterrupted and in a quiet atmosphere.

They see life in black-and-white terms, and once they identify an issue and determine a solution, they will be stubbornly dominating and intolerant of any other opinion on the subject. Deep within them is both a desire to rebel and a fear of the unruly side of their nature. Their aspiration is to be honest, fair, and good, but they also want things to go their way. Thus when crossed or overruled they will feel resentment but then repress it and harbor it for years.

Inner voice of criticism. Achievers' constant criticism of self is so intense that many of them say they even hear a voice in their minds, an "inner critic" who continually finds fault. Because this inner voice always has the final word – a disapproving one – Achievers tend to apologize often for what they see as their shortcomings. The voice will demand they say yes even when they want to say no, that they reinvestigate an issue rather than let it go.

This inner barrage may be so persistent that in conversations or meetings Achievers may be unable even to hear others and so may seem argumentative, picky, or irritated – objecting, qualifying, correcting, and questioning nearly every statement. Because of this critical inner voice, Achievers always have a difficult time evaluating their own performance, for they perpetually fall short of their own standards of perfection.

Aptitude for teaching. Achievers are intense, rather proper people who take life seriously. Because they want to call forth the best in self and others, they tend to be perpetual teachers. Developing self-sufficiency and independence is so important to them that they often preach rather than teach, going into such detail that others find them frustrating. They may take a critical or impersonal approach in their teaching, but they are always precise and balanced in the presentation of their material.

Decision-making style. Achievers are comparative decision makers who research and study previously effective plans, programs, and/or products, measuring the results against their own resources. They do not want to make a mistake, and, because time is money, they are not going to squander it trying to reinvent something that has already been proven reliable. They gather information and review it in detail so as to make the very best decision based on practicality and common sense.

Though this process can be time consuming, Achievers would rather pay up front than take a chance on having to pay later. They therefore engage in meticulous research, and it often helps them make sound decisions. On the other hand, the time consumed in this often tedious process can prevent them from taking advantage of opportunities available to those who are free to move quickly. Even when a decision is made, they have nagging doubts about it.

Achievers resent being given a "sales pitch" on anything. These independent people are looking for information only and simply refuse to be pressured by any outside source. They are, however, susceptible to pressures exerted by close associates – co-workers, colleagues, or family members.

Because of their many internal pressures, Achievers can, in a flash of anger or sudden loss of objectivity, make an impulsive decision that they later come to regret. The resulting resentment will lead them to become less and less communicative about pending decisions as a way of safeguarding their independence and personal dignity.

Leadership style. Achievers are natural leaders who at their best are inventive, original, and creative in the world. At their worst, they can be dictatorial and stubborn, driving others too hard with their rigid determination. When in this negative state they simply expect others to be as dedicated to achievement as they are. This intense focus of concentration and energy leaves little freedom for creativity or self-expression.

When operating in a positive vein, Achievers will simply and clearly state their expectations and deadlines and allow others the freedom to complete their projects in whatever way works best for them. They will, however, appreciate periodic reports and will expect projects to be completed on time. Achievers are self-reliant, dependable, hard-working, conservative people who value these same qualities in others.

Achievers make good leaders of meetings because they prepare ahead of time, keep the meeting on track so as not to waste time, and make certain that every person has the opportunity to state his or her views. They want fairness and justice to guide procedures, but because they attempt to keep things moving on schedule, they can also appear pushy, authoritative, and uncaring in groups. They also make accurate notes regarding the tasks and responsibilities assigned to each person and continue to follow up to ensure that everything has been completed.

Living with family and friends. Highly controlled people, Achievers are secretive and do not easily disclose their personal feelings or opinions. Fear that irrational emotions could overwhelm them causes them to keep a tight rein on their responses. This extreme self-control can extend from emotion into the realm of intuition, thus impairing their judgment regarding other people; this repression can, in turn, lead to a financial loss, or to a loss in relationship. They especially repress their anger, allowing it to be expressed only through passive-aggressive behavior, which can be particularly evident when they do not assert their own needs.

Loyalty. In love relationships Achievers will become totally dedicated, vulnerable, and loyal, thus developing a deep and enduring union. They are highly moral people who work hard to give their families every advantage and opportunity to grow physically, mentally, and spiritually.

Independence. Not wanting to waste time, Achievers do not like dependent relationships. They are self-starters, productive and resourceful people who avoid depending on others, for to do so would relinquish their control and independence. Neither will they allow others to become dependent on them, because they do not want another job that demands more of their precious time.

In their value system, time should be used for working, for achieving. These loners can easily become so protective of their time and space that selfishness develops and eventually cuts off the important and needed balance of social connections and personal relationships.

Social interaction. In social situations, even when plagued by a lack of self-confidence or feelings of inadequacy, Achievers will smile and radiate social charm. In more common, everyday life, Achievers show their inner anger toward the world in one of two ways. Some constantly look angry, scowling, or sad no matter how they really feel at the moment. Others present a happy, smiling exterior at all times, even though they may be experiencing anger as an intense slow burn. Both kinds of Achievers tend to have a look of neatness about them— every hair in place, never disheveled.

The value of reputation. Achievers have a continual inner struggle with a sense of being unimportant. This attitude causes them to place great value on the respect others have for them. Achievers appreciate it when others notice and admire them for the good qualities they have worked so hard to develop.

Their "inner critic" undermines the expressed admiration of others and prevents them from internalizing compliments, however. Outwardly they can graciously accept a compliment from someone while inwardly commenting that the person is not an expert, has lower standards than their own, or is just being nice; in any case, the compliment is rendered meaningless. They are constantly aware that they could have done better, they could have worked harder.

Quick judgments. They tend to make quick judgments about others' motives. Thus they often feel guilty for judging and finding fault. The inner voice of criticism, which is so harsh and demanding of Achievers, prevents them from evaluating relationships well. Their inclination toward pessimism is often revealed in their biting and satirical humor.

Positive qualities. Achievers, as they mature and move into the process of transformation, develop many endearing qualities. They are ambitious, resourceful, and stimulating people who will sacrifice time and energy to be faithful to others and to work. Full of energy and animated in conversation, they are natural leaders, kind and gentle, who have the vitality to inspire others with kindness and a belief in themselves.

Fairness, honesty, and directness are esteemed in their value system. High ethical standards make them well-balanced, moderate people who are impartial and honorable in their treatment of others. They have well thought out values and possess the courage to stand up for them even under extremely difficult circumstances. Their loyalty and integrity in personal relationships creates lifelong friendships that they and others treasure among the most prized gifts of life.

These born leaders establish a distinct identity through their creative and original response to life. Their ability to see reality clearly, combined with their vision for the future and their high energy, make them creators—pioneers of a new way.

Remember: All the negative qualities of Achievers are but distortions of this pattern's strengths and positive qualities.

Two: The Helper

The virtues of society are the vices of the saint.
—RALPH WALDO EMERSON

Questions

1. Are you so sensitive and responsive to the pain in people around you that others might good-naturedly refer to you as a "mind reader" or "psychic"?
2. Do you find it difficult to limit the time or energy you spend when others seem to need you?
3. Do you struggle with organization in your personal life—starting many projects but following through on very few?
4. Is it difficult for you to judge how much time is appropriate for yourself or others to focus on meeting personal needs without becoming selfish?
5. Are you a flexible, accepting person who seldom, if ever, finds strictly right or wrong answers to life's problems?
6. In personal relationships, does your dedication to finding creative ways of expressing your affection often collide with feelings of resentment over being taken for granted?
7. Do you quickly become agitated or "stressed out" when doing tasks that focus on theoretical, objective issues that are devoid of any interpersonal dimension?
8. No matter where you are—on the job, shopping, on vacation, at a restaurant, at a party—do you seem to attract people, even perfect strangers, who pour out their hearts or tell you their life stories?
9. Do you gain a sense of personal fulfillment at helping others achieve their goals?

Personal perspective. Helpers possess a well-developed energy for relationships that they focus outward on the feelings and needs of others. They see life as a challenge and feel completely capable of handling everyone's problems and difficulties.

They radiate the inviting warmth of a bright fire in a country kitchen during a blizzard. Rescued from the cold, a person relaxes, becomes vulnerable, and pours out his or her heart, only to discover that the moment the story is finished the Helper bundles up and heads out into the darkness to search for another lost soul.

Overinvolvement in the lives of others allows Helpers to avoid their own personal neediness. Their dysfunctional motivation results in a striving to feel needed by others. Their basic life issue is feeling self-sufficient, and their prime psychological addiction is pride.

Orientation to the world. For dysfunctionally motivated Helpers, the world is filled with people who have problems and needs to which the Helper is compelled to respond. The neediness they see in others is most often a mirror image of their own life needs, which they choose to ignore. Projecting all problems outside themselves allows them to deny their own vulnerability to life and people and gives them permission to avoid any culpability in problems that might arise.

Service. Helpers' emphasis on giving elevates service to the position of primary importance. They judge every activity by one criterion: how this activity will serve others. Consequently, they are often inclined toward a career with a service orientation or respond to their inner drive to serve through volunteerism. Though not all doctors, nurses, social workers, ministers, and counselors are Helpers, the penetrating genius Helpers have for seeing multiple solutions and choices will often direct them to choose one of these professions for their life's work.

Difficulty developing objectivity. Some say that Helpers are anti-intellectual. Many Helpers would simply describe themselves as "not heady." Of all the Enneagram patterns, this one experiences the greatest difficulty in activating analytical abilities. Rounding out the personality of a Helper requires a concentrated effort at grasping the "big picture" and developing the skills of objectivity.

They happily learn whatever can enhance the work of their chosen field, anything that can be used to benefit people. But because Helpers believe that giving is more important than thinking—or for that matter, more important than any other frivolous pursuit that might be undertaken merely for one's own self-aggrandizement—they do not spend any more time studying than is required for the proper and practical application of this knowledge.

Leadership style. Helpers often do not want to be in leadership positions; they are not comfortable with others' expectations that a leader should set goals and direction for the meeting. In Helpers' eyes these things are not important—individual people are.

They are at their best when in support positions. They prefer to stay in the background where they can use their talents of tact and cooperation to coordinate projects and focus on the practical aspects of keeping an organization going.

When positive, Helpers are dedicated to their work and to the people with whom they work. They make an art of being diplomatic in business dealings. When negative, they can get caught up in taking care of others to the point of smothering. Then, feeling overloaded and used, they can nurture negative feelings and completely lose sight of the job they were hired to do.

The one place Helpers will volunteer their time as leaders is in a project or organization devoted to the needs of people. They will put up with the frustration of details and organization if they know that ultimately their energy is going toward improving the lives of others. Even in these situations, however, they may minimize or pass off to others administrative and organizational responsibilities. Their prime concern is for the policies, insights, and helpful attitudes that make their organization beneficial to others. Before Helpers can become effective leaders, they have to learn how to work *with* others rather than *for* others.

Because of their lack of concern for impersonal policies and general planning, Helpers usually dislike and therefore avoid meetings. A group leader is doomed to frustration with Helpers, who are seldom interested in *Robert's Rules of Order* or business details. Instead, Helpers focus on the one with hurt feelings, the one who needs a glass of water, or the one who has not been understood. As a result, completing an agenda when a Helper is involved can be the supreme test of the leader's adeptness and ability.

Decision-making style. Helpers feel compelled to respond to the needs of the person directly in front of them and do not stop to weigh the consequences of their actions either personally or professionally. Because of this attitude they are often poor decision makers.

In general, Helpers would prefer either that another person whom they trust make the decision or that a group decision-making policy be implemented. Any decisions made in this manner will be loyally supported by the Helper. If a group process is used and dissension occurs, Helpers excel at mediating. Also, if any discord arises over a decision that is made, Helpers draw upon their notable powers of persuasion to convince the disgruntled person(s) of the rightness of that decision.

Often they put off making decisions either until a decision is no longer required or until, in total frustration, someone else makes it. In this way they can continue to tell the person in front of them whatever he or she wants to hear and are not responsible if the decision is hurtful to anyone. Their dysfunctionally motivated inclination is to base their decisions on what others want or need rather than on objective reality.

Living with family and friends. Helpers, who compulsively deny their own needs and desires, feel guilty when they are forced to admit they might lack something that only someone else could give them. Similarly, they secretly identify others as selfish when they attempt to have their own needs met. They flee from occasions for looking within themselves because they are afraid they might find nothing of substance or value.

If one asks Helpers what they need, they deftly turn the conversation to concern for the questioner. For, in truth, because their need is to meet needs, others' needs *are* Helpers' needs. Their ability to adapt to the person in front of them creates a nonthreatening and receptive atmosphere that opens the other to hear and ponder new possibilities. Helpers' have an innate ability to respond patiently to other people; their mastery of total focus on others becomes the cornerstone on which they build and justify their entire existence.

Saintly image. Helpers are admired by themselves and others for their generosity. People call them the "living saints." Helpers silently concur, because they take pride in always being available for others. This saintly image of caring and service camouflages Helpers' expectation that everyone forget any and all of their mistakes, faults, or weaknesses.

When people buy into this subtle manipulation, they suddenly feel guilty about their harsh judgments of this good person. The other person's guilt then becomes an open invitation for the Helper to forgive the ingratitude with one magnanimous gesture, thus adding a higher gloss to the Helper's already glittering halo.

One-way intimacy. Interpersonal relationships are all-important to Helpers, but they reserve an exclusive right to define the word *interpersonal*. By their definition, others share everything about themselves, and Helpers support and sustain them as they sort through life's difficulties.

In personal relationships they do not share reciprocally but maintain a distant, though friendly, manner. Others are encouraged to reveal all, and Helpers reveal little about themselves; the iron-clad rule for their interpersonal relationships is one-way intimacy.

However, because of Helpers' expertise at making others comfortable, most people never realize that Helpers have not shared themselves. Helpers also take advantage of the fact that most people are unconscious or egocentric enough to delight in having the spotlight focused solely on them.

Advice. Helpers, often finding themselves in situations in which they can give advice, do so without hesitation. They enjoy having influence in others' lives, which in turn inflates their own egos. In groups they will tend to be followers, not leaders, but in individual lives they want to be at center stage. Their help-turned-advice creates dependent relationships. In trying to make everyone feel comfortable, Helpers can become the stumbling block that will prevent others and themselves from doing the hard work of personal growth.

Manipulation. Helpers can use extremely subtle means to create dependency in others. They will find socially acceptable ways to minimize the achievements and gifts of others. If questioned about their attitude, they will softly proclaim that it was simply for the other's own good—for example, as a guidance tool, to prevent self-deception or to help them acknowledge reality.

They will use all their gifts of sensitivity to draw people to themselves in what seems to be a personal relationship. Then they will push them away, only to draw them back when they are sufficiently miserable or desperate for attention. The weaving of this spider's web increases others' dependency and elevates Helpers' self-importance.

Identity and self-worth. Helpers' self-esteem is defined both by the number of people who depend on their service and the intensity with which their service is needed. In return for their dedicated generosity, Helpers need appreciation, thanks, and gratitude from those they serve. In Helpers' minds, only these important words or signs of affirmation validate them as worthwhile, leaving them in a perpetual tug-of-war for their identity and self-worth.

Backlash of helping. Helpers are known for draining other people with flattery and compliments or with a lavish display of intense feeling. They say and do these things because they are on a perpetual quest to find someone who will shower them with that same interest and affection. Their unconscious tactic for winning love is to respond to others' needs, especially the needs of those who are impor-tant to them.

However, if someone they assist is not grateful, Helpers feel as if they had just been informed they don't exist. After receiving such a devastating blow to their self-esteem, they can easily slip into feeling martyred or hostile toward those whom they had been serving. Hostility often takes the form of backbiting or gos-sip. Because people confess their darkest desires and most secret faults to the com-forting Helper, Helpers often have more than enough ammunition for their gossip.

Focus on others. Their desire is to please, and they are deeply hurt when they fail in this regard. On the other hand, they are also deeply hurt when others fail to notice their help and thank them for it. Although they resist being taken for granted, they do not want others to be too obvious or gushy about their thanks; a quiet, private statement will do best. Helpers focus on others almost entirely, feeling protective and even possessive of the people they care for. This intense attachment to others creates a bond so strong that even distance or time often will not sever it.

Positive qualities. Helpers, as they mature and move into the process of transformation, develop many endearing qualities. Through their kindness and sensitivity they develop a deep understanding of human nature. Their tact and their expertise at gaining cooperation through open communication and their insight regarding human nature make them especially effective in arbitration, mediation, and diplomacy.

When they are able to give love freely, they make excellent counselors and loyal friends. They are gentle, naturally nonviolent people who do not judge or condemn and are singularly perceptive about other people's needs and concerned for their welfare. Warm people who like tactile contact, they often speak softly, drawing others into a sense of warm intimacy.

Personal growth, so elusive to them when their dysfunctional motivation is operative, can become their major strength as they listen to and follow the inner guidance that they have made so available to others. As they mature in a conscious way, their gentle nature is most effectively revealed through their loving respect for the inner workings of the human spirit and spirituality. This movement creates the potential for them to become visionaries who expertly guide others along their own inner journey.

Remember: All the negative qualities of Helpers are but distortions of this pattern's strengths and positive qualities.

Three: The Succeeder

If I blunder, everyone can see it; not so, if I lie.
—JOHANN WOLFGANG VON GOETHE

Questions

1. Do you sometimes think you're too cynical or suspicious because you intuitively seem to know the hidden motives of others—especially their dark, manipulative intentions?
2. Are you able to be positive, optimistic, and upbeat around others even though you feel pessimistic or desperate about your life when you're alone?
3. Do you guard against becoming too emotionally vulnerable or dependent upon even those closest to you because you fear being manipulated?
4. When your goals are unclear or you don't have any goals, do you lose your energy and find that life is suddenly dull and boring?
5. To avoid being rude or hurtful, do you often have to feign interest in a conversation you're having because a new idea or important current project is beginning to race through your mind?
6. Do you prize relationships that are free and undemanding and break relationships that become too complicated or time consuming?
7. Are you able instantly to hide your feelings of shock, disappointment, anger, embarrassment, and so on until you can deal with them in private?
8. Would you tend to err on the side of saying too little rather than saying too much?
9. Is it difficult for you to take time for yourself, to relax or to "do nothing" when there are still projects left undone?

Personal perspective. Succeeders repress their personal desire for relationships so that they can sustain a harmonious relationship between themselves and the world. They see life as a gamble, and they intend to hold the winning hand. They are masters of disguise who have made the "poker face" a fine art.

With an inner wardrobe that would rival that maintained by Universal Studios, they repress their personal feelings by donning the disguise that will create the image they intend to project. Because they fear becoming vulnerable, no one, especially those in authority, will see them without a mask.

Succeeders feel caught in, and so they want to avoid, a sense of personal failure. Their dysfunctional motivation results in a striving to feel successful. Their basic life issue is productivity, and their prime psychological addiction is deceit.

Orientation to the world. Succeeders are ever watchful of how others are perceiving them. As image-oriented people, they know a well-groomed, distinctive look is key to appearing successful. Above all else, they fear failure, and the greatest failure is to lose the respect and approval of others. For them, success lies in the appearance of success and is therefore ultimately defined by others' admiration and respect.

Flair. With their accent on appearance succeeders dress to be noticed or admired. They project an intensely masculine image if they are male, an intensely feminine image if they are female. Often they have good taste, but not always.

Even the most introverted Succeeders possess a readily available mask of extroverted sociability with which to create the illusion that they are people who can handle everything with flair and class. Continuously projecting an "on top of the world" air of confidence serves to give them an unapproachable quality that keeps others at arm's length, thus causing them to be known as the aristocrats of the Enneagram. This aura of aloofness is their protection against anyone who might want to get too close.

Political savvy. Succeeders are political people who believe that knowing when not to speak is just as important as knowing when to speak. They will never say too much—especially to those in authority. They have an extraordinary ability to read the hidden motives and intentions of others. This talent, along with an innate sense of cunning, gives them an edge in nearly any situation because they can always make the properly ambiguous political response.

Generally Succeeders are gracious to everyone. When other people act foolish, the Succeeder may continue to respect their personhood and freedom of choice but will discount their importance, for Succeeders lack the patience to tolerate another's prejudices or weaknesses.

Productivity. Succeeders see the world in terms of goals to be attained, jobs to be done. Although they continually look to the future and set new goals, they are motivated toward those goals by a system of immediate rewards from others that acknowledges and affirms their accomplishments. Within a short time after achieving a goal, no matter how exalted, their success will become empty, hollow. Like the song, they will ask, "Is that all there is?"

They list their short-term and long-term goals, verbally or nonverbally, consciously or unconsciously. For them, it is quite natural to sacrifice personal needs—even their health—to see that these goals are achieved.

These energetic overachievers fit almost too well into American society, where to produce is everything. They produce so that they will be admired and respected during their lifetime: the idea of posthumous recognition has little meaning for them. Because their identity lies in what they do, criticism of their performance equals rejection of their personhood.

Efficiency. Succeeders are organizers. They prefer to have everything in order before beginning a project and will then organize and reorganize, because they have a natural ability to discover better systems. Outstandingly efficient people, they have a low tolerance for inefficiency in others.

Leadership style. Leadership is a natural and integral part of Succeeders' drive toward success. They carry the potential for being especially effective with groups and can be excellent at building unity. In their drive for success, however, they often overlook other people's contributions to projects or ignore others' unique gifts. When they become aware of what they have done, they quickly call upon their charm and magnetism to smooth the feathers they have ruffled.

Succeeders are free thinkers who possess a special talent for ideas and communication. They have the intuitive know-how to expand on an idea and make it a success. They are risk takers and can become overextended both financially and personally. Because they are highly creative people who have almost too many interests, they can scatter their energies, lose their focus, and become ineffective.

Their ability to sell people on a project or idea springs from a contagious confidence in their product. This enthusiasm, along with their creativity and need for self-expression, makes them effective in advertising and promotions. Convinced that whatever they promote is the best, Succeeders exude a radiant, "all things are possible" attitude that inspires others and overcomes any resistance others may feel.

Succeeders have difficulty doing routine work and perform best when they have a good deal of freedom. Thus they can often do their most creative work alone. If interrupted while on "a creative roll"–no matter how important the matter–they become impatient and irritable with the intruder.

Succeeders have high expectations of themselves and others and are intolerant of inefficiency, carelessness, or laziness. Though they greatly admire people who are self-motivated, creative, and productive, unfortunately they seldom communicate their respect to the person with these qualities. Although their smooth exterior makes them appear to have a moderate, relaxed style of management, those who work for them quickly discover that these bottom-line people exert an intense, constant pressure to produce.

At their best, Succeeders' leadership style will encourage self-expression, freedom, productivity, and growth. At their worst, they are demanding, cold, impersonal, and extravagant to the point of leading an organization to ruin.

Decision-making style. With their goals ever before them, Succeeders find decision making not only easy but natural. They see their decisions as a logical consequence of all the circumstances surrounding the issue. In truth, however, their decisions are often impulsive. Succeeders become excited by possibilities and can take too many chances in the optimistic belief that Lady Luck is riding on their shoulder. Very often they are lucky–but not always.

Another reason Succeeders prefer quick decisions is that whenever something needs to be done they want it done yesterday. They hate putting things off because they don't want to get bogged down in details that could prevent them from moving ahead freely–and they value their freedom. Succeeders believe that when opportunity knocks you had better be ready to move, because if you don't someone else will. These highly competitive people know that the runner-up is quickly forgotten. They intend to be remembered.

All too often Succeeders find themselves having to resolve a backlog of difficulties in their relationships with other people. Because they are so busy being creative, productive, and free, they do not see resentment and frustration building among employees or colleagues until it has reached the boiling point. Taking the time to deal with it can be difficult for them; they dislike having to curtail their forward movement to face personal feelings. Moreover, they hear any criticism as saying, "You have failed."

On the other hand, Succeeders do not hesitate to tell others when they are wrong. They override other people's decisions on the spot when they believe there is a better way. Obviously, Succeeders will continue to create their own pain and tension until they develop genuine emotional responses in their relationships.

Effective communicators. Succeeders are talkative, optimistic people who love to communicate their new ideas in many words. Perpetual salespeople, they project so much confidence in their product that even the most skeptical person can become a believer.

Also, when it serves their purposes, Succeeders can be masters of sarcasm and double messages. With words and a smile that imply warmth and reason, they can subtly back a person into the proverbial corner and leave him or her with no choice but surrender.

These are competitive people for whom words are one of their greatest strengths and their first line of defense. Often good public speakers, they research their subjects thoroughly, reflect on their material, and present it with a charm and natural stage presence that can be irresistible to the audience.

Living with family and friends. Succeeders are deeply feeling people who repress their personal feelings because they fear rejection, which could become an obstacle to success. Thus they are complicated people in relationships. Only after others have become vulnerable will they dare to consider the possibility of the smallest personal disclosure. Even in relationship they remain guarded for fear their vulnerability may be used against them. They hear themselves as loving, warm, quiet, thoughtful, and assertive. In the same instance others may hear them as aggressive, loud, or abrupt.

Private emotional life. Because it is such a struggle for Succeeders to express their deep feelings, they will usually give up trying unless encouraged and affirmed. Fear of disapproval, another form of failure, causes them to perform in relationships and don the mask most acceptable in the situation.

When overwhelmed by feelings of hurt, rejection, or anger, they withdraw emotionally and increase their activity as a way of dealing with the pain or frustration. By thus putting people at a greater distance they reinforce their belief that no one really cares about them.

Live in the illusion of success. Because of the importance they place on other people's perceptions of them, Succeeders can believe the illusion that their lives are the way they appear to be. Having once convinced themselves of the truth of an illusion, they are easily able to promote this illusion as reality to others.

Engaging their natural and diverse talents for communication, enthusiasm, optimism, and social interaction, they can smoothly convince everyone that their marriages, families, or jobs are fantastically successful. In fact, all they may have is a facade of success. Thus, for Succeeders, the unmasking of illusions is a necessary first step toward wholeness.

Work orientation. Succeeders prefer work-oriented relationships. They mix their personal and professional lives by bringing their work home and always being on call. Lacking respect for their own personhood, they dedicate themselves to their public role, position, or image. They therefore find taking care of their personal needs difficult and can easily feel taken for granted.

Competitive and ambitious people, they make friends by sharing tasks, not feelings. Thus, Succeeders have many friendly acquaintances but few, if any, intimate friends. For some Succeeders, even relaxation is defined in terms of having the opportunity to talk about those work-oriented projects that they ordinarily don't have time for under the pressure of schedules and deadlines.

Fear of failure. Projecting an image of confidence and capability, Succeeders experience deep fears that they are unredeemable failures as people. Personal criticism is especially difficult for them because it confirms their own darkest suspicions about themselves. Thus, they have a driving need either to forget their failures or to find a way to turn them into successes so that everything can be remembered as positive. They would prefer that others do likewise.

Family standards. Succeeders' compulsive need to set goals extends into the family. They have definite ideas about what others should or should not do, should or should not say, because of the effect these activities will have on attaining the goals the Succeeder has set for them. They are intolerant of and embarrassed by any display of rudeness, poor manners, narrow-mindedness, or laziness because these attitudes damage the image of the entire family—which, of course, includes them. In the end, Succeeders take pride in, and even credit for, the accomplishments of those close to them.

Standards for friendship. With their emphasis on work and family, Succeeders look for and appreciate friendships that are free and undemanding. Most highly prized are friendships centered around work interests or friendships in which they can "pick up right where they left off" even though months or even years have gone by. They never put people on pedestals but treat everyone as an equal.

They rarely feel guilty in relationships because, for them, the first rule of a relationship is that it be unquestioning and respectful. When others become upset or angry Succeeders see them as becoming moody or throwing a temper tantrum, and they create an internal distance in the hope that the other person will come to his or her senses quickly.

Positive qualities. Succeeders, as they mature and move into the process of transformation, develop many admirable qualities. Their loving nature and idealistic optimism about people and life combine to make them strong leaders who motivate people toward unity and high aspirations. With their gifts for organization and efficiency they insist on clear goals, job descriptions, and standards.

Their enthusiastic, entertaining personalities and multidimensional interests and accomplishments make them attractive companions. They are unusual people who lose nothing of what life teaches them and thereby develop a great inner strength and wisdom. As they become faithful to their own emotional and spiritual life they manifest a true freedom and independence that evokes the deep respect of others.

Their success is surrendered back to the world through a dedication and generosity that delights and surprises and makes others happy. Succeeders possess an inherent affinity for spiritual philosophies, art, beauty, and romance, which motivate them to become deeply involved in life. Creative and imaginative people who do not like to worry about details, their energy is best utilized on expansive pursuits that include variety.

Remember: All the negative qualities of Succeeders are but distortions of this pattern's strengths and positive qualities.

Four: The Individualist

Confronted by outstanding merit in another,
there is no way of saving one's ego except by love.
—JOHANN WOLFGANG VON GOETHE

Questions

1. Would you say that being with people, nurturing personal relationships, and being intensely loyal to the people you love are the innate gifts that bring the greatest pleasure and meaning to your life?

2. Even in your closest relationships, does fear of loss or abandonment cause you to struggle against feelings of jealousy or possessiveness?

3. Do you tend to avoid or procrastinate over tasks that require focusing on details or paperwork, seeing them as tedious and depressing?

4. When presented with a new plan, idea, or project, do you feel that it's important to recognize flaws first so that the possibilities won't become unrealistic and therefore disappointing?

5. Is your sense of meaning and purpose in life best expressed through the symbols, stories, and traditions that connect you to people, to your faith, or to life in general?

6. Have you spent a great deal of time and energy on a quest to understand the meaning of your own life and history, hoping to understand your purpose for being on this earth?

7. When experiencing the beauty of nature—for example, a sunset or a budding flower—do you connect with something spiritual and even sometimes feel your heart will burst because of the sheer wonder of creation?

8. Do you often feel so many emotions at once that you become confused about which to express first and how to organize your thoughts?

9. Are you attracted to the dramatic or unusual things in life—in clothes, food, friends, art, decor?

Personal perspective. Individualists are emotional people who focus their sensitivity to needs and feelings on themselves. They cherish their deep feelings and continually nurture them as a means of reaffirming their specialness. This emphasis on feeling, however, leads to a catch-22.

Soon they become like a greenhouse filled with overfed and underpruned exotic plants. They have cultivated so much that eventually there is simply no room for anyone, even themselves, to admire the blossoms or smell the perfume. The plants grow wild, and the excessive greenery drains life from the blossoms. In much the same way, Individualists become so constricted in their overfed and underpruned feelings that they are unable to give expression to their own uniqueness.

Individualists feel caught in, and so they want to avoid, their own ordinariness. Their dysfunctional motivation results in a striving to feel special. Their basic life issue is attaining insight, and their prime psychological addiction is envy.

Orientation to the world. To stand up against the pressures and demands of the world, Individualists draw upon their abilities to relate with other people—

depth of feeling, range of emotion, and the ability to make a quick analysis of a human situation. Intensifying and overusing these prevents them from developing their natural qualities of self-discipline, practicality, and stability. In overemphasizing their own emotional lives, Individualists force their inherent strength of character into being expressed as a quiet but stubborn independence.

Attraction to the unusual. Individualists have clear values and standards, and they attempt to refashion the world by imposing their own design on it. They find drastic change exciting—the kind of change that wipes the slate clean and sets the stage for a new beginning. With it comes hope for improving the quality of life, hope for a better world. Individualists appreciate the new and unusual and are often attracted to people, styles, and experiences that others would consider offbeat.

Sensitivity. Individualists have enormous sensitivity, which is directed primarily toward themselves and secondarily toward others. Sensitivity is a rare gift, and in its most healthy and correct form it would mean being sensible, perceptive, receptive, and aware. In the dysfunctionally motivated Individualist, however, sensitivity has become heavily veiled by the common and shallow definition of sensitive: delicate, tender, high-strung, and touchy. By focusing on their own neediness Individualists develop this shallow side of sensitivity, thus convincing themselves and others to treat them with "kid gloves."

Tragedy. Individualists endlessly reflect on their past, which they identify as tragic. Because they see their lives as a series of disappointments and betrayals by authorities, they are hyper-aware of the situations in which their desires and needs have not been fulfilled. This perception compels Individualists continually to seek understanding of themselves by attaching some logical form or order to past events.

Having lost their true identity, they long for something or someone who will make them feel special. Unaware of their own strength, they come to believe that they have little if any power to effect change or influence situations. Seeing their lives as controlled by exterior forces leaves them with little faith in themselves, other people, or the future. As a result they easily identify with the role of victim.

Constant analysis. By continually sifting through the past they dissipate their considerable energies and become self-absorbed. Even when Individualists find resolution for their emotions and thereby resolve the past, it continues to live with them as a reference point for the present. The buried treasure in this ceaseless search lies in the fact that it leads to the development of highly complicated and creative mental processes.

Inner world of desire. Needing to balance the sadness of digging through past tragedies, Individualists escape from pain by fleeing into a fantasy world of desire. Reality creates disillusionment and propels them into the more familiar, comfortable surroundings of their inner world. Thus they have a difficult time living in the present moment as they drift back and forth between tragedy and fantasy.

Performers. Individualists, painfully aware that they are easily embarrassed and that they have choked their ability to be spontaneous, quickly master the art of inner dialogue. After examining upcoming situations and possible hidden conflicts, they devise and practice several alternative scripts or responses as a way of protecting themselves from the demands of living in the present moment. This well-rehearsed "spontaneity" can often cause them to perform rather than interact.

Individualists feel on stage most of the time, but they themselves are both per-former and audience. The perfect performance creates the illusion of adequacy and allows them to feel worthy of being loved. Thus they dress with a sense of the artistic or to fit a role but always to cover their sense of personal inadequacy.

Pessimism. Because of the tragedy they have experienced, Individualists come to protect themselves through pessimism–thinking fatalistically about them-selves and having gloomy expectations of others and of life. If bad things happen they are prepared, and if good things happen they are pleasantly surprised. Unfortunately, because Individualists are unaware of the extent to which pessi-mism has permeated their thought and speech, they would be devastated to learn that they have become known for their negativity.

Difficulty being accepted in groups. Being in groups may be difficult for Individu-alists because they are unable to control the varied responses that may be required. Moreover, without realizing they are doing it, they can use their natural protective tactic of preparing for the flaws in every situation to deflate the enthusiasm of an entire group.

Ironically, these people who long to be accepted by others set themselves up to be rejected. Their dread of feeling neutral–what others might call normal–compounds this dilemma as their mood swings from ecstatic joy to excruciating sadness. However, their best side can also be revealed in a nonthreatening group in which their multiple interests reveal them as fascinating conversationalists.

Artistic temperament. Because they can seldom express their intense emotions directly, Individualists become indirect and/or symbolic in expression. This preference often leads them into the arts. Many Individualists pursue artistic expression as their occupation or avocation–writing, performing, painting, music–but not all artists are Individualists, and not all Individualists are artists.

Decision-making style. Individualists use their skills in communication and their sensitivity to others to draw out the needs and opinions of those who will be affected by their decisions. They elicit others' ideas both because they are con-vinced of the value and importance of the individual and because they need to be supported in their decisions.

Their lack of spontaneity has made them deliberate people who need to exam-ine all their options. Therefore, they do not make decisions easily or quickly, but they do make them. If they feel threatened, their decisions will be based on an analysis of their own feelings and needs. If they feel secure, their decisions will reflect respect for the majority of people affected.

Having made a decision, they are, for a reasonable time, open to explaining their rationale to anyone who does not understand it. Prolonged dissension, however, is met by intense anger from the Individualist, who becomes impatient and feels rejected and misunderstood. Once Individualists make a decision, they stand behind it. Even in the face of adversity they are confident because they view their determination as based both in objectivity and in respect for the individual.

Leadership style. Individualists always strive for a unique style of leadership. Most often it will embody a mixture of personal relationship, sensitivity, crea-tivity, and explosive temperament. If subordinates learn to read and respond to the mood of the day, they will find their jobs to be challenging, exciting, and satisfying. If not, they might find life under the leadership of an Individualist rather difficult.

Individualists tend not to be oriented to detail and thus are quick–sometimes too quick–to delegate responsibility. If another person meets their high standards of performance, Individualists feel as if that person has complimented them personally by showing respect for their leadership. But woe to the person who accepts responsibility but fails or is unable to follow through! Because Individualists take everything personally, they experience other people's incompetence, carelessness, or slipshod work as a personal affront.

Being hyper-aware of expertise, Individualists want to be recognized and respected for their abilities. Similarly, they respect others in their areas of specialization. Difficulties arise, however, when their abilities are not recognized, or when people who lack their background want to deal with them on an equal footing.

Individualists tend to interpret facts through feelings; this personalized approach is an incomprehensible source of aggravation to those who function best on a nonpersonal plane. Being acutely aware of the emotional atmosphere of their surroundings can help Individualists to short-circuit many potentially explosive situations before they surface. On the other hand, if they are to use their leadership abilities to the full, they must learn not to take things personally and focus on developing objectivity.

Living with family and friends. Individualists–who want to be known and understood more than anything else, but who also fear the responsibilities and demands of personal relationships–share only carefully selected parts of themselves with various people. Later, they are left with a sadness that no one person knows them intimately. They seldom feel that they have communicated adequately or that another has truly understood them.

Adult peer relationships. A rare and magic moment of communion with another person fills an Individualist with a gratitude that can easily lead to a long and loyal friendship. Adult peer relationships are therefore treated as sacred. An opportunity to spend time with a friend, even if suddenly offered, is considered top priority and can easily bump the other plans and responsibilities of the day down a rung.

Standards for friendship. Individualists' self-protective stance, fueled by their fear of being rejected or made fun of, causes them to set such high standards of friendship that few ever meet them. Individualists' desire to re-create their friends in their own image–with the same intense feelings they experience–can cause difficulties that will severely test or even destroy relationships.

Should a friendship fail, Individualists exonerate themselves by thinking or saying, "If only you had understood how I feel, you would have agreed." Believing that life has been too hard on them and that the world already expects too much from them, Individualists are convinced that it is others who should do any necessary changing. If the other person is not sufficiently repentant, the Individualist reasons that the relationship is probably not worth continuing anyway. They console themselves with the certainty that the other person will recognize his or her great loss and be sorry long after ties are broken.

Importance of tradition. Individualists' ability and need to connect their past and present explain the respect and importance they invest in traditions. Traditions become the living evidence and reminder of their stability and strength. Their love for and understanding of history is clearly communicated through a value system that becomes a source of law, order, and security. When it is expressed in a dysfunctional way, this love of tradition is experienced by those close to the Individualist as a demand for unwavering obedience and loyalty.

Faith traditions—stories, art, music, and symbols—often become a source of strength on the personal journeys of Individualists. Their complete intolerance for a life lived in mediocrity will make that journey an intense one.

Sense of style. Whatever their standards or taste, the personal world of an Individualist will be elegant and refined within those standards. They arrange their personal space to be unique and beautiful, a safe haven from the world. Being regarded as sophisticated, genteel, and elegant is important to Individualists. Unfortunately, they can often appear pretentious, brittle, or unapproachable.

Being center of attention. Individualists feel most secure and loved when they receive the undivided attention of another person for lengthy periods of time. Only when liberated from the constraints of schedules and deadlines do they become free to share the intricacies of their inner selves. They have an excessive need to spend time with a person before they can believe in the possibility of being understood by her or him. This compulsive need to be known causes them to explain, reexplain, and overexplain their feelings and ideas about life.

Others can feel drained by their constant desire to be understood, which is sometimes expressed through complaining and whining or through demands to be heard. They also expect others to focus on them by continually admiring their gifts and talents. This desire to call attention to themselves, which arises from feelings of inferiority, can be one of the greatest stumbling blocks for Individualists to overcome.

Positive qualities. Individualists, as they mature and move into the transformation process, develop many remarkable qualities. They have a keen sense of and value for the beautiful and elegant. Charming people, they are loyal in friendships and have a deep compassion for others. As they invest the time necessary to develop their spirituality, they become acutely attuned to others, which allows them to understand the pain that the less perceptive might pass over.

They can inspire others to reach new heights of consciousness through their ability to clarify the thoughts and feelings of those who have become confused and can no longer make any sense out of their inner life. They are original, clear thinkers who can become wise and effective teachers. Their organized thinking, stability, and self-discipline can become anchors that others rely on.

Individualists are dependable people who like variety in their lives. These qualities, combined with their need to see progress, can earn them the financial success that is so important to them. Gifts of intuition and practical, sound judgment allow them to enter the business world through many different avenues. As they learn to be other-centered, they use their personal gifts to develop tangible, practical products that can potentially benefit humanity. These affectionate people need to spend time in solitude and relaxation to maintain a balanced perspective on life.

Remember: All the negative qualities of Individualists are but distortions of this pattern's strengths and positive qualities.

Five: The Observer

Our greatest pretenses are built up not to hide
the evil and the ugly in us, but our emptiness.
The hardest thing to hide is something that is
not there. —ERIC HOFFER

Questions

1. Do you relish and even require extended periods of time alone to ponder and sort out the important issues of life?
2. Do you have an unquenchable thirst for new experiences, new adventures, or new knowledge, and are you quickly bored by repetition?
3. Do you usually have a point of view different from everyone else's and find yourself amazed at the lack of rational thinking behind others' conclusions?
4. Do you enjoy talking about and planning a project for months, even years, but find your enthusiasm slipping away at the prospect of beginning the hard work of actually doing it?
5. In personal relationships, do you often feel frustrated and pull back because others misread your intentions?
6. Are you generally impatient with group decisions, becoming restless and irritated as others ramble on and on about unrelated, unimportant issues?
7. Do you tend to see the absurdity of life and enjoy throwing people off guard by pointing out the ridiculous with wit and humor?
8. Do you place great value on individualism, personal freedom, and space and become quickly interested by anything new, unexpected, or unexplored?
9. Are the social interactions of your life initiated primarily by others, even when you want to be included or want some form of communication?

Personal perspective. Observers are factually oriented people who focus their thinking and calculating on the world outside themselves. Their goal is objectivity; their method is to live in the world of ideas as if it were the outer world.

Peering out from their sacred ivory tower, Observers sit back and watch the world in a cool, dispassionate manner. They think distance creates an objectivity that allows them to discover the real meaning of any issue, person, or situation. This separation from the world disconnects them from their true inner strengths of communication, sensitivity, and versatility. After gathering data they withdraw to an interior cloister to consider, calculate, and finally reconstruct all they have observed according to a pattern that is logical to them.

Observers feel caught in, and so they want to avoid, a feeling of personal emptiness. Their dysfunctional motivation results in a striving to feel full of knowledge. Their basic life issue is knowing, and their prime psychological addiction is greed.

Orientation to the world. Observers experience the world as intricate and interesting, so they are inclined to observe reality without becoming involved in it. They want to observe, know, and comprehend everything and to see how it all fits together. Their identity lies in knowing and assimilating, thus making confusion and vagueness their enemies.

Need for privacy. From the perspective of Observers, their time is best used in observing, thinking, and calculating and in finding patterns of meaning. Other people can see them as stingy with their time and energy because they are slow to make commitments and they need what seems to others an inordinate amount of time to weigh all the possible consequences before they commit themselves.

Observers fear that commitments will draw them away from their passion for being alone to think or to focus on projects that not only interest them but also release their creativity. Treasuring their time and energy, they find it important to conserve them and not foolishly fritter them away. They may also find that, unless they spend a good deal of time alone, they become confused and quickly drained of energy.

Separation from the world. Observers are loners, detached from the world. They have little respect for ways of understanding that are not logical and analytical and therefore rarely use them.

They tend to isolate one moment from another, compartmentalizing all reality. Their chief way of relating to the world is not directly but through an elaborate perceptual system that they themselves create. This system is a grid of categories that they place over reality to understand it. No two Observers will develop the same system, and each one is confident that his or her system is the best.

Need for clarity. Observers are competent, careful planners who have a penchant for redefining the issues, always trying to achieve greater clarity and simplicity. In their continual mental search for precision, Observers tap their own wellspring of resourcefulness, which allows them to circumvent creatively any obstacle that might arise. This persistent search for lucidity makes Observers inventors and original thinkers.

Desire for knowledge. Observers take great pleasure in being known as wise. They hoard their knowledge and do not share it until someone asks the right questions. To offer information prematurely would be similar to wasting expensive perfume on the desert air. They value perceptions and knowledge for their own sake and have no need to put them to any immediate, practical use.

Observers are plagued by a sense of inner personal emptiness. Knowledge is the commodity that fills their hollow spaces. In their quest for knowledge they often collect huge libraries of books and other learning materials. Often they are driven to become experts in a particular area and amass a complete library in this chosen field of expertise. They are lovers of realism and collectors of facts on many subjects of interest.

Decision-making style. Although Observers make decisions all the time, they do not necessarily see themselves as decision makers. Instead, they think that all they are doing is stating the only logical solution to the puzzle at hand.

Observers will tend to avoid decisions in the realm of relationship, leaving those to people they deem more qualified. Their approach is impersonal, and they can tend to overlook others' feelings as they examine the pertinent facts. Facts will override feelings in the decision-making process when an Observer is in charge.

They research the facts thoroughly, methodically categorize the information, and reach logical conclusions. Because they complete this process quickly, they are generally impatient with the process of group decision making. In committees, for example, they think that others have not done their homework and so are wasting valuable time by rehashing old material and focusing on inconsequential details. One of the most difficult things for Observers is to learn to be open to examining and valuing alternative points of view.

When they are responsible for decisions, they plan ahead for any possible obstacle that might arise. Thus many people think they spend far too much time in the planning phase. Yet, once the project begins, it moves quickly, and there are seldom "clean up" or corrective measures that need to be addressed later. All the details are taken care of with a precision that is amazing to others.

Leadership style. Observers are headstrong people who would prefer to be leaders in an organization or on a project. They are confident that they either possess or can acquire the information, knowledge, and inventiveness to direct and lead or can hire someone who has the qualifications needed to do an excellect job. If they are not careful to avoid it, they can communicate this confidence in their abilities to others in a distasteful, patronizing manner.

A key element in Observers' ability to lead lies in their openness to doing new things. Although far from being rebels, they are thoroughly aware of the consequences of clinging to the past. They promote progress with logic and humor by inspiring others to have the courage to discard old, outmoded ideas or practices.

The most difficult and frustrating problems that Observers encounter in leadership stem from their undeveloped interpersonal skills. In general, they communicate too seldom. When they do, they often use a condescending and directive tone that can intimidate and breed resentment in others.

Observers are confident that their system of gaining knowledge is superior to all others. Because they seclude themselves to process the information they have gathered, their perceptions tend to be contrary to everyone else's, and they usually find fault with any plan or idea presented to them. This characteristic can prove to be frustrating to those who work with or for Observers.

For example, co-workers or subordinates who submit a proposal, believing that the issues at hand have been clarified, may receive it back in short order marked with notes and deletions that indicate an expectation for sweeping changes. Repeated experiences of this kind can cause co-workers to lose enthusiasm and pride in their work as well as diminish their capacity to use their initiative and creativity. Observers' full potential to lead is realized only to the extent that they develop their ability to relate interpersonally.

Living with family and friends. Observers maintain an inner distance from everyday family life. Although physically present, for the most part they preserve their status as objective third parties to any confusion or dissent that might be taking place. Baffled by the energy expended over unruly feelings, they find themselves incapable of bringing logic to bear. Remaining aloof appears to them to be the only sensible solution.

Family learning experiences. Observers plan and create interesting, educational occasions for spending time with either individual family members or with the family as a whole. These activities frequently involve travel and/or the outdoors, for such enterprises stimulate their own adventuresome spirit. The bonding with their families and the love that Observers have for them is most poignantly experienced and recalled through these shared adventures.

Impersonal interactions. Because Observers overemphasize factual information, in personal relationships they can seem remote, lost in thought, not present to others, or antisocial. It is difficult for them to express feelings; therefore, they seek refuge in superficial interactions in which they inquire into subjects that interest them. Though they can become excited about these interactions, their enthusiasm is not for the personal contact but for the knowledge they are gaining though it.

Disregard for feelings. If asked how they feel, Observers tend to report what they think about what they feel. They consider their feelings unimportant, leaving others confused about how to respond to them. When Observers see other people's hesitant or negative reactions toward them, they retreat inward, convinced that they do not have the social graces necessary to communicate with people.

Observers live in a world governed by ideas, reflection, and inspiration that keeps them from realizing the value of sharing their inner selves. They often compensate for feelings of emotional inadequacy by sporadically overindulging in physical pleasures. These binges can then be followed by short-lived bursts of strict self-discipline.

Initiating communication. In relationships Observers do not make their needs known or their desires felt. Unsure of themselves and reluctant to entangle themselves in personal relationships, Observers avoid the possibility of becoming vulnerable by simply leaving all social overtures to others. Many Observers would not think to call a friend, ask someone out, or initiate a social gathering. They may even give the impression that it is not important to them to be included — when, in fact, it is.

Cryptic communication. Observers are slow to speak, but when they do they say something only once; they regard repetition as boring and unnecessary. Appearing to be assertive and pushy in speech, they exacerbate their problems with others both by their ability to think out exactly what their position on the topic is and by the terse manner in which they communicate it. There is a finality to their logic, like a treatise complete with conclusion; if others do not appreciate this wisdom, Observers may simply consider them to be shallow.

Discomfort in social situations. Because Observers feel inept and awkward in social situations, they often conclude that they are unlikable and so avoid experiences that would force them or others into the proverbial Cinderella slipper — into a situation they feel they wouldn't fit into. Their rhythm of long periods of silence followed by assertive statements can annoy others, as can their emotional reserve and noncommittal attitude. When they are silent, others may become uncomfortable because Observers intentionally give the impression that they know more than they are saying.

Self-reliance. Observers think that with enough careful planning and proper follow-through a person can always be in charge of his or her own life. Therefore, when things do not go as planned or when the unexpected happens, they quickly determine that someone else's incompetence has mucked up the works. Feeling let down by others, Observers become more self-directed and look squarely to themselves for stability.

Because it is difficult for Observers to admit that they do not know something, it is almost unthinkable for them to ask for help. To prevent becoming indebted to others, they are determined to get beyond the obstacle of the moment by themselves; thus they become resourceful people. Although they will not risk intruding on an outsider's life for fear of rejection, those who are included within their close circle of friends or family will feel their strong, loving protection and will feel free to ask anything of them.

Positive qualities. Observers, as they mature and move into the process of transformation, develop many attractive qualities. They have an irrepressible curiosity and interest in people, the world, and the universe, which makes them perceptive listeners. Not threatened by new concepts or new ideas, they are the ideal candidates to promote growth and change because they can present progress in logical, acceptable terms with cleverness and humor.

Loving adventure and freedom and having great courage, Observers are excited and stimulated by experimenting with new possibilities. Yet they rarely are rebellious, for they have a deep respect for the past. These spiritual people accept others with a nonjudgmental attitude that becomes a channel through which they foster independence, delegate responsibility, and enable others to discover and act on their own inner wisdom.

Observers, who see the absurdity in life, either charm people with dry, intellectual wit or delight them with raw, bawdy humor. As they develop, they find themselves much sought-after companions, and, to their great surprise and delight, find themselves highly attractive to the opposite sex.

Remember: All the negative qualities of Observers are but distortions of this pattern's strengths and positive qualities.

Six: The Guardian

The greatest mistake you can make in life is to be
continually fearing you will make a mistake.
—ELBERT GREEN HUBBARD

Questions

1. As you get up in the morning, are you enlivened when you have a full schedule of diverse activities for the day?
2. Are you generally more at ease entertaining in the comfort of your own surroundings, even though it means more work for you?
3. Would you say that dedication to home, family, marriage, and/or community are the basic values out of which you live your life?
4. As a person who takes responsibility seriously, do you often resent and feel overburdened by the number of people who make irresponsibility a way of life?
5. As a general rule, do you need to gather the opinions of others—family, friends, co-workers—before making a decision?
6. Having strong opinions about life, do you mistrust and become upset with people who attempt to justify and expand the "gray areas"?
7. Do you feel more connected with people who are important to you when you know the details of what's going on in their lives on a regular basis?
8. Are you a hard-working, organized person who prefers to keep to a tight schedule, even to the point of scheduling your vacation or relaxation time?
9. Would you have more confidence in and loyalty toward an authority figure who laid down specific rules rather than one who was flexible and able to "go with the flow"?

Personal perspective. Guardians are factually oriented people who repress their ability to make decisions so that they can maintain a harmonious relationship between themselves and others. However, they are also social people who continually seek to connect with a stable group having well-defined values. They feel this need because they experience a pervading sense of insecurity. As a way of compensating for their lack of self-confidence and inner authority, they depend on the stability and values of the group.

Like bureaucrats, Guardians feel most secure when conforming to laws, rules, and regulations. The cost of conformity becomes apparent in their inability to make decisions or develop creative solutions.

Guardians feel caught in, and so they want to avoid, a feeling of deviance from the law. Their dysfunctional motivation leads to a striving to feel safe and secure by following the rules. Their basic life issue is risking, and their prime psychological addiction is fear, especially of not fitting in, of doing things wrong, and of displeasing those who are important to them.

Orientation to the world. Guardians see the world in terms of risk. Their need to be protected from life by the group leads them to assimilate standards that may or may not be their own. Eventually, as they fail to identify internal values and find no point of inner stability in their lives, every situation becomes a subtle occasion of fear.

Need for schedules. Guardians use activity to prevent themselves from thinking about their fears and apprehensions. Free time weighs heavily on them, and they avoid it by highly scheduling their lives. But their enjoyment of action can lead to overinvolvement and overcommitment. Some Guardians, when faced with the possibility of an open space in the calendar, will even double schedule themselves as a way of hedging against a last-minute cancellation.

Responsibility and overinvolvement. Guardians confront their constant, low-grade fear in two ways. First, they unthinkingly accept responsibility for people and situations, making them feel they are an integral and necessary part of any organization or group and thus certain not to be excluded. Moreover, with themselves in charge, they need have no fear that the proper thing will not be done.

Second, Guardians attempt to conquer the things they are afraid of; a Guardian who did not would soon become entirely ineffective and eventually a lonely recluse—the condition Guardians fear the most. What others consider a delightful challenge, Guardians will often see as threatening. Yet they must confront these inner demons and conquer their fears lest they be left out or found to be incompetent.

Cautious approach. Guardians take only calculated risks. Before they embark on a project, they determine that the chances are good they will be able to accomplish it. Similarly Guardians take a cautious and often skeptical approach to accepting new knowledge. Lacking confidence in their own ability to decide, they prefer to trust what is known and repeat what they have done before.

When a new idea is proposed, they will comment either that it has never been done this way before or ask why one should fix what is not broken. Knowledge can increase authority and responsibility; therefore, seeking new knowledge is a serious undertaking for these conscientious people who hold themselves responsible for everything they learn.

Lack of inner authority. When law, rule, custom, or tradition backs them, or when they are dealing with their own responsibilities in familiar surroundings, Guardians can be unshakable. Without support systems to back them up, they feel weak and indecisive. Lacking the confidence to express their personal observations and opinions freely, they depend instead on faith in authority rather than faith in self.

Sudden or rapidly emerging problems may be difficult for them to handle, because with no precedent to follow, the fear of criticism looms large. At such times they may express themselves haltingly as they question themselves inside about the appropriateness of the next word or phrase.

Ambiguous relationship with authority. Guardians have an ambiguous relationship with those in authority. To feel secure, they want to follow an authority's directives, guidelines, or procedures. They search for a source of authority and then look to that person to decide all the issues. Sometimes this "authority" is simply the other person in a relationship.

Having found an authority, however, Guardians can exhibit a contrary, stubborn streak, often expressed by the way they reserve to themselves decisions over which laws they will keep, which they will bend, and which they will break. They want the protection that authority affords, yet they are also angry at feeling confined by demands and expectations. Their angry defiance can erupt covertly, yet they expect the authority to guess what their problem is and take corrective measures.

If the authority fails to pick up these cues or chooses not to respond, Guardians can begin to undermine by gossiping and creating in-groups that wrest power away from the acknowledged leaders. Another solution the Guardian often opts for is simply to leave the situation abruptly, with no explanation or discussion.

Decision-making style. Guardians' group orientation leads to a natural preference for teamwork. Whether in the personal sphere or the world at large, Guardians will search out the opinions of others, using a dialogue style of decision making.

Although they respect and value other people's judgment, eliciting of their ideas is no guarantee that the final decision will be made in a democratic fashion. When people in the group disagree, Guardians' alternative approach may be to spend time using dialogue to bring dissenters around to their way of thinking. In general, they prefer to have consensus, for it provides them with the security and protection of group responsibility.

The strength of Guardians' dialogue approach lies in the sense of ownership and shared responsibility that naturally flows from personal participation. Its weakness is in Guardians' compulsive need to seek personal protection by either overtly or covertly making all decisions in dialogue. This need reveals the insecurity and lack of inner authority that drive Guardians to abdicate personal responsibility for their choices.

Whether decisions are made by the group or independently, Guardians carry them out slowly, carefully, and responsibly. This approach allows time to inform, explain, and discuss difficulties that may arise.

Leadership style. Guardians' leadership abilities are most fully expressed when responsibility is clearly defined and there are proven procedures to follow. They thrive on regularly scheduled communication with both superiors and subordinates. If the communication system breaks down, Guardians become frustrated and angry. The lack of connectedness triggers their insecurity and their fear that either they have done something wrong or the organization has lost its sense of direction and purpose.

Though some personality patterns on the Enneagram feel constricted by standardized systems, the experience of Guardians is the exact opposite. Systems free them to be flexible, objective, and relational. With clear parameters, Guardians can use their considerable energy to affirm and support others and encourage them to excel. In this kind of environment they become known for their dedication, justice, and honor. Even in the ideal situation, however, if sudden changes or unexpected problems or obstacles arise, Guardians can quickly become rigid and inflexible.

These super-responsible traditionalists trust what is known. They would rather adjust already proven techniques than look for new ways of doing things. If they run into any opposition, Guardians turn stubborn and hostile, detailing to anyone who will listen how effective their approach has been, how effective they themselves have been.

Interwoven in their self-righteous proclamations will be complaints about how others have failed to live up to their responsibilities or commitments. When gripped by insecurity and fear, Guardians' negativity prevents them from seeing possibilities or searching for creative solutions. Left unchecked, this self-defeating attitude can undermine and destroy what Guardians most value—communication, mutual trust, and connectedness.

Living with family and friends. Membership in a group or social circle affords Guardians a sense of the security they crave but assume they cannot find on their own. If Guardians do not feel firmly anchored with a person or a group, they become apprehensive, insecure, and anxious. Such feelings lead to a kind of frenetic activity as they search for a place to belong—which they believe is what they need in order to have inner peace.

Thus companionship, marriage, home, and family are important elements in Guardians' lives because they anchor them in the world. If opportunities for a family are not available, they will need to become anchored in a stable group or institution.

Rules of group membership. Guardians use the group standards and laws to keep others in line and, finding security in conformity, enjoy in-groups and cliques. With group approval they will activate their social skills and natural graciousness, placing them at the service of the group.

They will reach out to people on the group's fringes, drawing them into the inner circle. On the other hand, their confidence is so important and yet so tenuous that they can view groups other than their own—groups with different or conflicting norms—as enemies. Because they make law absolute, they can just as easily cast out people who deviate from the norms that are important to them.

Reassurance. Because Guardians want to fit in, they cannot be told often enough how accepted and valued they are. Some even report a preference for written affirmations so they can read them over and over. The more courageous Guardians regularly ask questions or make statements that require other people to evaluate the Guardian's performance in a particular situation or area of life. In reality they have already judged their response or performance as positive but want to hear reassurance or approval from a person whom they respect.

Wariness of others. The need Guardians feel both to be closely connected to the group and to maintain harmony creates a wariness that makes trust difficult for them. However, they trust completely the few who prove themselves to be loyal. Social charm masks their underlying caution until they feel confident that they can correctly read other people's reactions. Their desire for acceptance and their fear of rejection combine continually to keep them off balance.

Importance of commitment. Guardians are extremely loyal to their "family"—whether it be a traditional nuclear family, a community or an intimate social group, or an organization or business. In the family they are faithful teachers who both communicate and model high standards and moral values. Their commitment to family and their need to belong often unite to make them the guardians of family tradition and history.

Just as they need to be connected to family, they also expect their family members to remain connected. They impose this expectation in any way that will produce the desired response—for example, through complaining, nagging, cajoling, or making others feel guilty. Thus they often become the "gathering point" for the group—the instigators of family reunions, holiday gatherings, or social events. At the very least, they are the dispensers of the information that allows everyone to continue to feel connected.

Importance of information. Guardians love "inside information" about everyone they are connected with and can become outraged if important information is withheld from them. Knowing all the facts, real or suspected, makes them feel they have earned the status of trusted confidant. Being kept in the dark fills them with self-doubt, causing them to feel insecure about their acceptance in the group.

Complaining. Although being firmly connected to a group relieves their insecurity and fulfills their need to work things out in dialogue, Guardians also often become the chronic complainers of a group. Their complaints usually arise from the suspicion that they are not receiving the affirmation, recognition, or appreciation they feel they deserve. Thus if someone crosses them, they can be incredibly unforgiving, using silence or their social contacts as weapons.

In response to a real or imagined injustice, Guardians complain to everyone except the person who could correct whatever is wrong. By preferring to nurse their grievances, they can, to their inevitable discomfort, become the source of dissension.

Positive qualities. Guardians, as they mature and move into the transformation process, develop many endearing qualities. They are loyal and intimate friends—courageous, enthusiastic, wholeheartedly dedicated, and able to sacrifice for individuals and for the group. They expend their considerable energy for the betterment of others.

Morally good and respectable people who value status, they are hard workers who easily move to the heart of the community and put forth great effort to raise its standard of living. Their genuine love and compassion for others motivates them toward community welfare, teaching, or a middle management position that can make use of their gifts for networking and creating balance and harmony. They are also able to discover and verbalize the values that can draw the most disparate community together to pursue a common goal.

Guardians, who often have a well-developed sense of humor and infectious laughter, also decorate their surroundings with warmth and good taste. These assets, along with their love of people, make them the most frequent and charming hosts and hostesses. Though artistically gifted, they are often consumed with responsibilities or too locked into group values to release their creative potential until mid-life.

Remember: All the negative qualities of Guardians are but distortions of this pattern's strengths and positive qualities.

Seven: The Dreamer

Serious things cannot be understood without laughable things, nor opposites at all without opposites. —PLATO

Questions

1. When a situation becomes intense, do you get a nearly uncontrollable urge to laugh or to point out the absurdity of it all, often with a good one-liner?
2. When you hear about or see problems in the world or in people's lives, do you almost automatically start thinking of solutions?
3. Are you "turned off" when people tell you how gifted you are or what great potential you have because you know that underneath is the expectation for you to be doing something more meaningful or productive with your life?
4. Are you stimulated by intellectual sparring, by new and different experiences, or by the possibility of being on the cutting edge of a new venture but "turned off" at the thought of your life being stable, secure, and routine?
5. Do you prize flexibility and avoid making long-term commitments or plans "set in concrete"?
6. Do people almost universally enjoy your company but at the same time give you the feeling they don't see the deeper, more intelligent, more loyal side of your personality?
7. Do you see yourself as a good communicator with a broad enough range of interests that you can keep a conversation going with just about anyone?
8. Are you the kind of person who, if given the opportunity, can see the potential use of many things others might throw out as junk?
9. Do you enjoy mental challenges and find yourself seeking out these kinds of challenges to keep life enjoyable or to keep from being bored?

Personal perspective. Dreamers are factually oriented people who focus their thinking and calculating on planning ways to make their lives easier. Their minds are in perpetual motion, fitting life's pieces together in myriad ways. They are high-energy people, in constant motion, and can even be somewhat jumpy.

Highly intuitive people who are often ahead of their time in the realm of ideas, Dreamers are the creators of personal EPCOT Centers and Disney Worlds—realms of dreams, possibilities, and fantasies. Dreamers ceaselessly search for the pot of gold at the end of the rainbow—the flawless solution to end the pain of being human.

Dreamers feel caught in, and so they want to avoid, any kind of discomfort or pain. Their dysfunctional motivation results in a striving to feel good, to feel happy. Their basic life issue is making their lives better, and their prime psychological addiction is gluttony for anything that makes them feel good.

Orientation to the world. For Dreamers, the world is the place in which discomfort and pain are experienced, so they prefer to live in their heads. In this way they protect themselves from becoming entangled in the stress of daily life. Instead, they make plans to salve, solve, and save. These escapes into what others call fantasy carry the seeds of consciousness that can awaken their minds if and when they seek to penetrate the mysteries of life. In compulsion, however, fantasy protects them from having to live within the confines of reality.

Love of planning. Dreamers are compulsive optimists, not realists. If there is a problem, there must be a solution. If there is a pain, there must be a cure. In their desire that all of life be pleasant, they work their analytical minds overtime to devise a new plan that will make it so.

They are compulsive initiators of new ideas, actually thinking that the right plan will of itself make everything better. Their preoccupation with plans comes from their desire to be rescued from reality, and from the belief that a perfect plan for happiness must exist. Their task is to discover that plan.

Unrealistic attitudes. Others can see them as insubstantial and unrealistic people who entertain "visions of sugar plums" while their cupboards remain bare. No one is more aware of their failure to devise the utopian solution than Dreamers themselves. The pain this failure causes only propels them more deeply into the world of fantasy and planning, thus postponing development of the breadth and depth of their character—qualities that can yield true wisdom as their fruit.

Appreciation for challenge. Though Dreamers shrink from discomfort, they thrive on positive challenges. All of life is seen as a challenge, especially its painful side. Throw down the gauntlet, and their adrenalin starts pumping. Their minds are filled with visions of how to exceed any expectations contained in the challenge.

Just as quickly, however, the next challenge appears—how to get others to enact their plans. The thought of the hard work needed to accomplish their newly devised solution sends them once again into the solitude of their fantasy world.

Self-indulgence. The Dreamer's approach to life becomes a vicious devourer of self-esteem that is appeased only by self-indulgence. Dreamers cannot get enough of what is pleasurable to them. Their pleasure may or may not come from activities that others consider enjoyable or entertaining.

Their work can be their pleasure, for example, as easily as physical appetites. Their attitude is that there are few things in life that cannot be enjoyed if you just put your mind to it. On the other hand, if you can't enjoy something, why bother? This attitude can make the process of maturation difficult for Dreamers.

Attraction to new ideas. Dreamers' craving for pleasure is frequently expressed in the challenge of learning new things. They are usually attracted to the latest ideas; however, they often find themselves unable to apply their newfound knowledge to everyday living.

This attraction to the new and interesting leads to a vast diversity of interests. They become masters of trivia and jacks-of-all-trades, but their lack of staying power can prevent them from reaping any benefits from the success that could be so easily accessible to them. Life has a way of slipping through their fingers as they tenderly caress their multiple interests but fail to rest upon or bless any single one.

Persistence. When they have a plan they are convinced is right, they can be as subtle as a jackhammer in their attempt to ensure its acceptance. If other people continue to reject the Dreamers' plan, the challenge becomes one of refining it and finding new ways to present it so that eventually others will see its wisdom and embrace it. When all else fails, Dreamers have several backup plans. Hidden in these plans, however, will undoubtedly be the original plan in a disguised form. In any plan involving others, Dreamers expect the details to be obvious; as in a game, others need only fill in the blanks and carry the plan through to completion.

Leadership style. In social or civic organizations, Dreamers' preference is to leave the leadership—with its inevitable responsibility and headaches—to others. They do, however, lend their humor, creativity, and networking skills to the task of affirming and supporting the leader.

In the business world, they are partial to the concept of team leadership—for several reasons. First, they themselves have difficulty setting long-range goals and dealing with difficult situations; thus they rely on the team to accomplish these tasks.

Second, Dreamers have a great need to be liked by everyone and so under pressure will agree to things that are impossible to deliver rather than face rejection or conflict. In a team approach it is the team who takes responsibility for making the difficult decisions—the Dreamer is off the hook.

Third, Dreamers' minds are always actively searching for ways to improve the organization. In the belief that change equals growth, Dreamers advocate constant change, an approach that can be disconcerting to others. Aware of this liability, Dreamers expect the team to slow them down if they change too fast and to help accomplish the change if it is acceptable to them.

Dreamers' sociability, high energy, creativity, and need for personal flexibility often lead them to be entrepreneurs. Thus Dreamers often need to hire others to follow through on commitments that they make. Their love of people and ability to communicate with everyone make them ideal representatives of any forward-thinking organization.

Decision-making style. Dreamers like to explore every side of an issue before making a decision. Therefore, they prefer that decisions be made in dialogue. Because they have so thoroughly examined the situation, they are fairly confident beforehand what the final decision should be. Even so, they continue to remain open to possible new input or unexpected approaches that others might offer.

Dreamers are enlivened by animated, impersonal discussions that lead to negotiation and compromise before reaching a conclusion. In addition, their self-confidence is buoyed up when others support the conclusion that they have already reached.

If the process becomes personal or hurtful to anyone, however, Dreamers either shut down the entire procedure or, if in authority, make an immediate decision that will settle the matter. Their indirect way of approaching problems, along with their need to keep everyone happy, can leave many loose ends and make closure difficult. Because Dreamers do not like to be pinned down, their preferred style is to make short-term decisions that preserve flexibility.

Living with family and friends. Above all else, Dreamers value their relationships with family and close friends, and especially esteem long-standing friendships. They will drop anything or get around any obstacle that might prevent them from doing something interesting with a person they care about.

Naïveté. Because of their compulsive need to circumvent pain, Dreamers never want to confront ulterior motives in themselves or others. Even when they are perfectly aware that others are being intentionally hurtful or taking advantage of them, Dreamers prefer to excuse or overlook it. Instead, they draw on their irresistible charm in the hope that a friendly wind will blow away the clouds of dissension.

Because Dreamers want to believe the best about everyone, calculated deceit or deliberately destructive behavior can catch them on their blind side, especially if the deceiver is a family member or close friend. Moreover, the naïveté they project can tempt the more devious to take advantage of them.

Personal generosity. Dreamers tend to be generous to a fault. If possible, they usually respond to any hard-luck story—even when they do not believe the story and know the person is trying to get something for nothing. Dreamers know more than they let on, so it takes a mighty fine grade of wool to pull over their eyes. However, because their appreciation of the fine art of story telling is usually greater than their need to confront, others can see them as good-hearted and gullible.

Consistently cheerful approach. Dreamers are social, congenial people. Because they are optimistic and lighthearted, people are immediately attracted to them. They love to gossip about all the good things that others are doing. Every conversation is an opportunity to connect people through sharing others' marvelous qualities.

They are unaware that this constantly cheerful approach could cause difficulty for people who have problems and do not always feel happy. Eventually Dreamers become puzzled, even dismayed, if all their relationships remain on the level of friendly acquaintance and do not progress to more intimate communication.

Difficulty with emotions. Because they have highly developed clever, analytical minds, they especially enjoy and treasure friendships with those whose intelligence matches their own. They live life on the social but impersonal plane of ideas and opinions and have to work hard at enlivening their emotions and feelings.

Although their feelings may be sincere, they do not always have the ability to express them in words or meaningful actions. The frustration that this all-too-apparent inadequacy causes Dreamers leads them, for example, to spend hours trying to choose the right gift or greeting card. In their embarrassment over expressing intimacy, however, they will probably choose a humorous card or a symbolic gift more meaningful to them than to their friend.

Happy attitude. Dreamers, uncomfortable with intense conversation, put great effort into keeping things light and general. They enjoy comfort and luxury in their surroundings; however, if it is impossible to create such a living space, they will create an atmosphere of luxury with their personalities.

They are life's "happy happenings," easy to be with, entertaining, masters of small talk and fun; but their talkative nature, often quite delightful, can quickly turn sour and boring if they do not acquire the self-discipline needed to focus some of their energy on listening to others.

Importance of optimism. When Dreamers are filled with optimism, they carry themselves with the bounce and energy of an adolescent. When depressed they lose their vitality, becoming lethargic and introspective. The wise companion can help Dreamers recapture their optimism with a new challenge. However, Dreamers can be secretive about anything in their personalities that they do not consider upbeat.

Hidden seriousness. They have a deep love and great need for people who take them seriously and respond to them in a positive way, because they lack confidence in their own capabilities. But because they also love to be the center of attention and make others laugh, they can easily be labeled clowns, which decreases their self-confidence further and increases their frustration about the difficulty of finding someone who will believe in them and take them seriously.

Preference for indirect communication. Dreamers' inability to acknowledge the negative leads to being indirect in their relationships. For example, because anger directly expressed would create uncomfortable situations, Dreamers simply refuse to acknowledge it.

The most common way for Dreamers to express dissatisfaction in relationship is through humor. By hiding a barb in humor Dreamers let off steam without risking the pain of open confrontation or rejection. When pressed to the extreme, they express their anger succinctly in irony or sarcasm wielded as deftly as the foil of a fencer.

Further, they do not correct others directly; instead, they wait until the person does the opposite of the behavior of which they disapprove, and then they affirm that.

Positive qualities. Dreamers, as they mature and move into the process of transformation, develop many admirable qualities. Visionaries and idealists, they open up others to new possibilities. Their scintillating minds and depth of character, when combined with effort and determination, create the potential for them successfully and ethically to discover solutions to long-standing global problems.

In their optimism they can find the good in every person and situation. They become loyal and trusted friends who delight in making others happy, creating fun and play. Lighthearted entertainers, they have a cheerful good nature that helps others to loosen up and feel at ease. They are eternally youthful, often in physical appearance and always in attitude. They are unpretentious people who feel equally at home at a picnic or a formal dinner party.

Their multidimensional interests open the door to endless opportunities. Although naturally gifted philosophers, scientists, teachers, or mystics, they could be equally successful in a sales-oriented, entrepreneurial position in which they could experience the joy of power and the challenge of lighting up the world with new ideas, possibilities, and products to enhance the quality of life for everyone.

Remember: All the negative qualities of Dreamers are but distortions of this pattern's strengths and positive qualities.

Eight: The Confronter

In the war of ideas it is people who get killed.
—STANISLAUS LEC

Questions

1. Do you have clear and firm ideas about what is right and wrong in situations that are important to you?
2. Do you generally find that you need to be alert for people with hidden agendas?
3. Do you find that the most irritating and difficult people to deal with are those who beat around the bush and never directly say what is on their minds?
4. Would you agree that indecision is the greatest thief of opportunity and therefore a valid argument against getting caught in group decision making?
5. Are you at ease in leadership positions and find them falling naturally into your lap?
6. Do you find that others often simply expect or assume that you will take charge?
7. Do you think of yourself as a practical person who understands what it takes to get the job done?
8. Are you the kind of person who is unafraid to take a stand against injustice, especially injustice toward people who are unable to defend themselves?
9. Do you generally express your views just as intensely as you feel them and even feel exhilarated in a discussion in which everyone disagrees?

Personal perspective. Confronters focus their drive, stamina, and spontaneity on the world. They thrive on the challenge of life and become energized in their self-appointed role as the fighter against injustice.

Confronters live in the tension of medieval knighthood in the courtly tradition. A knight was a tough soldier, able to use great force and withstand formidable attacks to protect the interests of his king. Yet within this rough exterior the courtly knight hid a gentler man—a lover of poetry, for example, and a master of romance. Becoming proficient in and linking these two worlds was a fine art pursued with gusto.

Confronters feel caught in, and so they want to avoid, a feeling of personal weakness. Their dysfunctional motivation results in a striving to feel strong. Their basic life issue is control, and their prime psychological addiction is lust—lust for life and lust for power.

Orientation to the world. For Confronters, the world is a stage. They splash their energy lavishly in every direction. Confronters' inbred sense of power is easily identified; their presence is felt when they enter a room. Because they have no intention of ever attempting to justify their ideas or their attitudes, they carry a commanding presence. This attitude states more clearly than words, "If you have a problem with me, here I am. Deal with me."

Image of power. A Confronter's inner world is a maze of personal weakness and showy energy. They admire strength—their own as well as others'—and disdain weakness. Viewing their strength as a divine commission to overcome all obstacles, they deal with all of life's issues as power struggles. Confronters have definite ideas about what is just and fight to see that their ideas of justice prevail. When justice as they understand it demands change, they initiate conflict with any authority or institution—whomever they view as the oppressor—to bring about reform.

In group situations, Confronters instinctively evaluate each person and, immediately knowing who holds the power in the group, move toward that person as quickly as a magnet to metal. If they have no desire for the leadership position, they will probably have great respect for the person who has gained this place of honor and be delighted to have found a valued ally, or perhaps a friendly adversary.

But if they covet the position, the struggle is on. Once they have set their sights on something, they possess the stamina, perseverance, and cunning to maneuver—watching and waiting for years if necessary—to win the coveted prize. Once the prize is theirs, no one will wrest it from them.

Innate tactical sense. Confronters have an innate tactical sense by which they can retain the power position. Once the battle has begun and they are confident that they stand on the side of justice, they feel a sense of exhilaration. Though conflict may leave others drained of energy, Confronters often feel revitalized by it.

Ambitious people who have the perseverance to overcome all obstacles, they will rise to the top ranks in whatever field they choose. Because of their intensity and zest for living, the staid and dignified life of a country squire would feel to them like a prison sentence.

Manipulative use of sickness. Confronters, who are always on the go and ready for more, can simply refuse to be sick or tired—conditions that to them indicate weakness. When an illness overtakes them, however, they will use it to maneuver for control. With the blustering confidence of the lord of a manor, they may bark orders from their sickbed with the full expectation that their commands will be carried out. On the other hand, if it would be more advantageous to adopt a seemingly helpless air to get others to do their bidding, they will do so without hesitation.

Ambitious competitiveness. Confronters' desire is for power, not necessarily prestige. They prefer psychological power, which in their hands can be every bit as intimidating as physical force.

If provoked, they can bully others and, spotting a weakness, take swift and accurate aim to render the opponent ineffective. Instinctively they know how to protect themselves, and they come out of nearly any encounter relatively unscathed, while others may be mortally wounded. If their power is used in a self-serving way, they have the ability to destroy multitudes.

Personalized approach to justice. Confronters' first concern will be for justice for themselves, and only when it is achieved will others reap the overflow benefits. Tending to see issues in black-and-white terms, and being all-or-nothing people who intend not to be taken advantage of, Confronters believe they have not only the right but also the duty to get ahead.

Bold in dress. Even their choice of clothing reveals their rugged individualism and power. They dress for comfort, dress in bold colors, or simply dress to please themselves. Often heedless of fashion, they also enjoy dressing to make a statement.

Decision-making style. Confronters' stamina makes them extremely tough competitors who are able to make decisions easily and "let the chips fall where they may." Their preference is to be the person who has the final word. The idea of bringing everyone into a decision-making process so that they feel good is, to them, a ridiculous waste of time and energy. If necessary, they can work with one or two competent people.

Confronters love board rooms and other places where they find themselves at the center of the action. Intelligent and aggressive negotiation enlivens them. Compromise, however, is another story. They view it as watering down the original plan. Confronters need to be convinced that any changes will strengthen the plan, not weaken it.

When other people present ideas to Confronters, they had better believe in their proposals enough to stand up for them forcefully. A presenter who lacks confidence or appears timid or unsure does not stand a chance of convincing these tough-minded hagglers. Confronters will interrupt, override, and generally ignore people who are hesitant or unsure of themselves or their product. In general, Confronters find it easy to say no and difficult to say yes, for saying yes yields their power to another. Furthermore, their no is often final – closing off the discussion and precluding any future mention of new ideas on the subject.

Another kind of person might say that it is only good manners to let everyone have their say. Confronters would say that it is bad manners to allow fools to continue to display their ignorance.

Leadership style. From the cradle to the grave, Confronters' "in charge" attitude will be their trademark. Thus, if leadership is not natural to them it is nonetheless inevitable. High-profile leaders and direct, blunt communicators, they expect bottom-line answers to their questions.

Their "hands on" management style is laden with extremes, both positive and negative. When the positive factors are uppermost, Confronters possess the potential greatness of a Gandhi. Cultivating the negative factors, however, could create someone with the destructive force of a Jim Jones.

They have learned well the power of words. Used positively, this command of language affirms, energizes, encourages, builds up, and rallies people to almost superhuman dedication and achievement. Used negatively, their words criticize, humiliate, intimidate, and generally undermine other people's self-confidence.

Confronters are unaware of the way their overbearing behavior affects others, and they usually pay a high price for this ignorance in lost relationships and lack of genuine cooperation. Arrogance is their greatest obstacle to becoming effective leaders. Because Confronters can be so intimidating that others feel the need to relate to them through an intermediary, they must be diligent in developing their skills in personal relationships. With the development of healthy, respectful relationships, they can help organizations grow and flourish under their leadership.

Living with family and friends. It is in the family situation that many of the Confronters' finer qualities often emerge. Here tenderness reigns with children, the elderly, and animals. Here their love of nature is revealed. Confronters have strong family ties and are fiercely protective of those in their care. Friends will also find them loyal to the end.

Active involvement. People who are close to Confronters will find them involved in their lives. Because of their great zest for life, Confronters and those around them may be constantly on the go. They enjoy group events like vacation trips and sporting events. They work hard for and take pride in their environment—home, neighborhood, and community.

These are the people who take care of the disadvantaged in the neighborhood or community. They can be found checking in on the person who lives alone, visiting the elderly couple who can't get around as easily as they used to, taking invalids to the store or to church. They enjoy using their tremendous energy to give practical assistance to others. Also, if a member of the community whom they admire is wrongly accused overtly or covertly, that person will have no more loyal defender than the Confronter.

Dedication to family. Confronters freely and generously give of themselves in any way that will benefit the entire family. However, they are just as vigilant not to give in to the whims of any one individual. Neither do they believe in giving anyone a free ride. Instead these strong people will encourage other family members to become strong themselves by taking personal responsibility and by facing life's difficulties squarely.

Confronters will enforce clear standards of justice among family members, even among the youngest of the children! People must own up to their actions and, if they are wrong, pay the consequences. Similarly, Confronters will not stand for anyone becoming the scapegoat and may take on the top authority in the family to make sure that justice prevails.

Insensitivity to feelings. Not sensitive to their own feelings, Confronters find introspection difficult. They do not understand the value of sensitivity, nurturing, or relatedness in self or others. Instead, they interpret sensitivity as weakness or indecisiveness and indicate their feelings clearly. Anyone on the receiving end can feel attacked—helpless, manipulated, and angry. However, if the targeted individual is able to stand up to the Confronter and, while avoiding personal attack, remain logical and objective, he or she will be pleasantly surprised. Confronters admire and respect people who stand up for themselves while keeping their personal feelings in check.

Confronters often project all positive sensitive or caring qualities on one woman—their dear old (or dead) mother, a remarkable woman in history, a movie star, or a world leader—and confer upon this one woman the title of "saint." Because no woman they know could meet the standards set by this saint, Confronters, whether male or female, feel justified in using, abusing, or dismissing the value of feminine qualities such as sensitivity, vulnerability, and nurturing qualities in themselves and others.

Expectations for fame and fortune. Although Confronters dedicate enormous energy to correcting injustice, they also expect to acquire love, fame, and possessions along the way. They are materialistic people who need concrete evidence that they have reached the pinnacle of power. It would be a great danger for them not to develop their spiritual side, for it is only the path of the spirit that will lead them through and beyond their tangled maze of egocentricity and dysfunctional motivation.

Difficulty admitting being a Confronter. Some people of this pattern may find it difficult to own and appreciate their Enneagram number because of the negative perceptions other people may have regarding strength, anger, and power. Church and society contribute to this difficulty when they overvalue conformity and passivity and undervalue the vigilance required to uphold the rights of the individual.

Positive qualities. Confronters, as they mature and move into the transformation process, develop many admirable qualities. They are resourceful people who stand up for others, especially the oppressed. In addition, they have the ability to teach others how to stand up for themselves. Often just being in the proximity of a healthy Confronter encourages others to grow in confidence and strength. People who have been beaten down by life feel secure and protected around them.

Confronters are quick to see when authority is used for self-serving purposes. Potentially spiritual powerhouses, they have no fear of being hurt or rejected in the cause of justice, nor do they count the cost when so dedicated. As long as their spiritual strength is focused outward and used in the service of others, they can accomplish tremendous good. With the development of consciousness and compassion, Confronters exhibit fair-mindedness, good judgment, organizational skills, and broad vision solidly grounded in spiritual values.

They will inevitably rise to the top of any organization, where growth and expansion will be their forte. These are people who thrive in political or military arenas in which they are both feared and respected. They are truthful and direct realists, passionate people who can become compassionate leaders. They are interesting people–exciting, blunt, earthy, shocking, and fun–people who see to it that life is not boring.

Remember: All the negative qualities of Confronters are but distortions of this pattern's strengths and positive qualities.

Nine: The Preservationist

I have so much to do that I'm going to bed.
—SAVOYARD PROVERB

Questions

1. Are you known as an easygoing, affable, common-sense kind of person even when inside you may be feeling very different?
2. Is there a place in your home that you find comfortable and relaxing and to which you generally gravitate to think, read, or relax?
3. Do arguments make you so uncomfortable that you avoid them, even to the point of walking out of the room when they begin?
4. Are you greatly attracted to outdoor activities, and do you find being in nature an almost sacred experience of freedom?
5. Do you feel that the best way to prevent trouble is to keep your thoughts to yourself and let the other person do the talking, even if you don't agree?
6. Do you see yourself as an independent person who can do what you need or want to do and not be swayed by group pressure?
7. Would you agree that in general people create most of their own difficulties because they take life too seriously and get all worked up over very minor things?
8. Do you enjoy thinking your way through puzzling questions, and do you often find practical answers to intricate problems?
9. When given the option, would you avoid sophisticated political or social gatherings, choosing instead the quieter, simpler pleasures of life?

Personal perspective. Preservationists repress their energy and power so that they can maintain a harmonious relationship between themselves and the world. Experiencing life as a threat to their desire to remain calm, they protect themselves by wearing a perpetually passive face that says, "I'm easy to get along with."

In many ways Preservationists live like fairy tale royalty who can insist that their magic kingdoms be completely serene. Their edict is explicit: "For all time, tension and conflict shall be banished from this land." Their reasoning for this decree is simple—because it is impossible to please everyone, why bother at all, for the struggle is not worth the effort. Through the sheer force of their personalities, they evoke obedience from their subjects, who will neither whisper nor hint of any unrest.

Preservationists feel caught in, and so they want to avoid, conflict. Their dysfunctional motivation results in a striving to feel peaceful. Their basic life issue is energy output, and their prime psychological addiction is sloth, or laziness, principally in the personal realm.

Orientation to the world. Preservationists are often professionally competent people who perceive the world in terms of conflict. Compulsive repression of their basic energy and spontaneity has denied them access to their natural strength and capacity to deal with life. Unaware of their durability, these giants of the Enneagram appear to be weak and defenseless. They spend their lives sidestepping issues, ignoring problems, and hiding from reality.

Detached view of life. Preservationists experience people as caring little about them personally and therefore having no hesitation about making too many demands on their time and energy. Their response is to dismiss most of these demands, and most of life, as unimportant. They prefer living as if things will work themselves out if given enough time and space.

Repressing their strength leaves them with a low level of energy. They therefore shun emotional expression or attachment. By assigning the same value to every experience, they are able to respond by adjusting their needs to whatever is available. Unfulfilled needs or desires are therefore not important enough to get upset about. They prize detachment, noninvolvement, resignation, and even apathy.

Passive strength. Preservationists deal with the conflict in any situation by ignoring it. They entertain the belief that nirvana can be achieved with a few minor adjustments.

They also emanate a sense of rootedness, even stubbornness, however, which is invested in preserving the status quo. With these qualities they control their environment more surely than they would by raising their voices in demands. Silently powerful and stubborn people, they will cling to old ways with an immovable tenacity.

Passive aggression. If crossed, or if more is demanded from them than they are willing to give, their passive strength deteriorates into passive-aggressive behavior that sends those around them scurrying for a safe haven. If the object of a Preservationist's repressed anger questions the intentions behind the biting words or actions, he or she is often met with either a look of total innocence or a protective wall of silence.

Practical common sense. Preservationists are frequently down-to-earth people whose ingenuity can well be applied to practical matters. Resourceful and creative individuals for whom common sense rules the day, they enjoy occupying their minds with the intricacies of practical problems and solutions. They also easily repress these gifts and sink into a morass of inactivity and ineffectuality.

Disregard for important issues. Preservationists have a magician's knack for making important issues vanish. With a laugh they can dispel darkness as gracefully as a sorcerer waving a magic wand. They are secretive and reserved people who, in their attempt to negate the value of life's problems and questions, negate their own personal sense of worth and importance as well.

Lack of self-esteem. Preservationists tend to dwell on the past, wallowing in what was or might have been and causing upheaval that places their emotions and common sense in conflict. Their inability to resolve this conflict creates a creeping inner paralysis or apathy that leaves them confused. Soon they have little awareness of themselves, and therefore come to believe that anything they think or do has little, if any, importance. This compulsive denial of importance prevents them from developing the true gifts of service with which they are endowed.

Rejection of their own personal value is their justification for sloth in the interior life and in personal relationships. They can also infect a group with their lack of self-regard, even to the point that the group will abandon any attempt to strive toward excellence.

Value of reputation. Just as Preservationists deny the importance of their personal life, they also overvalue the importance of their public life. Because they live with little self-esteem, the respect afforded by a good reputation is essential to their well-being.

Though they avoid their own problems, they enjoy being problem solvers, giving advice to people with whom they feel no personal connection. They dislike being the center of attention, preferring to enhance their reputations by developing the image of a humble servant, or that of the affable and friendly companion who never demands too much from life or from friends.

Relaxed life-style. Preservationists enjoy routine: they like seeing the same people and doing the same things. Planting themselves in one place provides them with some measure of the peace they seek. They also enjoy pursuing trivial pastimes like games, sports, crafts, and hobbies that make life interesting. Participation in these activities provides the essential outer stimulation needed to distract them from their inner paralysis.

Mask of contentment. Preservationists are proud people who wear a mask of contentment to hide a past about which they can do nothing and disguise a future for which they have little energy. The present moment contains their only hope of tranquillity, so they simply flow with the stream of life.

Time passes them by as they sit for hours simply being, enjoying nature or just being alone. They both need and resent schedules and deadlines, have difficulty setting priorities, and tend to procrastinate.

Decision-making style. Preservationists do not tend to be decision makers. Especially in their personal lives they do not think ahead and make decisions but rather do whatever pleases them at the moment. Not wanting to be responsible for the outcome of decisions, they evade the issues until others are forced to take a stand.

Preservationists do not directly give decision-making power to another; instead, they allow others to assume responsibility by default. If Preservationists don't agree with the decisions that others have made they rarely say so directly. Instead, they abide by the decision when necessary, do as they please whenever possible, and feel no compunction to support others' decisions because they have not participated in making them.

In general, however, Preservationists are quite content to cooperate with decisions made by others. They will follow these decisions as long as doing so preserves their inner tranquillity.

Leadership style. In the business world Preservationists tend to gravitate toward middle management. Often quite competent in the professional world, they will choose a relatively tension-free position rather than accept the pressures, conflict, and responsibility of top management. Middle management positions provide the challenge, respect, and security that Preservationists thrive on while still allowing them to maintain their inner calm.

Seeming indifference and lack of response are the greatest obstacles that both superiors and subordinates have to contend with in dealing with these affable people. They are so determined to avoid any possible discomfort that even if asked a direct question that threatens them, they can remain totally silent—as if the questioner did not exist.

Most people find themselves becoming uncomfortable with this prolonged silence and in their uneasiness will often begin to chatter away, answering their own question by putting words into the Preservationist's mouth. Finally they leave, feeling like fools. Thus do Preservationists successfully use the power of silence to maintain control and preserve the undisturbed environment they prefer. Their silence forces others to deal with problems and conflict.

In social or civic organizations Preservationists also avoid top leadership. However, they can respond with enthusiasm to the leadership of a committee or to being chairperson of an annual project—especially if its purpose is to help a disadvantaged group. This acceptance of a temporary position increases their feeling of importance and enhances their reputation.

In both business and the social realm, Preservationists are easy to get along with and are usually well liked. However, when there is tension or turmoil, they will retreat into their noncommittal fortress of silence and, if possible, physically leave the premises. Learning and utilizing the skills of honest, direct communication will be their most difficult and most profitable growing edge.

Living with family and friends. Preservationists show little enthusiasm in individual relationships, even important ones, but can be affable and friendly in a group. Therefore, friends may have a difficult time realizing they are important to Preservationists, and their associations may not endure the test of time.

Gentle giants. Generally Preservationists display a kindness that, combined with their natural quietness and tendency to be loners, easily summons trust from those around them. They often seem like gentle giants who, though big and strong, could never hurt a living thing and whose passive good nature could leave them defenseless even if unjustly attacked. Others may even feel a need to protect Preservationists, who have so well hidden their treasures of power and strength that they appear vulnerable and unprotected.

Denial of serious issues. Because they have repressed their strength and their feelings in an effort to avoid conflict, Preservationists have difficulty concentrating on weighty matters. Their attention span in an important conversation is deliberately low; for them, discussion of serious issues is disquieting. They often avert their eyes from one who is speaking to them or respond with a self-deprecating laugh. If an argument seems imminent—or actually begins—they avoid it simply by leaving the room, even though they have a natural ability to allow others to argue while they themselves remain peaceful.

Constant and unexacting approach. Preservationists insulate themselves emotionally, staying low-key and circumventing the emotional peaks and valleys common to others. Their choice of this path causes others to experience them as one-dimensional people. People refer to them in one generally constant way: as always happy or always sad; as boring, unemotional, resigned, passive, or apathetic; or as pleasant, nice, kind, carefree, or gentle. Whatever the description, they will be known as constant and undemanding of self and others.

Unawareness in relationships. Preservationists tend to be forgetful—missing appointments, getting in a car and not remembering their destination, or arriving and forgetting why they are there. They may forget any occasion that would require planning or effort.

Rarely feeling guilty in these situations, they justify their faults and mistakes by saying, "I forgot," or, "I'm sorry," truly thinking that these statements will always take care of the problem. This selfishness is their major block to expressing their natural universal love and kindness. Just as they forget others, they are surprised and pleased when they are remembered.

Indirect communication. Preservationists prefer to avoid any conversation that would force them to admit the presence of pain or conflict. Their style of confronting others is to ask a question, or to give the other a mean or "dirty" look that the Preservationist does not have to own and that the recipient is left to interpret. They also find occasions of leave-taking uncomfortable, for Preservationists lack the skills to express their feelings. Their denial of feelings, energy, and importance, along with their tendency to assign equal value to every person or situation, prevents them from either giving or receiving true forgiveness.

Positive qualities. Preservationists, as they mature and move into the process of transformation, develop many admirable qualities. Their selfless compassion and universal love allow them to tolerate the ideas, views, and prejudices of others. The years they have spent pondering the mysteries of life now produce the philosopher who is ever-grateful for opportunities to teach and inspire others. Through the years that they have been painfully tested in the fires of life, they develop the pure gold of universal love and service, which they freely give back to the world with benevolence and patience.

They are even-tempered, nonthreatening, modest, and kind. Being just but impersonal, they make natural arbiters. Having a deep interior strength and a healthy detachment that gives others permission to be upset, they work well with difficult people. Nature always beckons as a place of respite and soul strengthening for these imaginative and receptive people. In this nondemanding environment, Preservationists activate their spiritual potential and release their innate gifts for healing.

Having learned the power of silence and tranquillity, Preservationists naturally slow others down with their inner peace. They are people who accomplish much by doing little. Because they value harmony in a group, for them, peace is always achievable.

Remember: All the negative qualities of Preservationists are but distortions of this pattern's strengths and positive qualities.

Reflections in Still Water

Have you ever walked by a store that was advertising the latest home video camera by leaving it on and aimed at the street? It's a strange experience to be caught off guard and on camera. Most of us are both tantalized and embarrassed by such a glimpse of ourselves. "Have I put on that much weight?" "I didn't know my new hairdo looked that good!" "I need some new clothes." "Who was that striking figure I saw on the screen?"

Our introduction to the nine patterns of the Enneagram can evoke somewhat similar reactions. "Did I really see myself there?" "That's not such a bad kind of person to be." "Who would want to be like that?" "Who would want to be any other way?"

The Enneagram tantalizes because it describes human nature accurately. For the same reason it is also embarrassing. Truly, however, both reactions to it are unnecessary. Seen objectively, none of the nine patterns is good or bad, right or wrong. Rather, each is its own combination of strength and weakness, beauty and ugliness. Not only are each of the patterns mixtures, none of them invites judgment.

You cannot help being one of these patterns. That is the state of things. In truth, the Enneagram pattern that belongs to any individual has been both a wellspring of gift from which that person has drawn and a mire of dark motivation in which broken relationships and failures have found their origin.

No pattern is better or best, worse or worst. At times each of us may feel our pattern is the best; at other times, the worst. At one moment we are in touch with a strength; at the next, a weakness.

Rather than attempt to balance ourselves on such a teeter-totter of ambivalence toward self, the Enneagram calls us to a simpler task— simpler but more difficult. That task is acceptance, the ability to say, "That's right. That's me. That is how I often respond and react. That is my motivation for many of my thoughts, feelings, and reactions." In such nonjudgmental acceptance comes many gifts.

One is the gift of freedom. You can be yourself if you accept knowledge of self—not running from yourself, not condemning yourself, not justifying yourself, simply receiving yourself as gift.

Another is the gift of forgiveness for others. With awareness that all of us live with these internal contradictions, compassion becomes easier, letting go of grievances more natural. Receiving whatever another can give becomes a gift in itself.

Another is the gift of love. All of us are searching for love, and most of us become cynical about finding it, or at least we compromise our ideals in order to live in the real world. Hidden in the descriptions of the nine patterns are the secrets to receiving the love that others so ineptly give and to honoring our own clumsy attempts to care sincerely.

All people are puzzles one to another; at times it seems as if even our closest family and friends are speaking a different language and have come from a foreign country. The truth is, all of us carry within ourselves a secret that even we do not understand. The Enneagram begins to reveal that secret, and with it the secret to communication, success, and creativity. By coming to know these sacred secrets, we come to understand the work we need to do to unleash the power of our real selves and unlock the prisons in which others keep their secrets hidden.

The ugly duckling went into hiding because he was convinced he had no beauty or charm, that he was too repulsive ever to be accepted, let alone loved. No matter how hard he tried, he couldn't find a place where he fit in, where he was acceptable. Only by accidentally looking in the pond one day did he discover in his own reflection the grace and elegance of a swan.

Similarly, we too can see our true beauty only by looking into the still waters within. Knowledge of your Enneagram pattern is the beginning of freedom from the cycle of death and the beginning of a new life that is open to freedom and creativity.

Beyond Survival

The Three Centers

CHAPTER TWO

A tremendous spiritual power is slumbering in the depths of our multitude which will manifest itself only when we have learnt to break down the barriers of our egoisms and, by a fundamental recasting of our outlook, raise ourselves up to the habitual and practical vision of universal realities.
—PIERRE TEILHARD DE CHARDIN

The comedian Danny Thomas used to tell a story of a man who emigrated from the old country to New York City. Because he did not know English, he relied on his friends to teach him. He found a warehouse job easily enough and from his friends learned the few words he needed to get by each day. Lunchtimes were another matter, however. Because he did not know how to order, he went hungry.

Finally he asked his friends for help.

"What do you want to eat for lunch tomorrow?" they asked.

"Apple pie and coffee," he responded in his native tongue.

So his friends taught him how to say "apple pie and coffee" in English, and he practiced all night and the next morning. Lunchtime came, and he went to the local cafe and sat down at a booth.

"Waddaya want?" the waitress asked.

Slowly and distinctly, the man said, "Apple pie and coffee." And quick as a flash it came. He was pleased.

For the rest of that week at lunchtime he went to the same cafe, said, "Apple pie and coffee," and got what he wanted, though the words meant no more to him than gibberish.

But after a while he became tired of apple pie and coffee for lunch and went to his friends again. "What do you want to eat instead?" they asked.

"How about a ham sandwich?" he replied. So they taught him how to say "ham sandwich," and he practiced all day and the next morning.

Happily he went to the cafe. "Waddaya want today?" the waitress asked.

"Ham sandwich," he said as distinctly as ever.

"Rye or white?" the waitress replied.

"Apple pie and coffee," the man blurted back.

Sometimes learning something new can be more difficult than it seems at first. If we are going to grow and change, however, the difficulty of learning new things is inevitable.

This chapter presents a new paradigm for human nature. It explains and amplifies the understanding of the nine patterns that chapter 1 presented. If you are beginning to wonder if the Enneagram is becoming too complicated for you, don't worry. It's not. But it will explain to you more than you ever thought you could know about yourself and other people.

A New Paradigm

Within each of us exists three centers of intelligence, each with its own *true purposes* and its own *functions*. The *true purpose* of these centers is wholeness, completeness, objective psychological consciousness, and spiritual awareness. Each center's *functions* describe the lower or common ways that we use the intelligence of each center.

Because we live most (or all) of our lives with merely a functionary use of our three intelligences, rarely do we wake up to reality, grow into maturity, become conscious, or develop our spiritual nature. We live and die and rarely make a difference to anyone, especially to ourselves.

It is thus important for us to take a close look at the centers of intelligence, their true purposes, and their functions. These centers are the Affective Center, the Theoretical Center, and the Effective Center.

The true purpose of the Affective Center's intelligence is to bring about connectedness, relating us in healthy ways with other people, the universe, and God. The true purpose of the Theoretical Center's intelligence is to develop vision and creative awareness, giving us clear sight regarding the meaning of life. The true purpose of the Effective Center's intelligence is to generate movement, to help us harness the inner power of effort and energy needed to act upon the vision and connectedness that the other two centers provide.

Until we wake up and begin to work at becoming conscious of ourselves and our hidden, self-serving motives, we will continue to live in the illusion that we are just fine and it is other people who create problems. Thus we will not use these three centers for their true purposes but simply operate on the level of mechanical functions.

On the functional level, we use the Affective Center to manipulate a small world of feeling, emotions, and relationships. We use the Theoretical Center for thinking, calculating, and deciding within our own worlds. We use the Effective Center to preserve our safety and to focus on our own instinctual reactions and being. In other words, we simply use our intelligences to get by—to function in a mechanical way.

At first the notion of three centers or kinds of intelligence may seem new. In general, the Western world has identified the word *intelligence* with mind, thought, and logic. Emotion is considered another component of the interior part of each person, but it is often deemed to be more irrational than intelligent.

The aspect of effectiveness or instinct in the West is often not even considered intelligence.[1]

From one angle then, the notion of three centers of intelligence is an entirely new way of understanding human nature—one that, like the Enneagram, comes from an Eastern perspective. Yet we find remnants of it in the West when, for example, the phrase "thoughts, feelings, and actions" is used to describe a person. It is common to analyze human personality in terms of what people feel, what they think, and what they say and do.

The notion of three kinds of intelligence, therefore, is old and pervasive in many societies and traditions. For example, the Bible speaks of the human being in terms of soul, spirit, and body, reminiscent of the true purpose of the Affective, Theoretical, and Effective Centers.

True Purpose and Destiny

In the study of the Enneagram it is important to be aware of the true purposes of the intelligence of each center, for together they contain that destiny from which we detour ourselves in our search for self-love.

The Affective Center, when it is used in a healthy and life-giving way, is symbolized by the ear, through which we receive personal knowledge of another, and the inner ear, which hears the deep movements of the human soul. This is the center of understanding and spiritual intuition. It is the center of desire. Its mastery is process—understanding the stages of human development that lead to maturity and wholeness. It is the receptive home of Divine Love.

The Theoretical Center, when used in a constructive and healthy way, is given symbolic expressions by the eye, through which knowledge and information about things outside ourselves are received, and the inner eye, which sees deeply into self as well as into the true nature of reality. This is the center of idea and mystical unveiling. It is the center of objectivity. Its mastery is consciousness—objective awareness of self and the universe. It is the receptive home of Divine Light.

The Effective Center, when given healthy expression, leads us to complete the work of being a person in the world. Thus its symbol is the mouth, through which we state goals and effect change, and the inner voice, which creates motivation for expenditure of energy. This is the center of expression and direct perception. It is the center of freedom. Its mastery is creativity—the ability to make actual, to produce. It is the receptive home of Divine Life.

Because everyone is created with all three centers of intelligence in balance, it would seen only natural to use all these available resources to live life in the best way possible. In fact, there is no question that a balanced use of the centers would be ideal.

---

1. Maurice Nicoll, in his *Psychological Commentaries on the Teaching of Gurdjieff and Ouspensky,* 5 vols. (London: Shambhala, 1984), teaches about four centers—Emotional, Intellectual, Moving, and Instinctive (see vol. 1, esp. pp. 68–87). It is said that Gurdjieff sometimes taught of three centers, sometimes four, and at other times seven, dividing the Emotional Center into Higher Emotional and Emotional, dividing the Intellectual Center into Higher Intellectual and Intellectual, and dividing the Instinctual into Moving, Sex, and Instinctual.

According to the Enneagram, however, the formation of personality begins in the *unbalanced* way these three centers relate within each of us and with a preference we each develop for using one center more than the others as well as for accomplishing the purposes for which the others were intended. This imbalance causes the centers to be used only on the functional level and not for their true purposes.

The imbalance causes us to lose awareness of the true purpose and destiny for our lives. No longer free to give expression to a true self, we must create a false self as a way to survive in the world.

Gurdjieff, the great teacher of the Enneagram, taught that every person is created with an essence. This essence is not a *tabula rasa*, a clean slate, but rather a true identity, imprinted with proclivities and inclinations but also containing blank spaces. These empty places are filled in through the maturation process if the essence is allowed to develop and is not squelched or extinguished.

However, during the maturation process, every one of us falls asleep, psychologically and spiritually speaking, and spends life in a sleepwalking state. This inner dullness is what most people call normal consciousness, and thus it is dangerous. If we are to understand how and why we fall asleep, we must return to childhood—the "scene of the crime"!

The origin of the sleepwalking state of many adults lies in the process of childhood socialization. Little children act with honesty and sincerity, truly reflecting what is inside them. However, as we grow we must engage with the world, and we find that our essence can no longer be given free expression but must be repressed for the sake of survival. Thus does our personality begin to form. Personality is the result of experiences, relationships, and education and therefore is able to interact on the worldly level. As children, we learn to adjust and restrain our true inner selves to accommodate to the world around us.

This is the "crime" that is committed—the murder of the psyche, mostly by others but also in part by ourselves! Because as children we are expected to be different, are not acceptable as we are, we put to sleep the truth of self in an attempt to conform. Soon we cooperate willingly, for we gain rewards for our efforts. More and more we see reality not in our own true selves, which are creative, positive, and free, but in that lesser self that finds acceptable ways to respond to those our existence depends on.

Dependency on adults during the prolonged childhood of human beings increases the destructive effect of these accommodations upon the essence, the true self. It is not that the essence is of itself all good and pure; no, it too must develop and mature. However, instead of maturing the essence, the process of rearing a child leads to the child's ignoring the essence and in its place developing an outer core of personality, and then of false personality.

As the inescapable result of this process, we acquire habits, traits, likes and dislikes, prejudices, preferences, beliefs, images of self both false and true, desires, and felt needs—all of which reflect more our environment as children than our essence, or true nature. Life is encased in a shell of unreality and falsehood. From the time of conception through the early years of childhood, we each undergo a slow murder of the psyche.

In many ways it is the "perfect crime," not only because the victim cooperates in his or her own demise and so confuses responsibility for the deed, but also because it all looks so normal. The sun rises and sets; everything looks fine; there is no blood, no corpse. Because all the evidence is secret, hidden in the psyche, the crime goes undetected. The whole affair is so typical that to suggest that it should be otherwise is, for the most part, unthinkable.[2]

Preferring One Center

In the language of the Enneagram, the process of developing a personality begins with learning to prefer one center over the other two. We feel imbalance at first as an asset, because it gives ready form to our individuality and free expression as children.

The center that we use more than the other two is called the Preferred Center. As children, we rapidly learn to use this center in the inappropriate ways mentioned above. Comfortable with the advantages we erroneously believe this center provides, we overuse it in sweeping, inappropriate ways. We also overuse a second center, but to a lesser degree. The third center is ignored and rejected as unimportant.

This broad range from overuse to underuse of our three centers of intelligence distorts our ability to perceive or understand ourselves, others, and life in general.

The Secondary Center, which we also overuse, supports the Preferred Center, augmenting the range of activities at which we are competent. Being somewhat comfortable with the functions of this center, we use these strengths to expand and give substance to our personalities.

The greatest difficulty comes with the Third Center. Because we prefer primarily using the functions of one center and using those of another to assist it, the Third Center remains undeveloped and is underused. Having largely rejected the use of this center, we live unbalanced lives.

Attempting to live without the third center of intelligence is like trying to balance ourselves on two legs of a three-legged stool. Although developing the Third Center is difficult, we need what this center provides if we are to become balanced, whole.

The Third Center remains relatively dormant and operates on an unconscious plane, causing its functions to remain mysterious to us. When we come across someone whose Preferred Center is our own dormant center, that person can become an object of fear, disdain, or even aggression, on the one hand; attraction or desire, on the other. In projecting a part of ourselves on another, we either automatically reject the thoughts, feelings, and behavior of the other as irrational and inappropriate or we are beguiled by them. This dynamic explains many negative relationships in people's lives, as well as romantic attractions.

The diagram entitled "The Centers" shows the nine patterns of the Enneagram divided according to their Preferred Centers. Note that numbers Two, Three, and Four prefer the Center of Affect, whose mechanical domain is feeling, emotions, and relationships. Numbers Five, Six, and Seven prefer the Center of Theory, which produces predictable patterns of thinking, calculating, and deciding. Numbers Eight, Nine, and One prefer the Center of Effect, whose egocentric

---

2. Kathleen Riordan Speeth, *The Gurdjieff Work* (New York: Pocket Books, 1976), pp. 80–83.

THE CENTERS

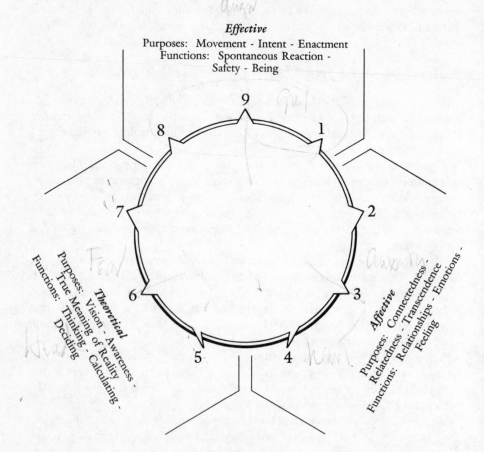

Effective
Purposes: Movement - Intent - Enactment
Functions: Spontaneous Reaction -
Safety - Being

8   9   1

7   2

Theoretical
Purposes: Vision - Awareness -
True Meaning of Reality
Functions: Thinking - Calculating -
Deciding

6   3

Affective
Purposes: Connectedness -
Relatedness - Transcendence -
Functions: Relationships - Emotions -
Feeling

5   4

The idea that those to the extreme right and left of each center have something in common with each other comes from lectures by O'Leary and Beesing (January 1986 in Denver, Colorado); the specific descriptions of that commonness are original to Theodore E. Dobson and Kathleen V. Hurley, as are the descriptions of the centers. Copyright ©1990 Theodore E. Dobson and Kathleen V. Hurley.

concern is being, safety, and instinctual reaction—spontaneous response that is independent of judgment or will.

Although all of us prefer one center and are both familiar and comfortable with its *functions,* we remain blind to its *true purposes.* Discovering the true purposes of the intelligence of each center demands increased consciousness; each center's functions are mechanical responses to life that continue to create egocentricity. The functions are seen as good by our sleeping selves simply because we are familiar with them. Waking up and realizing that living at the level of egocentric functions is inadequate is the shock we need to begin to grow in our humanity.

Before this work of consciousness can begin, however, we must become familiar with the various disguises worn by each center. Any astute sleuth realizes that a critical, unbiased examination of the evidence is the only lens through which to see that what appears to be reality may in truth be only an illusion. With this thought in mind, we can now begin to describe the general characteristics of people who prefer and therefore inflate each center.

People Who Prefer the Affective Center

People who prefer the Affective Center (the Two, the Three, and the Four) are concerned with feeling, emotion, and relationship. For them, the most important goal in life is understanding other people.

The Affective is the center of personal activity, and those who prefer it and overuse it believe that only interaction with people can allow a person— themselves or others—to feel worthwhile and alive. They pride themselves on their awareness of and ability to respond to people and their needs. They are relationally oriented people.

Affect-centered people appear to need others. Their need, however, is more for having others around them so that they can engage in personal interaction than it is needing to lean on others. Their other-centered behavior, therefore, is often rooted in their desire and need to have others perceive them in a positive way. They also want and need others to affirm them, and they define this as a meeting of hearts.

People who prefer the Affective Center analyze situations in human terms. When they are faced with a dilemma, they attempt to resolve it by being sensitive to the feelings of all the people involved and by analyzing motivations to gain understanding. Meanwhile, they ignore many of the objective facts, as well as issues of security and safety. They believe that analysis of situations at the human level is the only important kind of thinking that needs to be done, but they are rarely methodical in their analysis.

Instead, they are adept at instantaneously becoming aware of all the parts of a person and/or a personal situation and then simply "knowing" how they need to respond. If they were asked to explain how they came to their conclusions, either they would not be able to answer the question, or they would answer it in a long and complicated way, with a rationale more personal and emotional than logical.

These people can become extremely serious about life, human relationships, and human values. Because their entire perception of themselves arises from this aspect of life, they devote great time and energy to nurturing personal relationships. When their emotions come forth in a lighter vein, they are revealed to be sentimentalists and lovers of excitement, pageantry, and anything spectacular, for all of these feed their emotions.

People who prefer and overuse the Affective Center have a typical way of entering a situation. Consciously or unconsciously they focus on the people in the situation, but their concerns have more to do with their image than with the reality of the situation they face. Beneath their conversation and actions will be a desire to convey to others the appropriate outer appearance of themselves. They are motivated by an underlying anxiety about whether they are liked by the people they are with, whether they in turn like these people, how others are responding to them, and what others need from them. Wanting to be with the "right" people, whatever that term may mean to them in a particular situation, gives them added motivation and drive.

However, when all their powers of human analysis do not work—when they analyze a person or situation as well as they can and they still cannot deal with that person or situation comfortably—they pull away emotionally in self-protection. Such aloofness is painful and dangerous for them because of their need to respond to others and to be responded to in return. Yet to them, loneliness is preferable to learning a new way of approaching the person or situation.

Unconsciously then, affect-centered people are manipulators. They are hyper-aware on the feeling level, but they use their information for themselves, especially to manipulate people into liking them, responding to them, and/or focusing on them. Like any accomplished manipulators, they can be quite subtle in their tactics, so that usually other people, and even they themselves, are unaware of the motives behind all they say and do. They are deeply feeling people who use feelings for their own purposes.

People who prefer the Affective Center have a lifelong struggle with an underlying sense of being unlovable.

People Who Prefer the Theoretical Center

People who prefer the Center of Theory (the Five, the Six, and the Seven) are concerned with thinking, calculating, and deliberating. For them, the most important aspect of life is trying to get what they call the objective view. The Theoretical is the center of impersonal activity.

People who prefer and overuse this center believe that information and objectivity make any person, themselves or others, a valuable and worthwhile individual. They pride themselves on the breadth and depth of their knowledge. They are factually oriented people.

They need to see things in context; thus they often exude a sense of being distant from a situation, perched high above, trying to comprehend the situation from afar before becoming involved or commenting. When theory-centered people relate with others, it is often through an intellectual identification, through ideas devoid of emotional involvement; that is, they understand another person's experience in the abstract but remain unaware of the emotional pain involved. Relating in this way allows them to maintain a sense of objectivity by seeing the context of the situation. They perceive emotional involvement or spontaneous response as jeopardizing their pure objectivity.

Theory-centered people trust only abstract knowledge as authentic and untainted. They are the least personal of all the patterns because they approach life from a hypothetical and ideal perspective rather than a practical or relational one. Theory-centered people are attracted to abstract learning processes—for example, books, courses, and lectures. They learn principles and methods through these sources as opposed to learning practical matters through experience and involvement in human situations.

These people feel most secure when they can see the connections among different aspects of the object of their study or perception. They do not consider that they have understood a subject until they have recognized systematic relationships and underlying principles or found a logical, unvarying uniformity in the thought or events in question. Theory-centered people find a sense of meaning in systemization. When operating in a lighter vein, they are aware of the absurdity of life and the illogic of human behavior, which creates a distinctive approach to humor.

An enduring quality of people who prefer the Theoretical Center is their deep-seated unwillingness to accept information from the other two centers. More than people who prefer the Affective and Effective Centers, theory-centered people are stubborn about relying exclusively on the functions of their center—thinking, calculating, deliberating. They will relentlessly cling to their own perceptions, thoughts, and plans even when it is obvious to others that these do not match reality.

Their typical way of entering a situation is to stand back from it, reflect, and act with deliberation. They want to know the rules and do not refer to people, feelings, or other exterior realities but instead speculate on systems, general principles, and methods. These provide the structure that protects them from the human involvement that they fear will diminish their objectivity. When they approach a situation, they do so with an unconscious desire to extract from it all the nonpersonal data, which will provide them with the pure insight needed to evaluate and substantiate their perceptions.

When all their efforts at comprehending a situation objectively fail, however—when their intellectual structure fails to help them understand and deal with a person or a situation—they become even more stubbornly attached to their abstract point of view. The sense of disconnectedness that results is often painful and disorienting to them, but it feels better than entering the vague world of feelings and emotions or instinctual reactions.

Consciously or unconsciously then, theory-centered people feel superior to others. Their very stance in a situation—perched above it to see the entire context—supports this illusion. They feel that their objective and disinterested viewpoint gives them an edge on others in dealing with reality. They often hide their superior attitude under a cover of friendliness or false humility. They use their need to follow a deliberate, well-planned course of action and their inability to deal with emotional or gut reactions as protection from becoming involved in the world.

People who prefer the Theoretical Center have a lifelong struggle with an underlying sense of being incapable.

People Who Prefer the Effective Center

People who prefer the Center of Effect (the Eight, the Nine, and the One) are concerned with safety, instinctual reactions, and being. For them, the most important aspect of life is making others deal with them. The Effective Center is the center of physical energy and movement and of sexual energy; people who use this center primarily think that having power and influence in a situation is essential.

They believe that power and influence make any person, themselves or others, worthwhile and alive. Because their concern focuses on their security, survival, and energy, they pride themselves on the ability to stand firm in a situation and take control of it. They are instinctually oriented people.

People who prefer and inflate this center make demands on themselves as well as on others. They are exacting of life and of themselves, and this attitude creates more standards for them regarding how they *should* act and who they *should* be than people of any other center experience. Consequently, they easily ignore the importance of relationships and feelings, as well as the importance of being objective and deliberating. Their demands and expectations arise from an awareness of their own energy, their ability to control, and their ability to make an impact upon the world. When they take control they may be obvious about it, but as often as not they do so behind the scenes, or in a passive-aggressive manner.

They appear secure, emanating a sense of rootedness and therefore of being unable, unwilling, or unconscious of the need to move. Beneath this stoic outward appearance lie insecurity and a disquieting sense of unknown threat. Needing to know how they are measuring up to the demands of life causes them constantly to compare themselves with others, consciously and unconsciously, and to ascertain their relative power or authority in a situation. Once this assessment is made, their confidence and security are restored.

Effect-centered people are instinctual. Their knowing comes from the depth of their being, and they often seem unshakable once they have made up their minds. In this way they continue to exert power and influence—important words for people who prefer this center. By overinvesting in their instinctual reactions they wield such authority that others can easily be intimidated by them and therefore fear confronting or contradicting them.

By overusing their instinctual energy, spontaneous reaction becomes a way of life—a way that may suddenly surprise and overpower others. But when their spontaneity comes forth in a lighter vein, they can generate life in any gathering, creating excitement and play for themselves and others.

People who prefer the Center of Effect enter a situation with conscious and unconscious attitudes concerning their own safety and strength relative to others. Because their reputation is important to them, who is right and who is wrong in any situation are significant questions. In a conflict they want to be on the side of right, because only being right will guarantee them a platform from which they can broaden their sphere of influence. Their past performance gives them the right to demand and use power and influence in the next situation.

However, when all their attempts to gain power and control fail because they are not measuring up to their own expectations within a personal relationship or situation, they slide into deep insecurity. This insecurity may be expressed out-

wardly in anger toward others or inwardly in self-criticism an
other hand, when they believe that they are right, they refuse
chosen response. They will "cut off their nose to spite their f
cumb to what they view as weakness. As painful as all th
effect-centered people stubbornly wallow in them rather tha
to a different way of approaching people, situations, or life

Unconsciously, then, people who prefer the Effective Cei
tile toward everything, including themselves. They are rarely
the way they are, wanting them rearranged, changed, improveu. They see life in
terms of win and lose, right and wrong, good and bad, and they use their energy
for their own protection. They have a difficult time accepting the world as it is.

People in the Effective Center have a lifelong struggle with an underlying sense
of being unimportant.

The Balance Points

A special word needs to be said about three patterns: the Three, the Six, and
the Nine. These numbers are called the Balance Points, and they have a special
place in the Enneagram.[3] Because each of them is in the middle or the heart of
its center, it can be said that these patterns show in an especially intense way the
inner contradiction that is created by preferring and thus overusing one center.

These three patterns reject the appropriate use of their Preferred Center
because they tend to idealize harmony between what is happening inside and
outside themselves. They repress their center's energy, living with the illusion
that what is most important in life is being all things to all people. The path they
choose toward that goal is denying the strength of the functions of their Preferred
Center. Called Balance Points because their goal is to keep everything in balance
in their lives, these patterns never overtly go too far one way or the other in their
reactions.

Threes, or Succeeders (in the Affect Center), repress their sensitivity to feelings
and needs in self and others, using their sensitivity to people to create an aura of
accomplishment, self-assurance, and competence in life. Threes carefully balance
all reactions so as not to betray personal thoughts or preferences if doing so will
disturb others or harm their own chances to move ahead in the world.

Sixes, or Guardians (in the Theory Center), repress their ability to calculate
and decide, relying on others, especially authority figures or institutions, to give
guidelines and make rules for life. Sixes use their familiarity with abstract thinking
to see everything in the context of their group, carefully balancing all their reactions for the sake of the welfare of that group.

Nines, or Preservationists (in the Effect Center), repress their energy, especially in the personal realm, passively using their steadfastness of energy and presence on trivial matters. Nines carefully balance all reactions in life to ignore
tension or difficulties and instead use their energy to create an atmosphere of
peace and serenity.

---

3. In their book *The Enneagram*, O'Leary, Beesing, and Nogosek call these the Denial Points
(pp. 146–55).

thing Spiritual Power

Like a steady diet of apple pie and coffee, preferring one center of intelligence over the others will never provide the fulfillment and satisfaction that people seek. Everyone is impoverished by one-sidedness. Only the balanced use of all three centers of intelligence can yield the healthy nourishment needed to search for one's true destiny amid the glory and the rubble of one's present life.

Balance, however, can be achieved only through the hard work of becoming conscious, for in our limited ability to grasp or understand truth, we are not united within but divided. The struggle to become conscious, though often frightening at first, is a spiritual quest that will bring light into darkness and give meaning to life.

No one understood this struggle better than the psychologist Carl Jung, who said, "At first we cannot see beyond the path that leads downward to dark and hateful things—but no light or beauty will ever come from [one] who cannot bear this sight. Light is always born of darkness, and the sun never yet stood still in heaven to satisfy [a person's] longing or to still [a person's] fears."[4]

Regarding what he called "the miracle of reflecting consciousness" and the search to find meaning in life, Jung said, "The importance of consciousness is so great that one cannot help suspecting the element of *meaning* to be concealed somewhere within all the monstrous, apparently senseless biological turmoil, and that the road to its manifestation was ultimately found on the level of warm blooded vertebrates possessed of a differentiated brain—found as if by chance, unintended and unforeseen, and yet somehow sensed, felt and groped for out of some dark urge."[5]

In the wisdom of the Enneagram, simply gaining the knowledge of how our Third Center, our unfamiliar center of intelligence, operates is an exercise in futility if we don't apply this knowledge in our own lives. It would be like memorizing "ham sandwich" and reverting to "apple pie and coffee" when life presents an obstacle.

Three centers of intelligence all exist within each of us. Because two are overused and one is underused, none of them is doing its right work. That is why there is "a tremendous spiritual power slumbering in the depths" waiting to be awakened—waiting to become conscious.

4. C. G. Jung, *Modern Man in Search of a Soul* (New York: Harcourt, Brace & World, 1933), p. 215.
5. C. G. Jung, *Memories, Dreams, Reflections* (New York: Random House, 1965), p. 339.

Through the Magnifying Glass

A Closer Look at the Nine Patterns

CHAPTER THREE

Clad in this "self," the creation of irresponsible and ignorant persons, meaningless honors and catalogued acts—strapped into the straight jacket of the immediate.

To step out of all this, and stand naked on the precipice invulnerable, free: in the Light, with the Light, of the Light. Whole, *real in the Whole.*

Out of myself as a stumbling block, into myself as fulfillment.

—DAG HAMMARSKJÖLD

R ecent years have given rise to a national phenomenon that is quickly reaching the lofty position of a national pastime. The private lives of everyone in the public eye—politicians, sports figures, movie stars, religious leaders—are being meticulously scrutinized through the powerful magnifying glass of television. We have a front-row seat in our own living rooms.

News commentators and others have tried to find the good in these almost daily disclosures by speculating that the threat of public exposure might scare other potential public figures into cleaning up their acts. It would be lovely if somehow the national revelation of private addictions would help develop a healthy national conscience. Probably more accurate, though unlovely, is the reality that public figures will be forced to be more discreet about their indiscretions.

As Terry Kellogg has noted, *"The most common recovery for addiction in our culture is addiction.* We jump around from one to another, preferably finding an addiction that won't piss people off so much."[1]

Developing consciousness and conscience is the task of the individual. Until we begin to take that task seriously, unconscious motivations will continue to drive our lives, with the inevitable consequence of dysfunctional behavior and addiction. The lovely thought that exposing the foibles of public people might somehow give rise to a national conscience is simply another form of illusion—magical thinking by sleeping people.

A healthy national conscience will evolve only to the degree that, collectively, more of us do the personal inner work of growth and healing than, collectively, there are people clinging to the destructive forces of unconscious living. The place to begin using the magnifying glass is not on others but rather within our own lives.

---

1. Terry Lee Kellogg, *Broken Toys Broken Dreams* (Amherst, MA: BRAT Publishing, 1990), p. 16.

Getting Life in Focus

The Enneagram offers several enlightening tools to assist us in understanding our lives, tools that come to us in the form of categories of unconscious motivation. It is by understanding these categories and how they apply to each number or pattern described by the Enneagram that we come to understand the underlying structure of our unconscious minds.

Each number or pattern has three categories associated with it—a preferred center, a way of relating to life, and an approach to problem solving. No two numbers have the same combination of categories; the specific addiction of each number arises from the unique way it combines qualities from these categories.

Chapter 2 discussed centers of intelligence; in this chapter we focus on the ways people relate to life and the way they overcome life's obstacles. In the Enneagram there are three different ways to relate to life: the way of *subjugation* by meeting life head on, the way of *mediation* by negotiating with life, or the way of *reduction* by reacting to life. There are also three different ways to approach life's problems: by seeking expansive solutions in an *aggressive* way, by seeking temperate solutions in a *dependent* way, and by seeking enlightened solutions in a *withdrawing* way.[2] The diagram "Relation to Life and Approach to Problem Solving" summarizes this information for all the nine numbers of the Enneagram.

All of these attitudes are automatic, mechanical, and for the most part consistent. Thus they serve to keep us asleep, unconscious of our true selves. They create comfort zones of illusion that we call reality. Their illusory nature is especially clear in their consistency: in no life, for example, is an aggressive stance always appropriate, yet the people who take this approach do so consistently because they are blind to reality.

We develop these habits as a way to survive, as a way to cope with life and the demands people make upon us. Ideally, we would learn how to respond appropriately to every individual and situation. However, doing so would call for consciousness, awareness, and maturity—qualities not available to us in the early stages of normal human development. By responding automatically and mechanically, we lose the wonder of choice and the excitement of discovery, and in this way we fall asleep.

Consciousness is the only antidote that has the power to liberate us from the grip of these attitudes. The choice to examine our motives, thoughts, feelings, actions, and reactions—no matter how difficult, how painful it may be to do so, especially at the beginning—is the birth of the psyche into awareness.

Relating to Life

The three ways of relating to life in the Enneagram system are the way of subjugation, the way of mediation, and the way of reduction.

---

2. In *Personality Types* (Boston: Houghton Mifflin, 1987) Don Richard Riso says that these latter three categories have been adapted from the clinical observations of Karen Horney; her original terminology referred to those who take an expansive solution (aggressive patterns), those who take a self-effacing solution (dependent patterns), and those who take a resigning solution (withdrawing patterns). Riso does not clearly indicate if it is known who first saw the application of Horney's ideas to the Enneagram (pp. 7, and 321–25). O'Leary, Beesing, and Nogosek use these categories but do not indicate their origin (*The Enneagram*, pp. 105–10).

RELATION TO LIFE AND APPROACH TO PROBLEM SOLVING

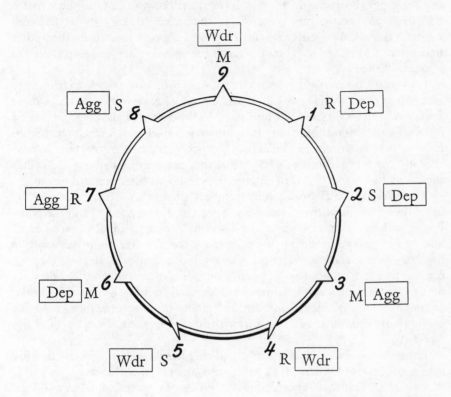

Relation to Life

S — Way of Subjugation

M — Way of Mediation

R — Way of Reduction

Approach to Problem Solving

Agg Aggressive

Dep Dependent

Wdr Withdrawing

The groupings of numbers on this diagram (2, 5, 8; 3, 6, 9; 4, 7, 1 and 3, 7, 8; 1, 2, 6; 4, 5, 9) are proposed by other teachers of the Enneagram. This explanation of those groupings is original to Theodore E. Dobson and Kathleen V. Hurley. Copyright © 1990 Theodore E. Dobson and Kathleen V. Hurley.

The Way of Subjugation. Three numbers attempt to subjugate life with the strengths available to them through their Preferred Center: the Two, the Five, and the Eight. People with this view look out at the world and see little that is unmanageable because they sense within themselves the capacity to deal with whatever the world presents to them. The world does not overwhelm them; they find a way to manage it. This attitude is the illusion they use to protect the interests of their egos.

Because the outer world poses no threat, such people display a kind of security that allows them to act in a self-possessed way. This very attitude keeps them from seeing the reality of their humanity and therefore of allowing the process of transformation to begin. They live with an inner sense that whatever they do is right, and this attitude reinforces the ego at the expense of the true self. Because they feel comfortable in the certainty that they can handle anything that comes their way, they see no need to enter into the hard work of personal growth.

The Way of Mediation. Three numbers attempt to mediate with life by using the strengths of their Preferred Center: the Three, the Six, and the Nine. People with this view look out at the world and, seeing themselves on an equal footing with it, are confident that they can make whatever minor adjustments that may be necessary to come up with the proper response. Because they are constantly aware of what is happening outside themselves, they decide their next move on the basis of what has just happened, or what is happening in the present moment. By negotiating with everything and everyone, they keep their equilibrium or balance, for they invest their egos in their ability to hold the world at bay.

Their illusion is that by constantly adjusting their stance in response to what is happening outside them, they will find contentment and meaning in life. If they admitted that they do indeed have a Preferred Center and began to use its functions properly, they could not always negotiate but would be forced to take a stand. However, because their ego investment is in keeping a balance between themselves and the world, they reject their truest abilities—those of their Preferred Center—and in so doing they deny their uniqueness and individuality. Instead, they become what others need or want them to be. Feeling comfortable this way, these people push down the deepest questions of life, thereby postponing the process of transformation and personal growth.

The Way of Reduction. Three numbers attempt to reduce the issues of life to a manageable size by using the strengths of their Preferred Center: the One, the Four, and the Seven. People with this view look out at the world and see a big and somewhat overwhelming reality. Sensing that their ego interests will be threatened in the world, they are wary. Though they are certain they cannot manage the big world, they are also confident they can manage their own little world. Therefore they carve the world down to lilliputian size so as to deal with it in a way that protects the interests of their egos.

As a result, these people abdicate responsibility for control and fulfillment of their lives to people and situations outside themselves. Because they believe they are not in charge of their lives, their own personal growth could take place only if things were different, only if they had the right guidance, only if . . . Comforted by such thoughts, they dull the pain of life and put off the hard work of personal growth. This attitude prevents them from seeing the reality of their humanity and entering the process of transformation.

Approaches to Problem Solving

In the Enneagram system there are three ways we can react to the situations that life presents. We can approach problems by seeking expansive solutions and being aggressive, by seeking temperate solutions and being dependent, or by seeking enlightened solutions and withdrawing.

The Aggressive Stance. The Aggressive numbers in the Enneagram are the Three, the Seven, and the Eight. Their goal is to restructure the world. They are project-oriented people whose goals create for them an ever-widening circle of freedom. They accomplish a great deal, and developing relationships with others is merely a means to that end.

They may or may not have well-developed social skills; they may or may not get along with other people. Whatever their goal appears to be outwardly, their deepest goal is to effect change, which will be evidenced only by results. They want to mold and shape reality according to their own notions of how it should be. In their continual attempt to enforce their ideas and plans, they may cause others to experience them as intimidating. The outer world becomes their arena of competence, for they know how to get things done.

The ego investment of those who take the Aggressive Stance is an obvious one. They set the rules and expect people and circumstances to fall in line. Whether the approach is overt or covert makes little difference. By their strength or their charm, by their power or their wit, they *will* accomplish what they set out to do. Preoccupied as they are with the growth and greening of the outer world, their inner world often remains parched and they themselves impervious to the importance of dealing with the real issues of life. It is this inner aridity that prevents the process of transformation from taking root within them.

The Dependent Stance. The Dependent numbers in the Enneagram are the Two, the Six, and the One. These are socially oriented people, who want to know what others are doing so that they will know what to do next. People who take the Dependent Stance feel, think, and act in relationship to others.

Thus they seek temperate solutions to life's difficulties. They need others to whom they can respond; they would not know how to proceed without first processing the reactions of people around them.

The ego investment of those who take the Dependent Stance is more subtle than that of those who are Aggressive. It is hidden in their motive for living in reference to others: they want to be accepted. Their desire is to be thanked, reassured, and liked. They do not perceive their worth or value outside this context. For this reason, they can often be generous to a fault. The price they pay for placing such high value on being accepted by others is diminished self-esteem. As a result of this trade-off, their freedom to deal with the real issues of life dries up, and the process of transformation withers before it can germinate within them.

The Withdrawing Stance. The Withdrawing numbers in the Enneagram are the Four, the Five, and the Nine. These people are overprotective of themselves. This self-protection is expressed in their independent way of retreating deep within to discover enlightened solutions to life's difficulties.

They consequently tend to be wary of others, which leads them to rely on their own inner strength on life's journey. Their independence, which is a by-product of their withdrawing stance, often separates them from others and isolates them from the world.

The ego investment of those who take the Withdrawing Stance is in their inner strength. They are people strongly committed to themselves and to the way they perceive things to be. Whether they present an exterior of friendliness or distance, whether they are introverted or extroverted, people whose tendency is to withdraw consider themselves to be the final judge in all matters that concern them. Though they can carry an aura of self-confidence, their preoccupation with going inward to find fulfillment and insight blinds them to dealing with the real issues of life. This inward overgrowth drains the nutrients from their interior soil, while the soil in their outer world lies fallow and can only be revitalized through the process of transformation.

Putting It All Together

The previous pages have detailed how the nine numbers of the Enneagram are divided into three groups of three, three different ways. The next step is to assemble this information. Notice that no number in the Enneagram has the same combination of characteristics. The special combination of characteristics for each number produces an individualized pattern of behavior, the unique foundation of each number.

The centers will provide the structure for our survey; the affect-centered numbers will be described first, followed by the theory-centered numbers, and concluding with the effect-centered numbers. This sequence for describing the nine patterns will be used consistently through chapter 7 of the book.

Affect-Centered People

Two: The Helper. People of this number are *affect*-centered people who focus their sensitivity to needs and feelings on others, not on themselves. As people who use the *Way of Subjugation* to relate with life, they think they can handle any needs presented to them by being sensitive to feelings. Taking the *Dependent Stance* allows them to look to other people's reactions before determining their own response.

Consequently, Twos find the interior world strange and confusing and so they avoid the inner journey. In gathering others under their protective wings, they purposely shield them from discomfort, especially from the confusion of looking within. Their aim is to make people comfortable even when discomfort may lead to growth. Looking outward and focusing on others' feelings and needs rises out of their affective orientation. These qualities combine to create the foundation of the pattern of dysfunctionally motivated Helpers.

Three: The Succeeder. People of this number are *affect*-centered people who repress sensitivity to their feelings and needs for personal relationships because they use the *Way of Mediation* to relate with life. Their *Aggressive Stance* makes them energetic, project-oriented people.

The energy of this pattern is softened by an awareness of the world of feelings and by a need to negotiate, even though Threes ignore the personal application of the affective functions. These qualities come together to construct a well-oiled machine with a powerful inner drive to complete with ease every project they undertake. They travel in the fast lane on cruise control because they have all the equipment to achieve their goal—energy, the ability to adjust, and some awareness of others' needs and feelings. These qualities combine to create the foundation of the pattern of dysfunctionally motivated Succeeders.

Four: The Individualist. People of this number are *affect*-centered people who focus their sensitivity to feelings and needs on themselves. By using the *Way of Reduction* they create a tea-cup-sized world of their own in which they can leisurely sip the elixir of their personal feelings and neediness. Further, they take a *Withdrawing Stance* by looking within themselves for what they value in life, which they discover in the bubbling springs of the Center of Affect—sensitivity, depth of feeling, and range of emotion.

Because they are focused inward, their pool of affect functions have inadequate outlets and therefore tend to stagnate. Their inner waters become polluted by personal neediness as their focus on the tragedy in their lives intensifies. Because they long to be understood, they lure others into sitting beside their inner waters with them, hoping that, given enough time, they themselves might find new meaning in their tragic past. These qualities combine to create the foundation of the pattern of dysfunctionally motivated Individualists.

Theory-Centered People

Five: The Observer. People of this number are *theory*-centered people who focus their thinking and objectivity on the world. By using the *Way of Subjugation* they attempt to analyze life in the hope of eventually comprehending it completely. Their *Withdrawing Stance* moves them deep inside, where they find the strength that they believe will carry them through life. They identify this strength as their power of reasoning—the strength of their preferred Theoretical Center.

Like hidden television cameras, they study, watch, and record, then analyze, their perceptions of everything that interests them. Although their secret camera records whatever enters its view, they fail to realize that someone else could film from another angle, thus gaining a different perspective and drawing different conclusions from the same data. As people who withdraw, they covet time alone to replay and ponder their treasured films in an objective, impersonal manner. These qualities combine to create the foundation of the pattern of dysfunctionally motivated Observers.

Six: The Guardian. People of this number are *theory*-centered people who repress their ability to think, calculate, or decide for themselves, especially regarding issues in their own lives, because they use the *Way of Mediation* to react to life. Their *Dependent Stance* increases their indecisiveness, because they wait to see how others respond before they can decide what to do.

Because their two major orientations are to negotiate and to relate, they walk on constantly moving psychic ground. These nomads wander the shifting sands of life with fear as their constant companion. Danger is palpable for these desert vagabonds because they do not trust their greatest strength—thinking and deciding. If they allowed themselves to sink into the sands of constant fear and indecision they would be buried, becoming entirely ineffective. Consequently, they gather with their group for safety and choose to walk into and through their storms of fear. These qualities combine to create the foundation of the pattern of dysfunctionally motivated Guardians.

Seven: The Dreamer. People of this number are *theory*-centered people who focus their ability to think and calculate on themselves. Consistently feeling overwhelmed by life, they use the *Way of Reduction* because they are certain that they can never comprehend all that the world contains. As a consequence, they fill their minds with plans and ideas that focus on what is pleasing to them, things designed to light up their magical world. Like moonbeams mysteriously dancing across the water, these people can be appreciated but never caught or pinned down. Their *Aggressive Stance* gives them the energy to remain in constant motion and the evasive stubbornness to get exactly what they want out of life.

Theory-centered people, they interpret acceptance of their ideas and plans as personal acceptance, thus casting shadows that keep the complexities of a personal life hidden from them. With their scintillating beam focused on the world of plans, their desire is to make things sparkle for themselves and for all who are important to them. These qualities combine to create the foundation of the pattern of dysfunctionally motivated Dreamers.

Effect-Centered People

Eight: The Confronter. People of this number are *effect*-centered people who focus their energy and spontaneity outward. Their *Aggressive Stance* focuses them on accomplishment, and their native ability to react to life with the *Way of Subjugation* causes them to meet life head on. Like a mother wolf who will lay down her life to feed her cub, they live with excessive demands on themselves and expectations of their environment.

They are as sensitive to justice issues as the she-wolf is to animals that invade her territory. Their preferred Center of Effect provides them with the energy to mold and shape the world according to their image of what is right. Seeing the Way of Subjugation as the only way, they will destroy everything that encroaches on their space while at the same time, with tender strength, supply the necessary maternal care that is essential to sustaining everyone's life. These qualities combine to create the foundation of the pattern of dysfunctionally motivated Confronters.

Nine: The Preservationist. People of this number are *effect*-centered people who repress their energy and spontaneity because their constant need is to negotiate with life by using the *Way of Mediation*. Like the chameleon, they change colors to blend unnoticed into their surroundings, thereby avoiding conflict or personal importance. They exercise this chameleon option most consistently in matters of personal growth and personal relationship, where difficulties can cause the most conflict. Their *Withdrawing Stance* causes them to retreat within themselves to slumber under the protective fronds of inner tranquillity.

The high price paid for this kind of peace is an inner deadness or paralysis leading to a loss of self-respect, intimate relationships, and self-knowledge. From this inanimate position they are irresistibly drawn to seek stimulation by watching those actively involved in life or by feverishly participating in pursuits that have little if any bearing on the true purpose of daily life. These qualities combine to create the foundation of the pattern of dysfunctionally motivated Preservationists.

One: The Achiever. People of this number are *effect*-centered people who focus their energy on themselves and their own world. They concentrate their energy, which they use to grind away at life the way a wood chipper grinds up piles of branches. Because they are forever feeling overwhelmed by life's situations, they react to life using the *Way of Reduction* and so feel unable to effect change in the outer world. They see and identify exterior limitations the same way one might see a tangle of jungle underbrush impossible to penetrate. Yet, by taking on the *Dependent Stance* of relating to their world, they let the world set their agenda while they set the standards for how they will fulfill that agenda. This inner dynamic is a cause of constant intensity and frustration for them.

Because they react to life's concerns they are constantly overwhelmed by the rapid growth of underbrush, and they feel driven to keep chopping away lest they become hopelessly entangled. The resulting seeds of frustration and resentment grow into weeds of anger, ever threatening to overtake their carefully manicured world. Their excessive expectations—natural to the Effective Center—serve as a magnifying glass through which their critical eyes discover even the tiniest mar on the landscape they intend to perfect. Imperfections loom large before them, activating their energy to attack any invaders who would destroy perfection and faultlessness. These qualities combine to create the foundation of the pattern of dysfunctionally motivated Achievers.

The Rewards of Turning the Magnifying Glass Inward

It takes courage to look through the magnifying glass at your own dysfunctional motivation. It's not always a pleasant sight. The ugly duckling didn't like being an ugly duckling either; he just didn't know he wasn't a duckling at all but a misplaced swan instead.

The Enneagram describes how the beautiful part of human beings gets "misplaced" too. How a swan's egg found its way into a duck's nest was a mystery. Similarly, most of us remain a mystery to ourselves as we search for that beautiful self that, every once in a while, tantalizingly peeks through the shadows. But the means by which we misplace our real beautiful self is all too obvious—strength, creativity, and personal freedom are hidden under layers of dysfunctional motivation and mechanical reactions. It is the personal work of consciousness that will peel back the layers of the false self and shed a light that can awaken this slumbering self.

This process of transformation or becoming conscious is not a matter of "cleaning up your act"; it is learning to live your life in honest, creative freedom. The magnifying glass called the Enneagram is a tool that assists you in this process.

Mind Maze

The Illusionary Systems

CHAPTER FOUR

Ignorant people do not seek after wisdom. For herein lies the evil of ignorance, that those who are neither good nor wise are nevertheless satisfied with themselves; they have no desire for that of which they feel no want. —PLATO

Stress has become a way of life for us regardless of age, gender, or occupation. Demands on every side—family, social, business—increase almost daily. Changes occur so rapidly that by the time you have learned enough to get one foot up in life, you find that you are nevertheless on the down escalator.

With all the pressure to study, categorize, and sort new information, our data banks are on overload. Is it any wonder that people lose count of their Excedrin headaches each week or that gathering at the water fountain becomes the social event of the day as Maalox Moments stretch into hours? Hurry, hurry, hurry. People hurry and get up so they can hurry and sit down, so they can hurry and eat to hurry to work, to hurry and get home to hurry and relax because they have to hurry to bed so they can hurry and get up . . .

The most puzzling aspect of all this is that we assume it's normal! Our crime is that we never question our assumptions. We sentence ourselves to life in a maze from which there is no escape.

Helping to create a pocket of sanity in the mind maze of our lives is another insight from the Enneagram: the illusionary systems. By describing an interlocking system of unconscious attitudes that form our prison walls, they clearly reveal how we continue to run up blind alleys and dash down dead-end streets. Seeing these illusionary systems for the first time may shock us enough to make us question our assumptions.

Is there any escape from this maze we find ourselves in? Perhaps. But those who simply *want* to escape have sentenced themselves to a life of futility. Only those of us who are willing to *take the truth inside ourselves* will stop long enough to search patiently for the secret passageway hidden at the end of every dead-end street.

Sadly however, few people will ever know what it means to be free, because they think they are free already. Believing they already live a decent life, they see little need to recognize how much they are controlled by worry, jealousy, conceit, negative thoughts, negative emotions, and the compulsive actions of themselves and others. In the end, their lives will have no meaning, because their real selves were never allowed to grow up and mature.

If you wake up and search for the truth of who you really are, the story is very different. You find your way out of the maze. You begin to solve the puzzle of yourself while at the same time gaining insight into the mystery of other people. Under the light of consciousness, the riddle of life finds multiple solutions. Every moment has meaning when you follow your destiny. You are free.

Blind Alleys and Dead-End Streets

Study of the illusionary systems can begin to reveal to us the intricacies of the maze we live in and help us tap the depths of the secret wisdom of the Enneagram. *Webster's Ninth New Collegiate Dictionary* defines illusion as "the state or fact of being intellectually deceived or misled, misapprehension." The illusions revealed by the Enneagram arise from several self-deceptions: that to feel good about yourself you must overuse a particular center; that to deal with the world suitably you must relate to life in a particular way, whether the Way of Subjugation, Mediation, or Reduction; and that to maintain the dignity of personhood you must approach life's problems seeking solutions that are consistently expansive, temperate, or enlightened.

We are easily ensnared by the illusion that unless we respond to life in these patterned ways, we will betray our real selves. Being thus deceived, we continue to strengthen our false personalities and rob ourselves of the creative force needed to move from mechanical to creative living.

The system of illusion for each pattern reinforces its prime addiction, operating consistently as a basis for mechanical feeling, thinking, and reacting. Operating by patterns and not by free choice dulls our inner sensibility, and we are easily seduced into believing that all is well when, in reality, our true personhood is being destroyed as we are led more deeply into our prime addiction. Little by little we fortify our illusionary system, giving our addictions ever-increasing power to dominate our lives.

Rising Above the Maze

When you are in a maze it becomes impossible to find out how close you are to the finish line. Only by rising above the maze and taking an aerial view, as it were, can you gain the objective perspective you need. Similarly, the secret wisdom of the Enneagram is revealed by taking an overview of each pattern's distinctive illusionary system through an examination of seven elements:

1. The **deception** is an experience that makes you believe that you have everything, when in fact you have nothing.
2. The **pseudo-deception** is an experience that makes you feel like nothing, when in fact facing it could open you to freedom.

3. The **antidote** is an experience that in fact can bring you new life but that feels as though it is bringing an inner death.
4. The **pseudo-antidote** is an experience that makes you feel alive but that in fact is leading you down a blind alley.
5. The **illusion of reality** is an experience of that state in which you most enjoy being yourself but that in fact blinds you to your essence and your true dignity.
6. The **personal statement of self-justification** is the often unconscious and unverbalized rationalization by which you lull yourself into living in illusion rather than facing reality.
7. The **orientation toward time** is what encourages an overemphasis on either past, present, or future to the exclusion of the other two, further reinforcing illusion.

Thus is revealed part of the hard work the Enneagram calls forth from us. We must face, accept, and embrace that which we most want to avoid if we are to discover the hidden passageways that lead to freedom. Furthermore, we find that opening ourselves to the experience that we avoid at all costs is a task that we must face many times each day. But to invite this wisdom inside yourself is to enter the treasure house of the secret wisdom of the Enneagram.

What follows is a bird's-eye view of the systems of illusion perpetuated by each of the nine Enneagram patterns. Using the order established in the previous chapter, it begins with the patterns of the Affective Center, moves to those of the Theoretical Center, and concludes with those of the Effective Center. This information is also summarized on the chart "The Illusionary Systems."

Two: The Helper

At the foundations of the Helpers' illusionary system is their dependent need to seek temperate solutions. Reacting to life with the Way of Subjugation, they meet life head on. Helpers want to associate with others on the basis of dealing directly with the human problems of the world, and because they are affect-centered people, they especially want to handle the personal needs and feelings of those with whom they relate.

The **deception** Helpers are caught in is the feeling that they are capable of han[d]... human problem, an attitude fueled by their prime addiction of prid[e]... s could be likened to two people living in one body. The outer person... uperior manner as Helpers take care of the world's needs; the inner person... martyr who gives and never receives, who loves others only to be taken for granted. Because the point of their martyrdom is egocentric, Helpers will complain, let their irritation with others flash briefly, or lash out at another person as a way of gaining sympathy for the pain of their martyrdom.

However, to cover the deception and keep it from being exposed, Helpers devise the **pseudo-deception** of personal neediness. They avoid experiencing their own needs, for doing so sends them into confusion and anxiety. Facing their need to both give and receive would cause them to admit a vulnerability too painful to bear.

THE ILLUSIONARY SYSTEMS

A) Deception   B) Pseudo-deception
C) Antidote   D) Pseudo-antidote
E) Illusion of Reality   F) Self-justification

	Relate to Life with the Way of Subjugation "I meet life head on."	Relate to Life with the Way of Mediation "I negotiate with life."	Relate to Life with the Way of Reduction "I am overwhelmed by life."
Self-justification	8	3	7
Approach to Problem Solving: Aggressive "I accomplish."	A) Need to conquer (Lust for life) B) Weakness C) Compassion D) Being strong E) Power F) "I will accomplish everything important."	A) Hide behind strength (Deceit) B) Failure C) Integrity D) Completing tasks E) Being recognized/admired F) "I will accomplish anything."	A) Feeling happy (Gluttony) B) Complexity of life C) Fortitude D) Boundless optimism E) Looking to the future F) "I will make the world happy."
Seek expansive solutions			
Project image of freedom			
Focus on the Future	Work to make the future just	Work toward future goals	Work on future plans

Approach to Problem Solving: ***Dependent*** "I relate." Seek temperate solutions Project image of benevolence Focus on the <u>Present</u>	**2** A) Capability (Pride) B) Neediness C) Humility D) Helping E) Winning love F) "I make others happy." Respond to the needs of the <u>present</u>	**6** A) Helplessness (Fear) B) Aloneness C) Courage D) Conformity E) Acceptance by the group F) "I relate to others." Make the most of the <u>present</u>	**1** A) Determination (Anger) B) Imperfection C) Patience D) Hard work E) Striving F) "I create order." Make the <u>present</u> the way it should be
Approach to Problem Solving: ***Withdrawing*** "I am satisfied." Seek enlightened solutions Project image of nonconformity Focus on the <u>Past</u>	**5** A) Superiority (Greed) B) Emptiness C) Generosity D) Gathering observations E) Being objective F) "I have found the key to satisfaction." Reflect on <u>past</u> experiences	**9** A) Indifference (Sloth) B) Distress C) Diligence D) Resignation E) Peace at any price F) "I preserve my satisfaction." Preserve the <u>past</u>	**4** A) Conceit (Envy) B) Inferiority C) Serenity D) Authenticity E) Developing singular identity F) "I have found the essence of satisfaction." Revere the <u>past</u>

If Helpers faced their neediness, it would open them up to humility, the **anti-dote** for their deception. Humility would allow them to look within and compassionately enfold the disturbing mixture of strength *and* weakness, success *and* failure, virtue *and* vice. Dwelling comfortably in this new interior home they would have the hearth around which they could gather mutual relationships and welcome divine logic and understanding.

Instead, Helpers avoid reality by developing the **pseudo-antidote** of helping. They run headlong into the lives of others, advising, consoling, assisting, encouraging—all as a means of escaping their dark and frightening inner world. They think their other-centeredness makes them good people.

The **illusion of reality** in which Helpers live, then, is winning the love of others. When others express love for them, Helpers feel complete. The illusion that caring for others will give meaning to their lives prevents them from knowing themselves as persons. The constant approval of others, like a temporary shelter in a storm, protects them from having to integrate their lives and distracts them from doing their own inner work.

Undergirding these illusions is an unspoken **personal statement of self-justification,** "I know how to make others happy." Thus Helpers also reveal their **orientation toward the present,** for they focus on the needs of the person in front of them. For Helpers, making others happy is simple: Give them what they need or want. They live with the attitude that if everyone were as other-centered as they are, many of the world's problems would be solved.

Three: The Succeeder

At the foundations of the Succeeders' illusionary system is their aggressive need to accomplish. Reacting to life with the Way of Mediation, they negotiate for equal footing with others and within a situation. Succeeders think that accomplishment is their entree to respect. Because they are affect-centered people, they believe they will be welcomed by others when their deeds are seen as sufficiently successful.

Thus the **deception** Succeeders are caught in is their ability to hide their real selves behind a show of strength, an attitude that is fueled by their prime addiction of deceit. Succeeders live in the illusion that their personal worth is derived from what they can do, from what they can produce, and from how they appear to others.

However, to shroud their deception and keep it from being laid bare, Succeeders fabricate a **pseudo-deception,** failure. Admitting ineffectiveness or a personal inadequacy is repulsive to them. Consequently, they deny, ignore, and avoid situations in which such self-revelation might take place, choosing instead to emphasize a well-polished, well-arranged veneer of warmth, graciousness or optimism. They avoid personal relationships or any activity that would require peering into their deepest selves, which they believe to be bankrupt.

If Succeeders honestly faced their failures, they could develop integrity, the **antidote** for their deception. Integrity emerges when the discipline of human struggle ignites the fire of truth. That fire would leap the carefully constructed backfire zones that protect their egocentricity, thawing the frozen ground of their emotions and illuminating the darkness that their repressed feelings have concealed.

Instead, Succeeders avoid truth by developing the **pseudo-antidote** of completing tasks. They prefer being task-oriented, not only because work uses their energy aggressively but also because they can be admired through their accomplishments and can hide behind them. With many projects and programs to complete, they simply have no time to enter personal relationships or to begin a process of personal examination.

The **illusion of reality** in which Succeeders live, then, is being recognized and admired. As far as they are concerned, if they look good, they must indeed be good. They come to think that the totality of life lies in receiving recognition. Being affect-centered people, they also have the ability to manipulate others into giving them the response they need so desperately.

Undergirding all these illusions is an unspoken **personal statement of self-justification,** "I will accomplish anything." Thus they also reveal their **orientation toward the future,** for their concern is focused on the goals yet to be realized, the victories yet to be won. For Succeeders, success has a simple formula: Sacrifice anything to attain the goal. They live with the attitude that if everyone accomplished as much as they do, many of the world's problems would be solved.

Four: The Individualist

At the foundations of the Individualists' illusionary system is their withdrawing attitude of being content within themselves. Feeling overwhelmed by the people and situations around them, they react to life with the Way of Reduction. Individualists see happiness as consisting of making their own world beautiful for themselves. Because they are affect-centered people, they believe that by focusing their gaze on the inner prism of personal needs and feelings, they will attain the happiness they seek.

The **deception** Individualists are caught in is their conceit, an attitude that is fueled by their prime addiction of envy. Forever examining and analyzing themselves in a self-conscious and self-absorbed manner, they simultaneously envy others for their abilities and blessings—whether material, personal, psychological, or spiritual. They want others' good fortune immediately for themselves.

However, to cloak their deception and keep it from being revealed, Individualists construct a **pseudo-deception,** feeling inferior—which reminds them that they are caught in the mire of ordinariness. Feeling like ugly ducklings, they are certain they will never be able to live intense and wonderful lives. Avoiding any gaze into the still waters of unfulfillment, they flap their wings continuously in dramatic expression and deep longing.

If Individualists faced their unfulfilled feelings and needs, it would open them to serenity, the **antidote** for their deception. In the calm waters of serenity, the ugly duckling would be mystically transformed into the beautiful swan. Serenity would enable them to see clearly their talents and strengths and discern how best to use the fullness of their personalities to live healthy, stable, balanced, and productive lives.

Instead, Individualists circumvent the strength that emanates from serenity by developing authenticity, the **pseudo-antidote** for their deception. By seeing only one half of their personality—feelings and needs—Individualists can only long for what they do not have—the fullest expression of their true self. They search within for the ability to express themselves clearly in the hope that one day they will find commitment with at least one other person who will understand them and give them all they desire.

The **illusion of reality** in which they live, then, is their need to develop an identity singular from all others, who will then acknowledge their unique place among human beings. Imagining themselves to be real only when life is intense, Individualists nurture the illusion that they *are* their feelings and needs, so that every feeling and need must be expressed if they are to be human.

Undergirding these illusions is an unspoken **personal statement of self-justification,** "I have found the essence of satisfaction," which, in a sense, is themselves—their personality, talents, and depth of emotion. Thus they also reveal their **orientation toward the past,** for they revere it as that which created them to be the person they have become. For Individualists, finding satisfaction is a simple matter: Express your feelings, fulfill your needs. They live with the attitude that if everyone meditated on themselves and experienced the fulfillment of expressing their feelings as they do, many of the world's problems would be solved.

Five: The Observer

At the foundations of the Observers' illusionary system is their withdrawing need to seek enlightened solutions. Their need to meet life head on flows from their Way of Subjugation. Observers relate with people and things through detached examination, and as theory-centered people, they consider life in an abstract and intellectual manner.

The **deception** Observers are caught in is a sense of superiority, an attitude that is fueled by their prime addiction of greed for knowledge and information. Observers think that gathering knowledge and distilling it into creative wisdom is the most important of life's tasks. Any other purpose in life is seen as inferior.

However, to camouflage their deception and keep it from being disclosed, Observers devise the **pseudo-deception** of personal emptiness. They are overwhelmed with their lack of all the knowledge that could make them self-sufficient. When faced with an unfamiliar field of knowledge, or if they do not comprehend something, they collect the nectar of knowledge through research and observation. Once it is gathered, they must withdraw to process this information into the honey of wisdom.

If Observers faced this sense of emptiness, it would open them up to generosity, the **antidote** to their deception. Generosity would lead them to shatter the narrow boundaries of individuality and become faithful to all of life through unselfish sharing of their abundant knowledge and wisdom. Their natural curiosity would lead them to explore possibilities for creating consciousness through clever and logical communication. To their complete amazement, life's greatest wisdom would be revealed through service and interpersonal relationships.

Instead, Observers avoid opportunities to share themselves by developing the **pseudo-antidote** of gathering observations. They avoid people, commitments, and relationships, choosing for their companions observation, objectivity, and the inner world of ideas. Even when they feel lonely or sense that others may have stumbled upon a happier way to live, they continue to withdraw.

The **illusion of reality** in which Observers live, then, is being objective. They believe they can and will attain the objectivity that will lay bare the secrets of the universe and yield answers to all of life's questions. Feeling safe in abstraction, quiet, and solitude, they live in a continual gestation period, rarely experiencing the wonder and joy of giving birth.

Undergirding these illusions is an unspoken **personal statement of self-justification,** "I have found the key to satisfaction." Thus they reveal their **orientation toward the past** as they must continuously reflect so as to gain knowledge and wisdom. For Observers, finding the key to satisfaction is simple: Ponder and be wise. They live with the attitude that if everyone deliberated as much as they do, many of the world's problems would be solved.

Six: The Guardian

At the foundations of the Guardians' illusionary system is their dependent need to relate. Reacting to life with the Way of Mediation, they negotiate with people and situations to find their place in the world. Guardians fit into the world by making all of their decisions through dialogue with members of the group—especially its authorities or leaders. By ingratiating themselves with groups, they relieve themselves of responsibility for personal choice.

The **deception** Guardians are caught in is a sense of personal helplessness, an attitude fueled by their prime addiction of fear. Guardians prefer relying on others' concepts and impressions rather than becoming aware of their own thoughts, opinions, and inner direction for life. When there are no group laws, norms, customs, or traditions on which to rely, they feel defenseless and vulnerable.

However, to veil their deception and keep it from being unmasked, Guardians fabricate a **pseudo-deception,** independence. Independent activity arises from a knowledge of one's own values, even if they are in conflict with the values of other people. To avoid independence Guardians blend into the conservative elements of the community and expect others to do the same. They view independent thought or action as stretching, possibly to the point of tearing, the fabric of society, and choose instead to rely on the rules or traditions of the group.

If Guardians could accept the importance of personal autonomy, they would develop courage, the **antidote** for their deception. By courageously resisting and overcoming insecurity, courage would penetrate their stronghold, breaking the chains that have held myriad freedoms captive. With their lost freedom restored, Guardians would stand fearlessly against anyone who might attempt to usurp that precious gift from them or from those they love.

Instead, they avoid their personal freedom by developing conformity, the **pseudo-antidote** for their deception. By harmonizing themselves with others' expectations of them, Guardians feel safe and secure, the approval of their group becoming their protection from self-investigation. They seek many opinions before they can finally make a decision and will do whatever is required to remain in good standing with their group.

The **illusion of reality** in which Guardians live, then, is acceptance by the group. They believe that being included in and welcomed by a group with whom they can share values creates the good life. The security of this way of life, however, is continually threatened by the hungry growlings of fear, an appetite that can only be appeased by constant reassurance from outside authorities, thus increasing their dependence on the group.

Undergirding all these illusions is an unspoken **personal statement of self-justification,** "I relate to others." They also reveal their **orientation toward the present** in their desire to make the most of it, resulting in being faithful to and responsible for upholding group values and norms. For Guardians, relating to others is simple: Ingratiate yourself by being gracious and responsible. They live with the attitude that if everyone related to others in the way they do, many of the world's problems would be solved.

Seven: The Dreamer

At the foundations of the Dreamers' illusionary system is their aggressive need to get what they want. Their sense of being overwhelmed by life results in the Way of Reduction. Dreamers relate with others through happiness. Being theory-centered people, they share happiness by discounting real problems and replacing them with planning how things could be more pleasant, especially for themselves.

The **deception** Dreamers are caught in is the need always to feel happy, an attitude fueled by their prime addiction of gluttony. They refuse the uncomfortable and consume whatever makes them content, cheerful, and lighthearted. If they are unable to turn aside difficult situations with a joke or gentle teasing, they will physically remove themselves from the target area.

However, to disguise their deception and keep it from being exposed, Dreamers construct a **pseudo-deception,** acknowledging the complexity of life. To admit that a problem cannot be solved, that an illness cannot be cured, or that a pain must be faced would be synonymous with defeat. With the battle thus perceived to be lost, the excitement of the challenge ceases along with the reason to go on. With this either-or orientation toward reality, Dreamers flee into the world of abstraction.

If they could face problems squarely, they would develop fortitude, the **antidote** for their deception. Fortitude would unlock the great wealth of dynamism that lies within them, for it would draw them into the oftentimes hard work of accomplishing their dreams. Fortitude would unite their Theoretical, Affective, and Effective Centers to accomplish a majestic work with the potential for elevating the consciousness of an entire community or nation, or even the world.

Instead, Dreamers run from such a realistic approach by developing the **pseudo-antidote** of boundless optimism. They maintain a high level of optimism because they deliberately refuse to acknowledge or even remember any reason to be gloomy or pessimistic. It is not that they are completely blind or deaf to difficult realities, but rather that they do not assign problems any importance or power.

The **illusion of reality** in which Dreamers live, then, is looking to the future. By dealing with life abstractly they can live in an abstract world. They are escape artists who use plans and constant activity to prevent reality from setting in and causing depression. They think of themselves as "sunshine pumpers" because their value lies in bringing to a gloomy world the joy and cheer that arise from the hope of a better tomorrow.

Undergirding these illusions is an unspoken **personal statement of self-justification,** "I will make the world happy." They reveal their **orientation toward the future** by not getting bogged down in the present and working on future plans. For Dreamers, the formula for happiness is simple: Accentuate the positive, eliminate the negative, and smile, smile, smile. They live with the attitude that if everyone tried as hard as they do to bring happiness to the world, many of the world's problems would be solved.

Eight: The Confronter

At the foundations of the Confronters' illusionary system is their aggressive need to be in charge. In reacting to life with the Way of Subjugation, they meet people and situations head on. Confronters persistently deal with every issue they find important. Because they are effect-centered people, they move through life with the force of instinctual energy, which allows them to stand staunchly, even defiantly, before anyone who obstructs their path.

The **deception** Confronters are caught in is their need to conquer every challenge laid before them, an attitude fueled by their prime addiction of lust for life and power. They have one idea of the way things should be, and although they call this idea justice, it would be more accurately described as gaining influence or rising to the top. Dynamic people, they have more than enough endurance to see that their expectations are fulfilled as they spontaneously splash their energy throughout the world.

However, to conceal their deception and keep it from being laid bare, Confronters devise the **pseudo-deception** of yielding to personal weakness. Admitting their uncertainty and feelings of vulnerability is a pain they refuse to endure, so they compulsively cover these delicate feelings with a show of strength, vitality, or enthusiasm. To reveal and thus face their impotence would disorient them. The ludicrous thought that they might need to submit to another person causes them to deny, ignore, and avoid showing any personal frailty.

If they could face their weakness honestly, they would develop compassion, the **antidote** for their deception. Compassion is the foundation upon which freedom and justice for all is built. It is the ingredient by which people can risk vulnerability to others. From the ashes of the Confronters' weakness, divine compassion would arise like the phoenix, bearing the possibilities of freedom, new life, and covenant love on its wings.

Instead, Confronters avoid the refining fires of compassion by developing the **pseudo-antidote** of being strong. When they are forceful, they feel safe, for no one can take advantage of them. With shrewdness and power they control their environment, overtly taking the upper hand in the physical world while covertly gathering psychological strength at every opportunity. Nothing is allowed to stand in the way of their idea of justice.

The **illusion of reality** in which Confronters live, then, is power. They equate power with goodness. They believe their power entitles them to dominate the world so that it will function in a proper and just manner. From this triumphal place of primacy, they take great satisfaction in dispensing their views on justice. They find security in power and so live in the illusion that dominance is what gives their lives meaning, worth, and purpose.

Undergirding all these illusions is an unspoken **personal statement of self-justification,** "I will accomplish everything important." Thus they also reveal their **orientation to the future;** they are concerned with the injustice that they must yet set right. For Confronters, accomplishing everything important is a simple matter: Speak loudly and carry a big stick. They live with the attitude that if everyone accomplished important things as they do, many of the problems in the world would be solved.

Nine: The Preservationist

At the foundations of the Preservationists' illusionary system is their withdrawing need to be content. Reacting to life with the Way of Mediation, they negotiate with people and situations to maintain their way of life. Preservationists merge into the world by being satisfied with it as it is, expressing contentment through inactivity and lack of awareness.

Thus the **deception** Preservationists are caught in is personal irresponsibility, which lives under the guise of contentment, an attitude fueled by their prime addiction of sloth. Their vibrant strength, veiled by a nonchalant attitude, is nonetheless revealed in their resistance to change. They value keeping things static, shunning exertion especially in their personal relationships and inner lives.

However, to mask their deception and keep it from being disclosed, Preservationists fabricate a **pseudo-deception,** distress. Their underdeveloped self-awareness demands that they avoid anything that would require their strength or presence. Therefore they can deny, ignore, and avoid any person or situation that would require a response. They avoid center stage, preferring the image of the kindly stagehand who makes others' performances possible.

If Preservationists could own the inner strength that would allow them to deal directly with life, they would develop diligence, the **antidote** for their deception. Diligence would evoke their natural vitality to create honest, mutual relationships and set goals that would affect the lives of others. Diligence would lead them on a mystical journey, teaching them how to become involved in life through a love born of understanding.

Instead, Preservationists avoid distress by developing the **pseudo-antidote** of resignation. Submissiveness deadens them to situations, feelings, or concerns both within themselves and between themselves and others. By capitulating to life's circumstances, they can maintain an easygoing exterior that prevents examination of their passive-aggressive motivations. Through resignation they live in the illusion that their goodness is derived from harmonizing with the world.

The **illusion of reality** in which Preservationists live, then, is preserving peace at any price. Yet below their easygoing affability runs such a powerful undercurrent of passive aggression that those closest to them get caught in the undertow. Preservationists, who live in the illusion that their lives are free of conflict and turmoil, are usually the last and most surprised to hear that anyone has a problem with them.

Undergirding all these illusions is an unspoken **personal statement of self-justification,** "I preserve my satisfaction." Thus they also reveal their **orientation toward the past,** which they preserve with great fondness, sentimentality, and denial. Refusing to grapple with the pain they have experienced, they don rose-colored glasses and invest everything in maintaining the seeming satisfaction they have found. For Preservationists, preserving the satisfaction of their conservative, static life is a simple matter: See no evil, hear no evil, speak no evil. They live with the attitude that if everyone would work at preserving the status quo the way they do, many of the problems in the world would be solved.

One: The Achiever

At the foundations of the Achievers' illusionary system is their dependent need to be validated for their goodness. Feeling overwhelmed by life, they use the Way of Reduction. Their hypersensitivity to the messiness of life compels them to make perfectionistic reforms in a world that resists reform, all the while trying to gain acceptance through their long-suffering efforts to make life better for others.

The **deception** Achievers are caught in is a personal sense of determination, an attitude fueled by their prime addiction of anger. Achievers become obsessed by the mediocrity they see in the world and are preoccupied with elevating everything to their standards. They feel constant agitation in their attempts to bring to perfection all the disorder, chaos, and evil that they see so clearly in the world around them.

However, to conceal their deception and keep it from being uncovered, Achievers construct a **pseudo-deception,** imperfection. Each morning they awake to discover that the perfectly constructed sand castle of the previous day's efforts has been washed away by the tide. In its place, the sea has spewed out weeds and debris that they must clear away. Unable to hold back the tide that creates such disorder, they feel the slow burn of resentment toward a world that never allows them to achieve the perfection they seek.

If they could tolerate even natural disorder, they would begin to develop patience, the **antidote** for their deception. With patience they could discover and appreciate the treasures that lie hidden in each day's commotion. With patience they would be able to enjoy themselves and others and appreciate the beauty that surrounds them. Patience would beget creativity that would eventually give birth to unbelievably beautiful gifts for expression and originality.

Instead, Achievers flee from the demands of patience by developing the **pseudo-antidote** of hard work. By concentrating on clearing away each immediate mess as soon as possible, they lay to waste their considerable energy. Their intensity, like blinders shutting out all distractions, confines them to an impersonal world. With this myopic and distorted view they relentlessly pursue the achievement of an unreal perfection.

The **illusion of reality** in which Achievers live, then, is striving. Achievers can breathe a sigh of relief and feel good only when, at the end of each day, they are able to point to the visible signs that a new and perfect sand castle has been painstakingly erected. They believe that striving to achieve, straighten out, and create makes them good people who are valuable to others and to society.

Undergirding all these illusions is an unspoken **personal statement of self-justification,** "I create order." Thus they also reveal their **orientation toward the present** as they allow each situation before them to tyrannize their lives. For Achievers, accomplishing order is a simple matter: Work hard, hope for the best, and be prepared for the worst. They live with the attitude that if everyone worked to create order as hard as they do, many of the world's problems would be solved.

Rising Above Illusion

Riding in a hot air balloon over your own hometown would allow you the leisure to observe the landscape below. With time to take in all the details, you could see relationships and draw conclusions that were never possible while you were actually living in a neighborhood and driving down its streets.

"I didn't realize how many trees there are in town!"

"Did you know that Main Street isn't straight? It curves slightly to the west!"

"Look how Johnson Creek creates separate neighborhoods on either side of its path all the way through town!"

The view from above is a very different view.

This chapter has looked from above at nine mind mazes to gain a new perspective on the illusions we live with and call reality. While we live amid the attitudes that entrap our minds we don't realize how they keep us going in circles. Each attitude in itself seems a perfectly reasonable response to a given situation.

The view from above puts a new slant on things, which yields greater clarity, precisely because when we rise above our illusions we become detached—no longer involved or invested. Looking objectively at the mind maze we call home, it's natural to wonder why we never saw it clearly before. You might ask, "How could I have been so blind?" It is the very nature of illusion, however, to deceive us into believing in what is not real.

With the objectivity of a new perspective, we are presented with choices to walk out of the maze of illusion and into the world of beauty, wonder, and freedom. In other words, once we see the maze for what it is, we have the power to choose not to live there.

Each of the destructive attitudes of our illusionary system is a primary wall that keeps us in the maze. Each time we give in to these attitudes we add a smaller wall that makes the maze more complicated. Objective vision becomes more and more difficult.

The solution, therefore, is not to give in to attitudes that continue building walls. What we learn from examining the illusionary systems is that what seems good for us truly is destructive, and what seems a hopeless waste of time will nevertheless lead us to freedom. Knowing that illusion has confused the magnetic needle of our inner compass, we can internally adjust our bearings so as to make decisions that will lead to life and freedom.

A new, objective perspective can also enable us to deal with the stress that is so prevalent in our society. Stress keeps us from seeing the illusion in our lives, gaining momentum and power as we continually accept, internalize, and multiply external pressures. However, though most of us would deny it, inside we like stress. It makes us feel like important, productive members of modern society. Until stress leads to serious physical, mental, or emotional problems, we wear it as a badge of honor.

As we look at the illusionary systems, it would be easy to put pressure on ourselves to hurry out of the maze and into freedom. However, doing so would simply hide illusion behind illusion. There are no quick fixes for dispelling illusion. By taking one step at a time, we can slowly gather strength, confidence, and wisdom.

Paradoxically, the momentum forward out of the maze increases as we slow down. Taking time to think and reflect prevents us from wasting time running down the blind alleys and dead-end streets of our self-created mind maze.

Trickster and Sly One

Intensifying and Neutralizing Prime Addictions

Try to apply seriously what I have told you, not that you might escape suffering—nobody can escape it—but that you may avoid the worst—blind suffering. —C. G. JUNG

N o one ever wants to admit being tricked. Even when it's a well-intentioned trick, like a surprise party, the recipient will often say something like, "Well, I thought this might happen when you said . . . But then I forgot about it." That statement may or may not be true. In any case, the well-meaning tricksters are left with the message that they were not quite as clever as they thought they were. So who tricked whom?

How much different this game becomes when the trickster devises a devious plot to rob another of position, power, wealth, or dignity! We do not then hear, "I suspected this was going to happen because ..." for the victim would be looked upon as a fool for not doing anything to save him- or herself.

How would you feel if today you discovered that a trickster had been pulling your strings ever since you were a child, making you dance faster and faster to a tune that didn't belong to you?

"Impossible," you say!

Do you feel stressed out? Are you running faster and faster and getting farther and farther behind? Do you have time for yourself? Do you get moody, touchy, depressed when things don't go your way? Do thoughts of revenge, resentment, envy, jealousy, fear, or worry occupy much of your day? Does your life have meaning? Are your relationships healthy and supportive? Do you like yourself? Do you *know* yourself?

Well now, let's look at this idea of a trickster from another angle.

The Shadow Dancer

Once upon a time, a very small child, Real Beautiful Self—a child who had come straight from God—fell into a deep sleep. While the child slept, Trickster tiptoed up to her bed.

Because it is the law of the universe that no one can harm Real Beautiful Self without being utterly destroyed in the process, Trickster tied invisible puppeteer's strings to the child's shadow. Then, quickly sprinkling a generous portion of sleeping dust on Real Beautiful Self, Trickster jerked her tiny shadow to its feet.

From that day to this, Trickster has been pulling these invisible strings with glee! Because the strings are invisible, this now grown Mechanical Shadow Dancer thinks she is a real person and therefore free to come and go and live as she pleases. Yet almost every thought, word, feeling, and action is a mechanical reaction to people and situations outside herself.

Meanwhile, inside Mechanical Shadow Dancer sleeps the child, Real Beautiful Self. Held captive, suspended in never-changing time, this lovely child can only be awakened through an effort made by Mechanical Shadow Dancer.

One day as Mechanical Shadow Dancer was spinning faster and faster, she suddenly dropped from sheer exhaustion. Trickster paid no attention because that was the plan. The older Mechanical Shadow Dancer became, the faster Trickster had to make her dance, for activity was the means by which Trickster convinced her she was real and living a real life.

Luckily Trickster wasn't paying attention this time, because as she fell to the floor, out of the corner of her eye, Mechanical Shadow Dancer spotted someone in the shadows.

"Who's there?" she whispered.

"Thank goodness you've finally noticed me! I've been trying to get your attention for years and was beginning to think you were a completely hopeless case!"

"What on earth do you mean?" asked Mechanical Shadow Dancer.

"Oh dear!" came the frustrated reply. "I have screamed and yelled, jumped up and down, whispered in your ear, held your feet, tripped you, and even hidden your shoes, and you didn't even notice me? Maybe you really *are* a hopeless case!"

"So it was *you* who stole my shoes! That was mean! Who are you, anyway, and why are you pestering me when I'm so tired?"

With a sweeping bow to the floor came the reply. "Allow me to introduce myself. I am Sly One, the clever, intelligent part of yourself that you have *obviously* been ignoring all these years."

"Be nice!" she said indignantly.

"Be nice, indeed! That is precisely the trouble! Why, you have been trying to be so nice all these years that you would dance to any tune you heard. You wanted everyone to like you so much that you'd start dancing when anyone snapped their fingers."

With a puzzled look on her face, Mechanical Shadow Dancer said quietly, "I don't even know what you're talking about."

"Well, perhaps I'm not as clever and intelligent as I thought I was," replied Sly One, calming down. "I will start at the beginning and tell you everything."

With that, Sly One began to tell Mechanical Shadow Dancer about Real Beautiful Self and about how Trickster had sprinkled her with sleeping dust. "Then," he said, "Trickster tied strings to her shadow (that's you) and made you dance to any old tune all these years."

When Sly One began to describe Real Beautiful Self, a look of recognition flashed across the face of Mechanical Shadow Dancer. It lasted only a second or two, but as it passed, silent tears began to slip down her cheeks. She tried to blink them back because she had decided long ago that crying was a waste of time. Besides, tears made her eyes all red and puffy.

When the story ended, Mechanical Shadow Dancer asked, "What happened to you, Sly One? Where have you been? How did you get here? Why do you remember Real Beautiful Self? In fact, how come you remember everything and I don't?"

"Slow down! I'm smart, but I don't remember *everything*. None of us remembers everything; each one of us remembers something. But I will try to answer your questions. On that fateful night, as Trickster was tying the puppeteer's strings to Real Beautiful Self's shadow (that's you), I quietly slipped into her shadow—into you. Ever since then, I've been trying to get your attention. I *need* you to help me wake up Real Beautiful Self."

As Mechanical Shadow Dancer listened intently, she became very sad.

"What's wrong?" asked Sly One.

"You are clever and intelligent, so you are important. Real Beautiful Self is . . . well, she is everything. She knows everything about how we got here, and, uh, you said she came straight from God! You can't get any more important than that! But what about me? I've messed everything up. I never even noticed that you were doing any of those things you said you did—except when you hid my shoes. But I didn't know who played that mean trick."

Then, very quietly she said, "You never once—not even once!—said I was important. What will happen to me? Will I just disappear? I'm not important like you or lovable like Real Beautiful Self. About the only thing I know how to do is dance, and now I find I've even been doing that all wrong."

"Not important!" Sly One shouted suddenly, standing in the middle of the room. "Now you listen to me! If it weren't for you, none of us would have survived. If you had stopped dancing and learning how to get along in this world, we would all be in sad shape. You have a lot to teach us, and we have a lot to teach you. We belong together, and together we'll be!—just as soon as we can figure this puzzle out."

"Even Trickster?"

"Yes, even Trickster. Now get some sleep," Sly One commanded. "We've got work to do, and I don't want to be stuck with someone who's half asleep. I've had enough of that for one lifetime, thank you very much!"

That night as Mechanical Shadow Dancer slept, she had dreams of a tiny Real Beautiful Self yawning and stretching and rubbing her little eyes.

The next morning as Mechanical Shadow Dancer opened her eyes Sly One knew that something was *very* different. With forehead furrowed and eyes squinting, Sly One crept very close to her face and looked right into her eyes. Suddenly startled, Sly One jumped backward three feet and stood perfectly still!

"What's wrong?" cried Mechanical Shadow Dancer.

But Sly One was speechless for the first time ever. For, as Sly One looked into Mechanical Shadow Dancer's eyes, looking back were the laughing, dazzling, sparkling eyes of Real Beautiful Self.

Puppeteer's Playtime

We all have had an experience in which someone knew how to "pull our strings." In our automated society, we might say "push our buttons," but it's the same thing.

In truth, it would be no use to pull anyone's strings or push anyone's buttons if those strings or buttons did not connect to something inside. When someone sees a string hanging out and gives it a good yank, the person begins to dance. Think about it. Haven't you ever seen someone's strings hanging out and felt a certain satisfaction at giving them a good yank or two? More often, however, we simply keep tripping over or stepping on one another's strings without intending to.

In this chapter we will begin to identify the clues that help us recognize when we are being manipulated by Trickster and thus *intensifying* our prime psychological addiction, and when we are working with Sly One and *neutralizing* our prime psychological addiction.

Examination of the nine patterns of the Enneagram has revealed that dysfunctional motivation has put the human personality to sleep. Without reflection, consciousness, and self-understanding, we give in to a prime psychological addiction, a distorted inner structure of reality.

This prime addiction is not so much about the way we are perceived as it is about the way we perceive; we automatically interpret reality through the distorted lens of our prime addiction. We inevitably live in the cycle of illusion until, like Mechanical Shadow Dancer, we have an inner dialogue with Sly One that puts a new slant on life and inaugurates new possibilities.

It is when we neglect inner awareness and fail to reflect on our own motives that our personalities deteriorate, intensifying our prime addiction. But when we do the hard work of becoming self-aware, our personalities evolve, and we neutralize our prime addiction. Neutralizing your prime addiction is cutting the strings being pulled by Trickster and awakening your full human potential.

Intensifying the Prime Addictions

To understand how the Enneagram describes the process of intensifying our prime psychological addiction, we must examine the arrows that connect the nine numbers. Although to the casual observer these arrows may appear random, in truth they have a consistent direction and meaning.[1]

In the diagram "Intensifying Prime Addictions" each number has an arrow that points to another number. Each number worsens its condition or intensifies

---

1. As was stated in note 2 in the introduction, the order of the arrows has a mathematical basis in the mysterious laws of recurring decimals. The first is known as the Law of Seven: 1 divided by 7 equals .142857142857; 2 divided by 7 equals .285714285714. If you divide any number under 7 by 7, these same digits turn up in the same order and repeat into infinity. Notice that the order of the digits is the same as the order in which those numbers are connected in the Enneagram. The second is the Law of Three: 1 divided by 3 equals .3333333333, 2 divided by 3 equals .6666666666, and 3 divided by 3 equals .9999999999; these are also recurring decimals, and the numbers that result are the numbers that are left out of the sequence that results from the Law of Seven. Notice that the 3, 6, and 9 are connected in the Enneagram by a separate set of lines, a self-contained triangle. By using both laws, all nine numbers are represented. See John G. Bennett, *Enneagram Studies* (York Beach, ME: Samuel Weiser, 1983), pp. 1–5.

INTENSIFYING PRIME ADDICTIONS:
MOVING WITH THE ARROWS

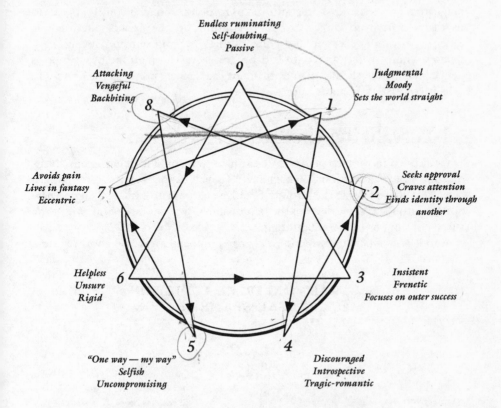

Copyright © Theodore E. Dobson and Kathleen V. Hurley.

its prime psychological addiction by "moving with the arrow," or, in other words, taking on the worst qualities of the number to which its arrow points.

Before we go any further, it is important to recall a fundamental principle of the Enneagram: namely, that each person has the prime psychological addiction of only one number, always has had that prime addiction, and always will have that prime addiction. Therefore, when we state that in moving with the arrows a person takes on the worst qualities of the number to which the arrow points, we do *not* mean to imply that he or she takes on the prime addiction of another number.

Although students of the Enneagram may at times use a phrase like "moving to your negative number" as a kind of shorthand, one does not actually take on the prime addiction of another number. All it means is that the individual in question is manifesting the worst qualities of the number that reinforces his or her own prime psychological addiction.

This is the work of Trickster. Unfortunately this nocturnal "movement with the arrows" has a natural, steady rhythm. When we are caught in dysfunctional motivation, this rhythmic beat lulls us into believing that we have found answers for our questions and solutions for our problems.

If anyone dares to suggest that we try a different rhythm, the reaction will range from consternation and confusion to revulsion and rebellion. It appears to us that we have no choice except to continue in the existing metronomic cadence. Without reflection and consciousness, we will remain dancing marionettes whose strings are controlled by Trickster. The metronome's tempo is inevitably, relentlessly increased until at last the dancer crashes to the ground in exhausted frustration and failure.

Neutralizing the Prime Addictions

Choices to move into personal freedom are presented in the diagram "Neutralizing Prime Addictions," which reveals what happens when each pattern begins to "move against the arrows." Creative energy is unleashed, bringing new options into focus as we develop the best qualities of the number from which the arrow pointing to our number originates.

Again, remember that we do not change numbers or take on another prime

NEUTRALIZING PRIME ADDICTIONS: MOVING AGAINST THE ARROWS

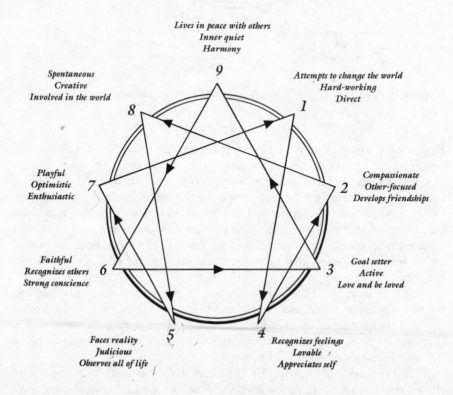

Lives in peace with others
Inner quiet
Harmony

9

Spontaneous
Creative
Involved in the world

8

Attempts to change the world
Hard-working
Direct

1

Playful
Optimistic
Enthusiastic

7

Compassionate
Other-focused
Develops friendships

2

Faithful
Recognizes others
Strong conscience

6

Goal setter
Active
Love and be loved

3

Faces reality
Judicious
Observes all of life

5

Recognizes feelings
Lovable
Appreciates self

4

addiction. Rather, we find that the best characteristics of this positive number begin to neutralize the prime addiction or sever the strings of the dysfunctional motivation of our own pattern.

Notice that each pattern always retains its individual identity; it is only the addictiveness of the pattern that needs to be dealt with. As invisible strings are consciously severed, we can begin to live a life of creative freedom. So great is the task of neutralizing the prime addiction of one number that it demands the efforts of a lifetime.

This is the work of Sly One. The "movement against the arrows," the most difficult, has a spiritual quality that demands the self-control of a dedicated dancer. This disciplined movement is the core of the hard work that the Enneagram presents to each of us. As the rigorous task of stretching and toning unused muscles begins, we will feel inept and inflexible. Perhaps we will long for the easy and familiar tug of devious Trickster's strings and ask whether, after all, Mechanical Shadow Dancer might be who we are meant to be. The tendency to misidentify your true nature at this point is still common; you are still blind to your essence, your Real Beautiful Self.

When we choose to commit to this difficult process, however, discipline and hard work form the scissors that snip the strings of control and set the dancer free. In light and freedom the dancer follows the inner rhythm of his or her Real Beautiful Self, giving clear and creative expression to the revitalizing dance of life.

The rest of this chapter describes how each pattern intensifies and neutralizes its prime addiction. Following the format set in previous chapters, this section begins with the patterns of the Affective Center, moves to those of the Theoretical Center, and concludes with those of the Effective Center.

Two: The Helper

Intensifying the prime addiction. Helpers intensify their prime addiction by moving with the arrow and taking on the worst qualities of the Confronters (Eights). When those whom they have helped do not appreciate them, when all their helping does not make the situation better, when they are rejected or treated roughly, they become vengeful toward others.

Helpers attack, often through backbiting–going from person to person telling them about the ungratefulness of those whom they have helped. If the backbiting meets resistance, Helpers still hold on to judgmental attitudes, rarely revealing them clearly in words but instead through innuendo.

Neutralizing the prime addiction. Helpers neutralize their prime addiction by moving against the arrow and developing the positive qualities of the Individualists (Fours). Awareness of their own feelings and needs begins to grow, and they spend time alone processing their feelings and analyzing their own lives.

As Helpers begin to develop the strengths of Individualists, they discover that there is more to life than helping and service. By identifying the real personal needs that only they can meet, they come to cherish their times of solitude.

They discover that they have feelings other than compassion–that, for example, they are angry at those who take them for granted, and that they care deeply about people and issues. Solitude becomes their gold mine of self-discovery as they unearth the nuggets of their own value, self-respect, and worth.

As doing is balanced with being they are able to embrace all of life—beginning with their own.

Resistance. Helpers may easily resist taking time alone for fear of becoming selfish. Nothing could be further from the truth, for their energy will always flow outward to help others. With the added dimension of interior work that leads to self-awareness, they will recognize the importance of learning to nurture themselves in a healthy way.

Reward. In their lifelong desire and need to "be there" for everyone, Helpers have placed themselves in the position of being taken advantage of by others. Now, with their newfound self-respect, they will not only treat others with greater respect but will be rewarded by being treated with dignity and valued as persons. The most priceless gold nugget for Helpers will be found in mutual relationships and in seeing the big picture—no longer seeing isolated portions but seeing each portion in relation to the whole.

Three: The Succeeder

Intensifying the prime addiction. Succeeders intensify their prime addiction by moving with the arrow and taking on the worst qualities of the Preservationists (Nines). When they cannot accomplish their goals, when they feel like failures, when they do not have the admiration of others, they lose any sense of direction, retreat, and do nothing.

This inactivity can be physical (for example, not working, wasting time on frivolous things, doing only the minimum), or it can be interior (for example, refusing to look at failures, to deal with personal faults, to grow, or to work on relationships). Feeling empty, consumed with self-doubt, self-criticism, and a silently growing passive-aggressive anger toward the person(s) who stood in their way or pointed out their faults, they sink into hopelessness. They do not trust themselves or their feelings, and they despair of ever experiencing the personal fulfillment of love and friendship.

Neutralizing the prime addiction. Succeeders neutralize their prime addiction by moving against the arrow and developing the positive qualities of the Guardians (Sixes). Guardians are preeminently aware of the group's integrity and are protective of individual rights, conscience, and respect for order and process.

Healthy Succeeders will work for the success of all concerned, not just for self. Maturing in loyalty frees them to include others in their projects and programs and to share the glory of success.

As their priorities shift from accomplishing goals to valuing people, the hard edges of their personality are made smooth. In their newfound respect for individuals and process, Succeeders grow more aware of their own dignity and goodness. With this new awareness, they begin to set aside time for relaxation and to "waste time" on developing personal relationships.

Resistance. Working with the group may threaten Succeeders, for they will fear becoming lost in the crowd and fading into oblivion. Nothing could be further from the truth. They are such highly accomplished people with so many skills that they will always be admired for their charm, their competence, and the knowledge they are able to pass along to others.

Reward. The gift of directing their energy toward inspiring, motivating, and uniting others is genuine intimacy and friendship. As Succeeders live their destiny, they unearth their vital gifts for building community. With their lifelong flight from vulnerability ended, the wounded and accessible friend and lover within them is irresistibly exposed.

Four: The Individualist

Intensifying the prime addiction. Individualists intensify their prime addiction by moving with the arrow and taking on the worst qualities of the Helpers (Twos). When they have not received enough attention, when life makes them feel ordinary and dull, when they have not been able to own and cherish the qualities that make them unique, Individualists cling to another person, hoping to become the center of the other's life.

They attempt to manipulate the other by sharing deep feelings of love and caring. These emotion-filled expressions carry the unspoken message and expectation that a similar response be forthcoming. Clothed in the aura of wounded fragility, they endeavor to impose guilt on the one who fails to care for them.

Neutralizing the prime addiction. Individualists neutralize their prime addiction by moving against the arrow and developing the positive qualities of the Achievers (Ones). Achievers are preeminently doers, doggedly persevering against all obstacles. It is through striving to overcome inner conflict and turmoil that Individualists enter the narrow passageway to perfection.

Healthy Individualists get involved in projects that turn their attention outward. As they focus on other people and the world, their own energy is activated. No longer expecting to be the center of the universe, they become involved in the betterment of society. This effort releases their natural strengths, heretofore held hostage by their myriad feelings. Self-sacrifice allows them to achieve goals that benefit both present and future generations. From their inner storehouse of emotions and perceptions, Individualists can provide the insightful analysis and clarity needed to resolve difficult problems and improve existing structures.

Resistance. Getting involved in the world frightens Individualists, for they lack confidence in their ability to accomplish, and they fear the world will make them compromise their standards and settle for mediocrity. Nothing could be further from the truth. Their creativity and their original approach to life will only be enhanced as they develop their practical abilities to accomplish and contribute.

Reward. The gift of becoming involved in the material world lies in the energy it creates. As Individualists focus on work that has practical, usable value, they establish a solid foundation, becoming thorough and realistic planners who excel in administration and management. Accomplishment yields the satisfaction that eluded them in compulsive introspection.

Five: The Observer

Intensifying the prime addiction. Observers intensify their prime addiction by moving with the arrow and taking on the worst qualities of the Dreamers (Sevens). When demands for involvement threaten to compromise their freedom, when outside circumstances begin to devour their thinking time, or when they feel prematurely coerced into sharing their prized resources, Observers quickly retreat and become more firmly entrenched in their preferred Theoretical Center.

With the focus on their mental constructs, they move farther and farther from reality, until their point of view becomes so eccentric as to be almost completely removed from reality. Others reject their vision because it is more a self-indulgent intellectual fantasy than a helpful or practical reality. But even when their idiosyncratic way of thinking isolates them from others and the world, Observers deny their feelings of loneliness, rejection, and pain. They remain unaware that the only locks on the door of their solitary cell are their own lack of feeling and refusal to become involved in life.

Neutralizing the prime addiction. Observers neutralize their prime addiction by moving against the arrow and developing the positive qualities of the Confronters (Eights). Confronters are known for their ability to accomplish. They spontaneously splash their abundant energy in every direction in an attempt to make things happen.

Healthy Observers become involved in the world around them. By imparting their knowledge and wisdom freely to others they often become highly valued teachers. In using their knowledge in ways others can appreciate, they find the fulfillment of having an effect on the world and making their mark in it.

In activating the energy of their repressed centers they find that spontaneous relationships soon yield a life of fulfillment. Their ensuing gratitude reveals a deep sensitivity to the people and issues important to them.

Resistance. Becoming involved with others and with the world may threaten Observers, for they do not easily risk giving up their independence or freedom. Instead, they convince themselves and others that they have nothing of distinctive value to contribute. Nothing could be further from the truth. As theory-centered people who have a natural curiosity about and love of life, Observers are always insightful. Their wealth of wisdom and ideas benefit those who cherish the beauty of truth as they integrate it into their daily lives.

Reward. The gift of becoming involved in life will lead to true freedom. In no longer isolating themselves to protect a freedom they do not possess, Observers can direct their energies toward transforming objective knowledge into the wisdom of experience. Former superficial social interactions become relationships of choice, respect, freedom, and unity.

Six: The Guardian

Intensifying the prime addiction. Guardians intensify their prime addiction by moving with the arrow and taking on the worst qualities of the Succeeders (Threes). When unexpected changes take place, coveted groups reject them, or normal security systems fail, Guardians' fear rises, gripping them in a stranglehold of resentment and rigidity.

Using worry, they control people and relationships to the point of smothering. Their frenetic behavior becomes a demand that remaining groups or individuals fulfill their needs for the security and connectedness that give their lives meaning. Their sense of self-worth decreases as their insecurities feed patterns of frenzied behavior. This destructive cycle prevents them from attaining the inner connectedness and grounding that would set them free. Consumed with insecurity, they shove their interpretation of loyalty and law down others' throats.

Neutralizing the prime addiction. Guardians neutralize their prime addiction by moving against the arrow and developing the positive qualities of the Preservationists (Nines). Preservationists are preeminently peaceful people who have an inner sense of their own power and who use it in quiet ways to achieve their purposes.

Healthy Guardians learn to live in peace within themselves first and then with others. By taking time to be alone, they learn to acknowledge their own thoughts and opinions without defensiveness and to face their fears squarely. They settle down, rest, and look within. There they discover the mystery that diversity, respect, and unity have all been cut from the same cloth. With this profound understanding guiding them, harmony, love, and service become their newfound companions.

Resistance. Withdrawing from the group to spend time alone may threaten Guardians, for they fear that others will question their loyalty and imply unfounded reasons for their absence. They fear something important will happen while they are gone, leaving them on the outside, forgotten. Nothing could be further from the truth. Their energy will always flow outward in a social way, connecting them to others, and others will be drawn to their vivaciousness. Discovering the treasure house of their interior world will yield a confidence, graciousness, and inner peace that will draw them into the heart of any group.

Reward. The gift of solitude and interior reflection is a knowledge of one's personal self-worth and an acceptance of one's strengths and talents. Thus newfound confidence releases Guardians' inner power to set a direction and follow their destiny, giving purpose and meaning to their lives. Guardians then come to trust and value their own thoughts and opinions and discover that the secrets of security were hidden in their own hearts. Free at last, they can live in peace with all people.

Seven: The Dreamer

Intensifying the prime addiction. Dreamers intensify their prime addiction by moving with the arrow and taking on the worst qualities of the Achievers (Ones). When their plans are not accepted, when the negative side of reality is thrust upon them, or when they cannot avoid painful realities that disrupt their personal lives, Dreamers lash out with a force that can be startling.

Ordinarily easy people to be with and fun to be around, they become moody and hostile, falling into self-pity and expecting someone else to take care of them. They stop making decisions or plans, their energy and vitality dry up, and they use their aggressive abilities to attack ideas, not people, and to protect themselves from outside advice.

Neutralizing the prime addiction. Dreamers neutralize their prime addiction by moving against the arrow and developing the positive qualities of the

Observers (Fives). Observers are preeminently appreciators of all reality, not wanting to judge or evaluate but simply to know everything as it is.

Healthy Dreamers will spend time in quiet reflection pondering both the positive and negative sides of themselves and reality, thereby recognizing that both are complicated and that there are no easy solutions. These quiet times will become safe opportunities for them to identify and experience the painful emotions that they have spent a lifetime repressing and denying.

As they develop a broader vision of reality, they discover the satisfaction of being taken seriously and of having their secret serious side and love for other people respected. As Dreamers develop the courage to embrace the total reality of life, they will mature in their ability to discern—a gift available only to clear-sighted, balanced realists.

Resistance. Looking at all of life, not only the bright side, will frighten Dreamers because they feel threatened at the thought of giving any power to the negative and thus becoming negative themselves. Nothing could be further from the truth. They always radiate light and good cheer to the world. However, with the added strengths of honesty and objectivity regarding themselves and life in general, they embody a solidness and balance that makes them even more appreciated as contributing members of society.

Reward. The gift that comes with solitude and reflection is the ability to balance interior and exterior reality. Thus do Dreamers discover how to deal creatively with life. Then, as not only the creator of plans but also a willing participant in the execution of their plans, Dreamers' full creative potential is released. Practical expertise gained through experience proves to be the final missing ingredient needed to liberate the intellectual prowess within them. They are then able to reach new heights of enlightenment that can benefit all of humanity.

Eight: The Confronter

Intensifying the prime addiction. Confronters intensify their prime addiction by moving with the arrow and taking on the worst qualities of the Observers (Fives). When their strategy for moving ahead is halted or blocked, when neither negotiation nor intimidation will break through a barrier, or when people they have counted on undermine their efforts, Confronters stop and redirect their enormous energies toward a new and unexpected plan of attack.

Everyone who stood in their way will be left in the dust to regret that decision. Still confident, they now have an inflexible determination to get what they were after and more. Convinced the world has chosen to self-destruct, they allow it to fall apart while showing only disdain for those who could have seen it coming but did not.

Neutralizing the prime addiction. Confronters neutralize their prime addiction by moving against the arrow and developing the positive qualities of the Helpers (Twos). Helpers are preeminently gentle and compassionate people. They express their heartfelt care for others through intimate sharing, personal vulnerability, and selfless action.

Healthy Confronters grow in compassion through valued personal relationships, in which they struggle to understand woundedness, emotions, and sensitivity to people and life. The struggle is intense, because they previously identified all these qualities as weakness.

Through eyes of compassion they now see that everyone is *not* created equal—some are stronger than others. This understanding is the lever that shifts the emphasis of personal justice to collective justice through nonviolent means. With the release of their Affective Center, Confronters' tenderness and strength unite to produce the merciful justice that contains the hope of peace on earth.

Resistance. Becoming gentle and caring will threaten Confronters, who often fear having their own safety compromised and their strength rendered impotent. Nothing could be further from the truth. Their strength is always a vital force, but with the added dimension of compassionate understanding, its destructive, insensitive side will gradually wear away. Their new relational abilities will make them even more effective in accomplishing the goals that are important to them.

Reward. The gift of energizing the Affective Center lies in the awakening of spiritual insight. Through this spiritual awareness Confronters discover and live out the destiny that will give meaning to their lives. They have always possessed the ability to attain personal goals, recognition, and material success. Now added to these abilities are spiritual awareness and emotional sensitivity, thus making of them life-giving people for individuals and for society.

Nine: The Preservationist

Intensifying the prime addiction. Preservationists intensify their prime addiction by moving with the arrow and taking on the worst qualities of the Guardians (Sixes). When they are faced with conflict in personal relationships, when they feel pressured to accomplish undesirable tasks in the personal sphere, or when too many expectations are placed on them, Preservationists' grounding gives way to uncertainty and stubborn inflexibility.

Unable to deal with the tension of their repressed emotions and feelings, they become rigid and legalistic. They look to the laws or to another person to resolve issues and to make decisions. Their resourcefulness and practical thought processes having been immobilized, their repressed pain and turmoil express themselves in behavior that destroys relationships and further devalues their already precarious self-esteem.

Neutralizing the prime addiction. Preservationists neutralize their prime addiction by moving against the arrow and developing the positive qualities of the Succeeders (Threes). Preeminently goal setters and accomplishers of tasks, Succeeders work hard and sacrifice themselves to get the job done right and on time.

Healthy Preservationists set and accomplish goals. They reflect on their lives, deal with their feelings, and acknowledge the importance of both self and others. With the growth of their self-esteem comes the formation of relationships of lasting value and unshakable commitment.

As their Affective Center opens, Preservationists experience the freedom and the pain of loving and being loved. With a newfound dignity they discover the difference that the exhilaration of accomplishment and intimate relationship makes to themselves and to the world.

Resistance. Expressing emotions and accomplishing goals will threaten Preservationists because they think that they cannot handle the turmoil and confusion such activities necessarily cause. Nothing could be further from the truth. These remarkably resilient and unflappable people have the inner stamina to move mountains once they have made a decision to do so. Because emotional turmoil creates confusion and causes them to lose their sense of direction, their initial work is to identify and deal with the causes of turmoil.

Reward. The gift in dealing with outside pressures and inner emotional turmoil lies in the many personal strengths that must be developed to do so. Thus is practical wisdom forged in the inner being of Preservationists. The depth and intensity required lead them on a quest for spiritual knowledge that expands their thinking and reveals their destiny. Thus others are drawn to Preservationists because of the freedom and selfless service manifested in their lives.

One: The Achiever

Intensifying the prime addiction. Achievers intensify their prime addiction by moving with the arrow and taking on the worst qualities of the Individualists (Fours). When they feel restrained by circumstances or people, when they are not the best at whatever they do, or when the significant others in their lives consistently fail to meet their standards in relationships, so narrow does their vision become that they slip into a morass of self-pity and self-criticism.

Soon they become overwhelmed by the tragic state their lives are in. Hopelessness blinds them to their gifts or talents and to seeing any options for the future or possibilities for things to be different. By impatiently and incessantly insisting on their perfectionistic perspective, Achievers develop a razor-sharp edge on their personalities that keeps others at a distance, especially if it is accompanied by an equally developed razor-sharp tongue.

Neutralizing the prime addiction. Achievers neutralize their prime addiction by moving against the arrow and developing the positive qualities of the Dreamers (Sevens). Dreamers are preeminently happy and optimistic people. They look at the bright side of life and create fun, laughter, and cheer wherever they are.

Healthy Achievers lighten up on themselves and on the world. They develop a playful attitude about life and even about work, giving up their dogged striving for perfection to become more enthusiastic about life and living. Their gift for seeing foibles in themselves and others is transformed into humor that delights and invigorates with its lighthearted approach to human weakness.

As they open up to their Theoretical Center, they see their need to focus on developing the gifts and talents that will give them the freedom to express their individuality creatively. By seeing the "big picture," they buy the time needed to both develop their gifts and enjoy life. Exercising self-control helps them fix their attention on the goal without becoming discouraged by the little obstacles along the way.

Resistance. Letting up on themselves and others threatens Achievers, for they believe that without constant vigilance their unruly side will take over and their lives will never amount to anything. Nothing could be further from the truth.

When they begin to accept actual responsibility for their lives and reject the illusion of their being responsible for keeping everything running smoothly, they become free to focus creatively on personal goals and relationships, and through relaxation they find new energy to accomplish their deepest dreams.

Reward. The gift of taking charge of one's own future lies in the development of creative leadership qualities that actualize one's unique destiny. No longer depending on others to unlock the doors to life frees Achievers to develop practical wisdom that can benefit many others in everyday living for years to come. By developing optimism they lend their vivacity to every relationship and thus find themselves excelling not only in carrying out projects but also in friendship and community living.

Living the Good Life

Trickster, Sly One, Mechanical Shadow Dancer, and Real Beautiful Self all have important lessons to teach us. Knowing there is a Trickster in each of us wakes us up to the constant possibility of living with illusion. The trick is making illusion seem like reality so that we never hope for or work for anything else. It becomes even more devious when it veils the goodness of reality and truth under the guise of illusion, thus deceiving us into believing that things are not worth the effort we know they will require. In making friends with Trickster we're taught the secrets of spotting even the most subtle of deceptions.

When we befriend our Sly One we learn the way of silence, patience, and dedication to truth and timing. Knowing Sly One tells us that there is cleverness at work in the universe, a cleverness that can make the difference if we will only make the effort.

To Mechanical Shadow Dancer we can only be grateful, for through this part of us we've been educated, learned to survive, and strengthened the muscles that will carry us on our journey through life. Living much of our lives as Mechanical Shadow Dancer will never have been a waste of time if we wake up, see the patterns we need to escape, and begin to live according to our own inner rhythm. Similarly, by stretching and straining our imaginations to see and believe the descriptions of our best selves, and by remembering times when Real Beautiful Self has appeared in our lives, even for only a moment, we begin to develop a vision of all that we can become.

The questions can now be asked once again: Do you feel stressed out? Are you running faster and faster and getting farther and farther behind? Do you have time for yourself? Do you get moody, touchy, depressed when things don't go your way? Do thoughts of revenge, resentment, envy, jealousy, fear, or worry occupy much of your day? Does your life have meaning? Are your relationships healthy and supportive? Do you like yourself? Do you know yourself?

If you are running faster and faster and feeling more dissatisfied with your life, Trickster is at work, and Mechanical Shadow Dancer has taken center stage. It's time to stop and look for and listen to the clever wisdom of Sly One in you. The Enneagram can assist in revealing you to yourself—with even more clarity than you might ordinarily care to have.

Who knows? It could be that Real Beautiful Self is waiting to be revealed when you peer beyond what is often referred to as "real life." Stretch to experience what your deepest self has always known, hoping and dreaming that it would be real: You were created good, you are good, and the dance of your life is indeed worth celebrating.

Wings to Soar

Balancing Centers and Wings

CHAPTER SIX

Every soul is pregnant with the seed of insight. It is vague and hidden. In some people the seed grows, in others it decays. Some give birth to life. Others miscarry it. Some know how to bear, to nurse, to rear an insight that comes into being. Others do not.
—RABBI HESCHEL

H ave you ever had the painful experience of watching a bird with an injured wing wildly flapping its good wing while running, frantically looking for a place to hide?

While visiting friends in California, we watched in spellbound silence along with everyone else at the breakfast table as the following scene unfolded across the street. On the ground was a bird with an injured wing in the state just described. Running behind the bird on tiptoe in slow motion was a man with a broom rake. Every little while he would make a sudden turn and, yelling, shake his rake in a menacing manner. Then turning back, he would resume his rather humorous Pink Panther routine.

It was quite obvious that the man had forgotten himself in every way and was focused solely on protecting the injured bird. What was not at first obvious was the reason he made his sudden turns, yelling and shaking his rake. Soon, however, the rationale behind this rather strange behavior became apparent when, turning with the swift fury of an avenging angel, the man swept a stalking cat halfway across the yard with his rake.

Meanwhile, the bird was in such turmoil that everyone watching was certain it would die of fright. Not so. The cat, after facing the wrath of the avenging angel, skulked off into the bushes. The man then dropped his rake and, falling to his knees, approached the injured bird and became totally still. After a moment, he slowly reached out his hand, gently picked up the now quiet little bird, and, placing it in a cage, locked the door.

Only outside intervention saved the panic-stricken bird from certain disaster.

From Panic to Power

Rarely do we (or any living creature) have an avenging angel protecting us from facing the harsh realities of life. If we depended only on external aid to deal with life's difficulties, we would inevitably become chronic victims. Sadly, chronic victimization is all too common in the world today. As it was for the injured bird, a safe, secure environment is available only at the outrageous price of personal freedom.

It's doubtful that there is even one of us who has not had an experience of feeling victimized, helpless, caged. If we don't want to take up permanent residence in a bird cage, however, it's important to investigate alternative living arrangements. The secret wisdom of balancing the centers and wings, the next step in exploring the Enneagram, can be a guide to this new way of living.

Our study of centers began in chapter 2. There we learned that everyone has three centers of intelligence. We are created with these three centers in balance so that we are free to respond with the appropriate intelligence at any given time. This freedom is soon lost, however. Only to the extent that we exercise and develop our God-given right of choice will we move from the confinement of panic to the freedom of inner power. The path to inner power is called balance.

Consider, for example, a man who is walking alone down a city street at night. Suddenly he is accosted by another man who obviously intends to rob him and inflict physical harm. Which intelligence should dominate at that moment? Naturally, the Effective Center's intelligence needs to be activated. This is the center of safety, action, knowing how to move, taking care of oneself, and getting by in the world. At this moment the man must think with the intelligence of survival.

If another center of intelligence were to dominate the situation, there could very well be disastrous results. If the man were to allow his Affective Center to reign, he might either burst into indignation at being violated or use deep feeling, sensitivity, and understanding to dissuade his would-be accoster. We might seriously doubt whether the offender would be detoured from his original intention by either approach.

By the same token, primarily using the Theoretical Center at this moment will get the potential victim nowhere. Explaining the legal consequences of the accoster's action to him at this moment will hardly evoke restraint. In such a moment, logic is of little use, for it is not uppermost in an accoster's list of priorities.

Only the Effective Center of intelligence can be allowed to dominate in this situation. If the Effective Center is not available for immediate use, it is inevitable that the man will become a victim.

Does this mean that the intended victim must be able to subdue the attacker physically or to outrun him? Not necessarily. Consider what happened when an elderly woman was accosted by a well-built young man in his mid-twenties. The man, roughly pushing her backward, demanded her money.

The woman quickly regained her balance, and pulling herself squarely up to her full height of five feet, two inches, asked in a firm voice devoid of accusation, "Young man, how would your mother feel if she knew you were doing this?"

The young man was so taken aback that he just stood for a moment in silence. Then in a half-embarrassed voice he replied, "She'd be real hurt, real disappointed, ma'am."

"I know you'd never want that to happen, and neither would I," said the woman as she walked by the young man with a smile and a nod.

The woman used the intelligence of the Effective Center, the solid, "here I am, deal with me" approach. That confidence was supported by the logic of the

Theoretical Center and the depth of feeling and concern of the Affective Center. Together, her three centers of intelligence were in perfect balance.

After such an example, you may ask whether we are saying that no harm will come to a person in whom all three centers are in balance. No, we are not. In life there are no guarantees—people and circumstances are unpredictable. Perhaps the ability to use effective intelligence would prevent you from being in an obviously dangerous place alone. Perhaps nothing you could do would prevent certain things from happening. The balanced use of all three centers can, however, assist you in dealing with the unexpected in a more positive, creative way.

In any case, the reality is that there is an appropriate intelligence to use in every situation and circumstance, and the appropriate intelligence will be equally supported by the intelligences of the other two centers. With willingness to do the inner work required to balance the centers of intelligence, we begin to access the freedom to make choices that will eventually lead through panic into power.

Building the Cage

One of the most beautiful sights in all of creation is a bird in flight. With effortless ease it rides the unseen winds with exquisite grace and beauty. Quick as a flash, a bird can dive toward the earth or soar to the heavens and disappear from view.

From the beginning of time a soaring bird has triggered flights of fancy in human beings, arousing our deep inner longings to be free. Echoes of this universal cry of the human spirit have been carried through song, poetry, and literature and even into the work of the Wright Brothers and our flights into outer space.

Just as a bird in flight mysteriously touches some long-forgotten memory of true freedom, the distress of seeing a bird with an injured wing touches the all-too-familiar pain associated with the struggle to survive. Both the mysterious unconscious awareness of true freedom and the conscious awareness of pain can be understood symbolically through the healthy bird and the injured bird.

Because all of us have been created with the three centers of intelligence in balance, we have an intrinsic understanding of true freedom. In perfect balance and harmony, we arrive in an imperfect, unbalanced world. Sounds of discord soon overpower the original harmony. Before long, as children, we learn that survival, having our needs met, means learning to act at variance with our true nature. With continual action, reaction, and interaction, we find that a particular way of behaving simply works better. Thus do children learn how to play the game of life.

The particular response that each of us as children discovers works best becomes our survival strength or Preferred Center. The Preferred Center can be likened to the body of the bird—the primary part that sustains life, digests input, sings happily, and screeches because it feels the pain.

For every action there is an equal and opposite reaction. Survival in an imperfect world with imperfect people demands that a child become unbalanced—imperfect—as well. This movement destroys the natural balance and conceals the child's true nature or essence. The resulting damage can be symbolically understood through the injured wing of the bird.

The injured wing, though still intact, is useless and a source of pain when accidentally bumped. Wounded in this way, if it is to survive, the bird must remain confined in a safe environment.

This, then, is the condition of the Third or Repressed Center of intelligence in individuals. In the bird, avoiding use of the injured wing is not a conscious action but rather a learned, mechanical reaction to pain. In human beings, the avoidance of the Third or Repressed Center of intelligence is also a learned, mechanical reaction to pain and discomfort.

Meanwhile, the good wing flaps and flaps. Like the Secondary or Support Center of intelligence, this wing is in good condition and can be used at any time. It is often even overused in the bird's attempt to fly again.

One strong wing is not enough to compensate for the injured wing or alter the imbalance that the injury has created; therefore, even the strong wing cannot fulfill its purpose. Likewise, the Secondary or Support Center is unable to compensate for the Repressed Center or to fulfill its own true purpose. Thus, like the bird, we are not free—unconscious pain prevents us from giving free expression to our true identity. We have no wings to soar.

It is important in this illustration to understand that though only one wing is injured, the entire bird is wounded, unable to fly. The same is true with people. When one center of intelligence shuts down because of pain, the whole person is affected. Like the bird, we too remain earthbound, not free to soar, to follow our destinies. Living in a self-protective stance, we overcompensate by using and distorting the centers of intelligence that we do have accessible.

By balancing the centers we can find wholeness. Wholeness is founded upon our ability to grow in consciousness so that the centers will be brought back into alignment, each one being used in the appropriate situation for its appropriate purpose. Only personal consciousness will bring about such healing, and healing arises from a soul-stirring mixture of stimulation and pain. Only to the extent that we are healed will we be free to fly.

Broadening the Wingspan

When talking about the Enneagram, people often refer to the idea of having "wings." The intention is to explain in specific ways how we pick up some of the qualities of one of the numbers next to our own number on the Enneagram circle, thus expanding our own pattern in a unique way. When people say, for example, "I'm a Nine with a One wing," or, "I'm a Seven with a Six wing," they mean that specific qualities of the number named as a wing are directly affecting the way their Enneagram compulsion is expressed.

Though people find such statements helpful in explaining their experience, there is one important shortcoming to this way of understanding wings, namely, people's "wing qualities" are confined to one of the numbers directly alongside their own number. If this were the only way to understand wings, three of the numbers—Three, Six, and Nine—would be limited to qualities from only one center of intelligence. Threes would have access only to characteristics of the Two and Four, thus confining them to emotional or affect-centered functions; Sixes only to attributes of the Five and Seven, restricting them to thinking or theory-

CIRCLE OF HARMONY:
CONSISTENCY, DIVERSITY, AND BALANCE

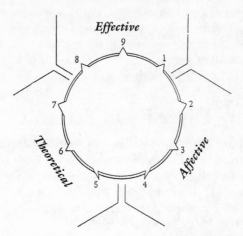

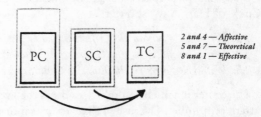

Wing Numbers

2 and 4 — *Affective*
5 and 7 — *Theoretical*
8 and 1 — *Effective*

PC - Preferred Center
SC - Secondary Center
TC - Tertiary Center

Balance Point Numbers

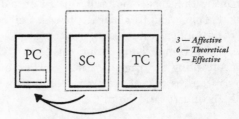

3 — *Affective*
6 — *Theoretical*
9 — *Effective*

The division of the nine numbers into Wing Numbers and Balance Point Numbers is proposed by O'Leary and Beesing in *The Enneagram: A Journey of Self-discovery* (the Balance Points they name Denial Points). This diagram and this explanation of how the centers relate to Wings and Balance Points are by Theodore E. Dobson and Kathleen V. Hurley. Copyright © Theodore E. Dobson and Kathleen V. Hurley.

centered functions; and Nines only to qualities of the Eight and One, restricting them to safety or effect-centered functions.

However, there is another way of understanding the diversity in each pattern that avoids all the limitations and dilemmas of this approach. It not only embodies the commonly understood approach to wings, but also gives greater breadth, depth, and diversity to *all* of the nine patterns of the Enneagram. This understanding of individual diversity, though initially more challenging to comprehend, has proven in hundreds of seminars to be more reliable in helping people identify and understand the subtleties of their own pattern.

Understanding Diversity in Patterns

There are three ideas at the foundation of this understanding of pattern diversity. First, no one *has* wings; rather, each pattern is either a *Wing Number* or a *Balance Point Number*. Second, the notion of *centers* is basic to this understanding; thus it is important for people to identify their Preferred Center. Third, Wing Numbers and Balance Point Numbers are treated differently in this understanding, which requires that they be explained separately.

Wing numbers. The patterns called Wing Numbers are on the outside edges of each triad of patterns, or on the outside edges of each center. The diagram "Circle of Harmony" shows that

The Wing Numbers in the Affective Center are Two and Four
The Wing Numbers in the Theoretical Center are Five and Seven
The Wing Numbers in the Effective Center are Eight and One

The center in which a number resides is the Preferred Center for people of that pattern or number. Overuse of that center is indicated in the diagram by the large dotted-line rectangle that inflates that center. Their Secondary, or Support, Center is the center that is *next to* their own number. Its overuse is indicated in the diagram by the smaller but still inflated dotted-line rectangle that encases this center. Finally, their Third, or Repressed, Center is the center *farthest* from their pattern or number. Underuse of this center is indicated in the diagram by the tiny dotted-line rectangle lying within this center.

By consulting the diagram "Circle of Harmony" and the chart below, people whose pattern is one of the Wing Numbers will be able to identify their Preferred, Secondary, and Third Centers.

PATTERN NUMBER	PREFERRED CENTER	SECONDARY CENTER	THIRD CENTER
Two	Affective	Effective	Theoretical
Four	Affective	Theoretical	Effective
Five	Theoretical	Affective	Effective
Seven	Theoretical	Effective	Affective
Eight	Effective	Theoretical	Affective
One	Effective	Affective	Theoretical

Of what benefit is it to know which is your Preferred, Secondary, or Third Center? It has many advantages; indeed, the secret to transformation itself will be found here.

To begin with, it explains how attributes from several patterns can seem to be your own. Again, we must recall that each of us is one–and only one–pattern. Though you have only one underlying motivation and therefore *one prime addiction* dominating your life, you can express *qualities* from other patterns. These traits round out your personality, acting like a lens through which the personality shines. Wing characteristics shade your use of your own pattern.

Because you prefer an *entire center,* you have available many of the characteristics of one or both of the other two patterns in the Preferred Center. Likewise, you have available some of the attributes of one, two, or even all three patterns in the Secondary Center. Few, if any, of the qualities of the patterns in your Third Center will be evident in your life, however.

Developing the Third Center. Only in understanding the necessity for reclaiming and developing the intelligence of the Third, or Repressed, Center can we regain the balance needed to live a healthy life. Without it, we can only overuse and therefore distort the gifts of both Preferred and Secondary Centers. As these consciously used centers attempt to compensate for the absence of the intelligence of the Third Center, they can create only a pale shadow of the real thing.

For example, no matter how strongly Individualists (Fours) feel about a project or how hard Observers (Fives) think about a project, that project will not be completed without the actual physical energy that can be found only in their repressed Effective Center. If they resist using their Repressed Center, their only other option is to convince another person with logic (distorted use of the theoretical functions) or to manipulate someone by taking advantage of their relationship (distorted use of the affective functions) to accomplish the project for them.

Resolving the dilemma. Understanding how people can include the attributes of several patterns also resolves a dilemma that has been a source of confusion for many people who study the Enneagram. The confusion arises when after having identified their pattern they continue to recognize in themselves many qualities of a pattern that apparently has no connection to their own.

For many people, the common teaching that we have only one wing not only proves easy to understand but also describes accurately their experience of themselves. Many others, however, unable to identify with either of the patterns next to their own, continue to question for months and even years whether they have accurately identified their pattern.

Without the confidence that you have correctly identified your pattern, the wisdom of the Enneagram is useless for personal growth and transformation. One Individualist (Four) might clearly recognize how qualities of the Three (Succeeder) modify his or her personality. Another Four might find more evident in him- or herself the positive characteristics of the Two (Helper), another number in the same Preferred Center (Affective).

Similarly, though a Four might identify with many traits of the academic, somewhat reclusive Five, a Four may also display attributes of a Six or a Seven, because these numbers also lie in the Secondary Center (Theoretical). For example, one Four may find that fear or the need to keep everyone in line with laws, rules, and regulations–aspects of the Six–predominate. Another Four may find that the Seven qualities of attraction to new and exciting experiences, lack of staying power, or enjoyment of the humor and stimulation of superficial social contact seem to predominate.

The supplemental characteristics acquired in the Preferred and Secondary Centers in large part account for the myriad expressions of every patterns' prime psychological addiction. These acquired characteristics support but do not dictate the underlying motivation; there are many factors in everyone's life that could partly explain the differences among people with the same pattern. Parents, upbringing, birth order, social environment, educational opportunities, introversion and extroversion, would only be a few of the many modifying influences in a person's life.

The complexity found in human nature reemphasizes the importance of discovering your own *motivation*. The importance of the acquired traits that expand and influence your personality versus the driving force of your prime addiction can be sorted out by only one question: Why do I do the things I do and say the things I say? Two people can appear to respond to a situation in a similar manner, but the underlying motivation for each one's response can ultimately be understood only through the prime addiction or Enneagram pattern.

Balance Point Numbers. As we proceed to a discussion of the Balance Point Numbers—Three, Six, and Nine—it is important to restate two of the concepts of this understanding of pattern diversity. First, no one *has* wings; rather, each pattern is either a *Wing Number* or a *Balance Point Number*. Second, the notion of *centers* is basic to this understanding; it is important for people to name their Preferred Center.

The Balance Point Numbers are named so because they stand in the middle of each of the three Centers.

PATTERN	PREFERRED CENTER
Three	Affective
Six	Theoretical
Nine	Effective

Two things distinguish the Balance Point Numbers from the Wing Numbers. First, although Balance Point Numbers have a Preferred Center, *they repress their Preferred Center*. Second, because of this peculiarity, *they have equal access to all three centers*. Thus, they are able to use their Preferred (but Repressed) Center, but they only use it at the lowest level of function and only when the qualities of that center will serve their own egocentric purposes.

Succeeders (Threes), in the Preferred (but Repressed) Affective Center, use their congenial charm and knowledge of relationship to maneuver others into being productive and into getting a job done.

In the personal realm they have little knowledge based on experience and therefore do not understand intimacy. They take all the credit and acclaim for successful production and interpret adulation as love and good relationship. By living in the illusion that success and love are synonymous, they easily convince themselves that everything they do emanates from a loving concern for others.

Guardians (Sixes), in the Preferred (but Repressed) Theoretical Center, use conceptualization to visualize negative possibilities that feed both worry and fear. They can apply their abstract thinking capabilities only to solving impersonal problems.

In the personal realm, they themselves have been totally removed, extracted from their abstract thinking processes. Because they cannot even see themselves in the larger scheme of life, it is impossible for them to see how to fit in or to make decisions regarding their own life. Therefore, marriage, home, family, or belonging to a stable group anchor them in the world and give them the reason for being alive. In addition, their negative mental visualizations give rise to their opinionated ideas about right and wrong and explain why they place laws, rules, and regulations above anything else, including people.

Preservationists (Nines) in the Preferred (but Repressed) Effective Center, use their creativity to actualize the ideas and possibilities sketched on a drawing board in the professional or social realms only. A good reputation continually shored up by peer acknowledgment becomes the single source through which they can believe in their own value or importance.

In the personal realm, having completely devalued themselves, they see no choice but to use their power and strength to close out everyone and everything that might reaffirm the terrible conclusion they have already reached. They will enter into activity or impersonal interchange only when they are confident it will remain lighthearted. The majority of their time and effort must be spent protecting and nurturing the little inner peace they experience; consequently, they use their effect-centered stamina to hold the world at bay, preventing turmoil from disrupting their lives. They must use all their available power and stubborn determination to ward off disrupting influences against tension and turmoil.

Secondary and Third Centers. Balance Point Numbers do not have a fixed Secondary, or Support, Center. What is fixed is that their Third, or Repressed, Center is also their Preferred (Repressed) Center. That is the center where focused effort to grow in consciousness must be directed so that their centers can come into balance.

Both of the other two centers could be called Secondary Centers. Again, remember that these Balance Point Numbers have equal access to all three centers. Although some of the qualities of any or all of the numbers in those two Secondary Centers are available to them, they will have few if any of the true qualities of the patterns in their Preferred (but Repressed) Center; these attributes can only be developed through hard work.

These three numbers each place great emphasis on manifesting what might be called the outer shell of their Preferred (but Repressed) Center but find its true purposes elusive. Threes are experts at the image orientation and manipulation that emanate from a lower use of the Affective Center or emotions. Sixes have many opinions—the lower use of the Theoretical Center or logical mind—but will not claim them as their own unless they are assured that in doing so their security will not be jeopardized. Nines have the great stamina and energy common to the Effective Center or instinctual self but use these qualities in a lower way to prevent things from happening rather than to make things happen.

For each of the Balance Point Numbers, the repression of the Preferred Center has its roots deeply embedded in the personal realm. Rather than being like the bird with the injured wing, these three patterns have had their wings clipped. Although they are free to hop around to all three centers of intelligence, they cannot get off the ground. Only when they put the hard work and effort into opening up their Preferred (but Repressed) Center and experience the pain of growing in consciousness will they receive their flight feathers and be free to soar.

Out of the Cage and into the Sky

A bird can live in a cage and, with proper care, live a relatively long and happy life. Yet, after being confined for a good length of time, if the cage door is left open the bird will fly away. It can't help but follow its natural instincts.

We too have a natural inclination to be free, to be good, to be relational, to be healthy, to love and be loved. Why, then, do we so often do or say the very things that lead to separation, isolation, alienation, and violence?

Perhaps it's because we've forgotten who we are and the true self lies sleeping behind walls made by survival mechanisms. We've built our own cages day by day, moment by moment, choice by choice.

Most of the time our walls of self-protection are so high we can't see beyond them. Every so often life knocks one of our walls down, and we panic. Suddenly we feel vulnerable and helpless. We can't imagine that these seemingly devastating moments are gifts—invitations to reclaim the freedom that was long ago forsaken.

Once in a great while we stop and look up—we see the sky, the stars. In those sacred moments our souls are stirred, and we remember who we are, where we came from. With split-second clarity we touch our greatness, our Real Beautiful Self, our true or best self, and understand that all the expansive beauty and mystery of the universe lies within us in microcosm.

But who dares to say aloud, "For a moment I remembered who I really am!" The kindly smiles, the raised eyebrows, the inevitable snickering are too much to take. So we tuck the memory away and keep the secret. Perhaps we also forget it ever happened, and our Real Beautiful Self falls asleep again. We know that everyone, including us, can easily identify the negative parts of ourselves that have no home like the ugly duckling. But what do we do when suddenly—even for a fleeting moment—there's a swan in our midst? Power, grace, beauty, freedom are very threatening indeed.

Remember that for every ugly duckling there is a swan waiting to emerge. Remember who you are, and remember that for the swan, the sky is the limit.

The Flight of the Swan

The Process of Transformation

CHAPTER SEVEN

One evening, the sun was just setting in wintry splendor when a flock of beautiful large birds appeared out of the bushes. They were dazzlingly white with long waving necks. . . . They spread out their magnificent broad wings and flew away from the cold regions. . . . The duckling had never seen anything so beautiful. —HANS CHRISTIAN ANDERSEN, "THE UGLY DUCKLING"

L ike the ugly duckling, cygnets or young swans show little if any of the majestic grace and beauty that will come with maturity. They have large bodies and tiny wings. Although they quickly master the waters of the northern climate in which the eggs are hatched, flight is much more difficult.

Cygnets have slightly more than three months to develop their wing strength to the point that they can lift their bodies off the water. If for any reason their wings aren't developed by the time of the southern migration, they are left behind and freeze to death in the harsh, unforgiving winter storms.

Therefore, cygnets spend many hours each day traveling back and forth on the water. By flapping their wings vigorously while their feet paddle furiously under the surface, they work each day and grow stronger. Instinctively they know the power of flight is essential to a swan's survival.

From this perspective, Andersen's tale of the ugly duckling becomes a penetrating metaphor for human experience. Symbolically, the duckling's quest for belonging, acceptance, identity, purpose, and a place in the world epitomizes the first half of every person's life.

The duckling, who had done nothing wrong, was an outcast simply because he was different. Scorned by his siblings, he had no one with whom to play and practice flight, no cheering section to encourage him or teach him how to fly. One day, lonely and filled with sadness, the duckling looked up, mesmerized by the sight of a flock of magnificent white birds. A short time later a bitterly cold winter storm swept over the marshes. Because he couldn't fly, the ugly duckling had to keep flapping his wings day and night to keep the water from freezing over and trapping him. As the slushy water got heavier, the ice crept closer, until his pool of water became so small that he could no longer move. Weary and frightened, he was frozen fast into the ice.

Like the duckling, most people are doing the best they can, but life keeps closing in around them until, exhausted, they can only surrender to what seems to be the inevitable. At that moment of emptiness the only alternative seems to be surrender to a Higher Power or, as in the duckling's case, the Hand of God disguised in the hand of a peasant. What seems to be certain death—physically, emotionally, financially, spiritually—is the essential element needed to begin the process of chipping away at whatever holds one in bondage.

It's amazing how success or power or personal advantage diminishes in importance when your life has been painfully turned upside down and inside out. It is as if you truly understand what life is all about for the first time.

If you allow yourself to be seized by this sacred moment, inevitably, you will begin to search for a new direction, to embark on a spiritual quest for meaning, destiny, and the Real Beautiful Self within.

Breaking Through

We have many "Breaking Through" experiences in our lives—invitations and opportunities to grow and change. Unfortunately, more often than not, we respond to them by doing only what is needed to stop the pain. Products of modern society, we treat the symptom but refuse to look for the source of the pain.

Once the pain has reached a tolerable level, we may go right back to living our lives in exactly the same way we did before the miraculous breakthrough. Before the pain subsides, however, fear may prompt us to give at least lip service to the importance of growing in consciousness and dedicating ourselves anew to spiritual values.

The value of both psychological and spiritual principles cannot be underestimated. Uncountable numbers of lives have literally been saved through the wisdom and guidance of professionals in both fields.

The difficulty lies not with the various systems but with people who simply learn the language. Believing they understand, they then use the words to protect themselves from doing the hard work of personal growth, the tedious work of strengthening their wings for flight. Like sleepwalkers, they only appear to be awake.

Generally people learn just enough to alleviate their pain or to manipulate others. They never understand that the only lasting benefits of knowledge come from applying it to one's own life. The news media give witness to this sad fact in every report of corruption through misused power, abuse of all kinds, and violence in every imaginable form in society and its institutions.

It has been said that a little knowledge is a dangerous thing. If a "breaking through" experience is to have any lasting meaning, we must do more than dabble in change. We must use such experiences as occasions to rethink and reinterpret all present ideas, values, beliefs, actions, and words with ruthless honesty—in light of a new consciousness.

Painful experiences that are not dealt with in a manner that will bring about healing must be repressed. This unconscious material then becomes the weapon of division, violence, and war within individuals and among peoples and nations. No one, regardless of profession, education, status, color, creed, or gender, is exempt from the often humiliating struggle and pain of becoming a conscious human being.

The signs of repressed, unconscious pain are everywhere. Jails are overflowing. Mental hospitals are full. Stress and stress-related illness are at an all-time high. Addictions of all kinds are on the rise, and new forms of addiction are uncovered every day. The population of homeless people continues to increase. Drug use and drug dealing defy control. Child abuse and spouse battering rise moment by moment. Divorce rates rise, and one-parent families struggle to survive. People of the First World have more material possessions than ever before, and depression is their number-one mental health problem. The world seems constantly on the edge of self-destruction as national revolutions and regional conflicts threaten to erupt into global war.

In the face of all this, isn't it bordering on the ridiculous for most people to think they are doing just fine? If there is still any doubt that people are asleep, unconscious and mechanical, just greet the next person you meet with, "Hi! How are you today?" The automatic response will probably be, "I'm fine, thanks–doin' just fine!" The mechanical response says it all. If you still doubt people are asleep, listen to yourself the next time someone asks you how you're doing!

Approximately two thousand years ago, Jesus of Nazareth was trying to wake people up to these same realities. "Do you still not understand, still not realize?" he once said to his disciples. "Are your minds closed? Have you eyes and do not see, ears and do not hear?" (Mark 8:17–18). Notice that he doesn't ask them if they have knowledge but instead inquires about *understanding*.

The world is filled with knowledge and knowledgeable people. Understanding, on the other hand, can only be gained through personal experience, through applying knowledge to everyday life. Knowledge is theoretical; understanding is practical.[1]

Understanding comes as we recognize the truth of our own duplicity, negativity, self-serving motivations, and petty jealousies. Only then can we recognize and understand the same struggles in others. Awareness of self creates compassion, forgiveness, and healing–gifts that are *first given to self* and create a new sense of identity. Then we *become* compassion, forgiveness, and healing for others.

The weakness that we do not embrace in ourselves, we despise and attempt to destroy in another. Individual conscious understanding is the only neutralizing force for violence and hatred. Any other solution necessarily precludes the will, conscience, freedom, and dignity of the individual.

Breaking Free

It will be apparent to anyone who reflects on his or her life that "breaking through" is never the problem. Most everyone has an abundance of invitations or opportunities to grow. However, these invitations are often ignored or refused,

1. See Maurice Nicoll, *Psychological Commentaries on the Teaching of Gurdjieff and Ouspensky* (London: Shambhala, 1984), vol. 3, pp. 1039–41. Much of the material in this chapter has been influenced by Nicoll's thinking.

either because we are more comfortable with familiar patterns of living or because we really don't know how to respond–how to go about changing. When a "breaking through" experience *does* produce consciousness and transformation, then "breaking free" from the restraints of mechanical, unconscious living will become the gift of freedom.

The Enneagram clearly describes how every person has unwittingly but necessarily exchanged inner freedom for survival in an egocentric world. The advantage of recognizing your psychologically patterned way of living is that it provides another opportunity to begin consciously *thinking for yourself* by showing you where and how you have not done so in much of life. By knowing your Enneagram number, you recognize there is an unconscious *predetermined* set of issues you will focus on and a *predetermined* set of responses you will make to those issues. The Enneagram describes how we respond mechanically, how we do not think for ourselves.

However, most of us probably believe we already do think for ourselves. This is not true. If it were true, we would neither have patterned, mechanical reactions to life nor think that our own view of life is the only valid one. The truth is that we don't think for ourselves.

For example, many people have strong opinions about different things and fully believe that their opinions are valid. Where did these opinions originate? In the family? In school? In the neighborhood? In the latest political speech? Yes! All of the above and more. All people are a complex blend of the thoughts, ideas, prejudices, and opinions of the people and experiences that have influenced their lives. True freedom is inevitably limited by our automatically accepted values, likes, and dislikes.

Notice how people surround themselves with things that support their accepted value system. Our choice of a neighborhood, social activities, reading material, political preferences, and religious practice all reinforce already accepted opinions, ideas, prejudices, and values.

When faced with someone who has a different opinion or value system, most people's automatic reaction is to negate or attempt to disprove the validity of the other's ideas and beliefs. Blindly accepted, unexamined values are always threatened by ideas and beliefs that differ. People who fear looking within and taking responsibility for their own faults will always attempt to curtail the freedom of others. Their minds close down and, consciously or unconsciously, they allow judgments, rumors, and half-truths to rule the way they live their lives. The result is that unthinking, unconscious people get other unthinking, unconscious people to join causes that none of them understands.

Always being against someone or something is a negative use of energy. Nothing positive can grow in the diseased womb of negativity. Likewise, negativity can never grow in the light of truth and consciousness. Jesus of Nazareth said it another way: "A sound tree cannot bear bad fruit, nor a rotten tree bear good fruit" (Matt. 7:18).

Inner freedom–the only freedom that can never be taken away–will reemerge only when we begin to think for ourselves. Without clear, original thinking about our own values, our lives will forever remain the same. Unless we think for ourselves–unless we seek to understand clearly what we do and why we do it–life will be a never-ending cycle of repeated experiences. If we never examine our mental attitudes but carry them unquestioned throughout life, how can anything be different? The same prejudices, ideas, opinions, and rules—if never evaluated or scrutinized—will automatically and severely restrict our freedom.

There can be no greater bondage, no greater evidence that we are unfree than the inability or refusal to examine ourselves objectively, without condemning or justifying. As Socrates said, the unexamined life is not worth living. What a terrible waste it would be to live and die and never touch or taste or feel the liberty to be the person you were created to be!

Freedom is first and foremost an internal reality. Most of us spend the first half of life chasing an illusionary external freedom. Thus, it will take the whole, if not more, of the second half of life to reclaim the freedom that was our inheritance from the beginning. We must stand guard like a sentry at the inner gates of freedom. "Breaking free" requires the vigilance to make choices that will allow us to live and grow in the light of consciousness.

Within the secret wisdom of the Enneagram lie the hidden clues that begin to reveal the possibility of neutralizing our prime psychological addiction and breaking free—not from our personality but from its destructive dimensions.

Transformation: An Uncommon Choice

Transformation is a choice—a common-sense choice that is not made by everyone. Transformation demands hard work and constant vigilance. Because its value is veiled by deception and illusion, many people avoid it, ignore it, sidestep issues that would cause it to begin, and otherwise reveal their preference for remaining asleep. Psychological and spiritual sleep allows us to maintain the comfort of routine, fortifying the illusion that psychological addiction and dysfunction is truth that gives life rather than deception that leads to death.

If habitual mental attitudes lull the spirit to sleep, conscious artistic living is the only force that will awaken it. Reacting to life is easy, but a well-thought-out response is far more difficult because it means waking up and being free.

Creative living is not a matter of being an artist with paint or dance or music. Instead, it is a matter of living your own life in a creative way—examining your life, thinking for yourself, choosing consciously and taking responsibility for your choices, finding new solutions to old problems, and expressing your Real Beautiful Self with integrity.

Because Western civilization since the Industrial Revolution has speeded up life, we no longer feel we have time to waste on things like beauty, wonder, and questions about life itself. Instead we have instant relationships, disposable values, and fast-food commitments. Because creative living is a tough job, many people choose to live safely.

Living is like driving: the faster we drive, the narrower our focus must become to keep the automobile safely on course. Living in high gear means that we can't risk looking at the scenery or at a breathtaking sunset for fear of losing control. Living in the fast lane demands treating life as a problem. With such an attitude, even the desire for transformation remains a mystery.

But safe living is also dysfunctional living. People who never take chances, never ask for a raise, never tell their friends they are dissatisfied with the relationship, go to church every Sunday just in case, repeat old patterns of behavior just because they don't want to rock the boat, play bridge every Tuesday evening out of habit, watch TV every night just because it is on—these people are *asleep*. They are not thinking, feeling, or doing anything creative. They are mechanical people who have found a safe way to live.

People who repress their thoughts, opinions, and emotions and allow them to marinate in the unconscious are dangerous. They become the perpetrators of hatred and division. Sleeping people like these are hazardous to their own health and to the health of society.

Waking up and living creatively means surrendering to the process of thinking, feeling, and doing. In other words, it means learning to use your Theoretical, Affective, and Effective Centers together in unified action. Safe living means repressing your thoughts and feelings, commenting negatively about self and others aloud or within, affirming your unimportance, unlovableness, or incapability, envying others instead of imitating the qualities in them that you admire.

Whenever we say (with no intention of following through), "I wish I could . . . " or, "Someday I would like to . . ." we do so because we are asleep. Whenever we express negative thinking by saying, "I can't . . . " or "I wish . . . " or "I don't have the time to . . ." or "If only . . ." or "I don't have what I need to . . . " we are allowing our prime addictions to erode the foundation of our truest and deepest selves—the Divine Child within, Real Beautiful Self.

Each of us is created with a spark of the Divine within—a Divine Image or Attribute that is the core of personhood. This view of humanity, common to the religious traditions of the world, is clearly expressed in the creation story of the Hebrew Scriptures, in which God says, "Let us make humans in our own image, in the likeness of ourselves" (Gen. 1:26).

However, just because this Divine Attribute or Divine Image is present, it is not necessarily expressed. It is a person's *choice* whether to express it, repress it, or distort it. Because this Divine Attribute is that part of ourselves that is open to divine influence and higher consciousness, the choice of expression, repression, or distortion takes on magnitude. When we are caught in dysfunctional motivation we repress our choices in the misguided belief that our destinies will be magically revealed. Addictive mental attitudes lead us to misuse our freedom and distort the Divine Image within for egocentric purposes.

T. S. Eliot, a master poet of the modern era, described the contemporary inability to live creatively:

The Eagle soars in the summit of Heaven,
The Hunter with his dogs pursues his circuit.
O perpetual revolution of configured stars,
O perpetual recurrence of determined seasons,
O world of spring and autumn, birth and dying!
The endless cycle of idea and action,
Endless invention, endless experiment,
Brings knowledge of motion, but not of stillness;
Knowledge of speech, but not of silence;
Knowledge of words, and ignorance of the Word.

All our knowledge brings us nearer to death,
But nearness to death no nearer to God.
Where is the Life we have lost in living?
Where is the wisdom we have lost in knowledge?
Where is the knowledge we have lost in information?
The cycles of Heaven in twenty centuries
Bring us farther from God and nearer to the Dust.[2]

As long as we deceive ourselves into believing the illusion that we are free and "doin' just fine," psychological addiction to a myopic point of view is inevitable. Creative freedom to explore the endless possibilities for developing human potential remain buried. Negative, self-justifying, self-righteous attitudes are mounds of dust that become foundational material for dysfunctional living. When the winds of life blow, the dust scatters and the foundations crumble.

How do we break through mounds of negative attitudes and break free to make the uncommon choice for transformation? Why do some people appear to wake up and make this choice but in a short time return to the sleeping state? Why do others run from one spiritual experience to another, one seminar to another, one religion to another, in a seemingly endless pursuit of transformation?

What is the secret element that causes some people to make the uncommon choice and tenaciously move through all obstacles toward consciousness, wholeness, and holiness? The secret lies in each person's inner commitment to work toward developing positive attitudes toward self, others, and life.

Transformation: An Eternal Love Affair with Freedom

On the physical plane the opposite of freedom might be described as bondage, slavery, or imprisonment. In the spiritual realm, the opposite of freedom is more accurately named negative mental attitudes, for these severely confine our ability to make free choices.

Attitudes—which by their very nature are unconscious—are the survival kits of egocentricity. Negative attitudes toward self, others, and life dominate and tyrannize everyone. Unless we break through these barriers of negativity, transformation is impossible.

Because attitudes are unconscious, we don't believe we have attitudes, much less negative attitudes. Instead, we believe that we simply like or dislike certain people, things, and situations. We don't stop to think that likes and dislikes are born out of unconscious attitudes based on prejudices, opinions, ideas, limited information, and a small amount of knowledge and life experience.

Negative attitudes about self sound the death knell for creative energy. We need only ask people what they believe about themselves to understand how easily and quickly creative energy is lost in negativity.

---

2. T. S. Eliot, "Choruses from 'The Rock,'" in *T. S. Eliot: The Complete Poems and Plays 1909–1950* (New York: Harcourt, Brace & World, 1962), p. 96.

Do most people believe they deserve to be failures? To be unloved? To be rejected? The automatic response would most likely be, "Of course not!" Why, then, is no amount of success, love, or affirmation ever enough? Why, when we feel like failures, that we are unloved or rejected, do we fall into self-pity, anger, moodiness, or resentment?

If we didn't have a powerful negative attitude controlling us, we would not accept failure or another person's definition of us as a definitive statement about our personal value or dignity. It is because we *do* have negative attitudes about ourselves that we develop an insatiable need for outside affirmation.

What about negative attitudes toward others? Do we judge, condemn, hate, gossip, ignore, control, or abuse one another? Is there any jealousy, envy, selfishness, lying, or pride operating in our lives? Because we see everything in life through our own attitudes, beliefs, prejudices, and illusions, it's apparent that unconscious negative attitudes have a firm hold on the lives of most of us.

According to the dictionary, transformation is a change in composition, structure, or character. Obviously then, transformation doesn't mean cosmetic outer changes but rather inner work on oneself. We can't advance in the transformation process unless our attitudes change. Positive attitudes lead to understanding, which is the only force strong enough to neutralize these prime addictions that create violence not only in individuals but in society.

Until we are willing to die to self by letting go of negative attitudes, there will be "no room in the inn" of self for the positive to be born. The light of consciousness is the star heralding the birth of positive attitudes and understanding. Choosing to remain asleep in the inn of self, we miss the wonder of birth, of rebirth, of new life through transformation.

If life is a cycle, as Eliot said, transformation is the return journey, the journey home that leads us back to the child, Real Beautiful Self—the person we were created to be. Transformation is bringing the light of consciousness into the dark, hidden places within ourselves where negativity breeds and multiplies. Negative attitudes shrivel when exposed to the light. Transformation is about life, about reclaiming the truth of ourselves and exposing the lies that we came to believe about ourselves in order to survive.

To put it simply, transformation is the process of falling in love with freedom, and thus with yourself, others, and life. Transformation is an eternal love affair with freedom.

Developing Positive Attitudes

If love is to grow, it must be nurtured. For transformation to continue to grow, it too must be nurtured, for you must love it and desire it with all your heart. There are five positive attitudes that you can work on developing that feed the soul on the return journey, the journey home. These five attitudes, faithfully pursued, will become the spirit driving you to defy logic and discover Truth:

Self-observation
Self-remembering
Metanoia
Forgiveness
Blessing the past

These positive attitudes are progressive, building on one another, creating new energy through awareness and honesty.

Self-observation

Self-observation is learning to become an objective witness to your own thoughts, feelings, words, actions, and reactions, as well as to the reactions of others to yourself. The intent is to develop an internal vision of self that does not condemn, criticize, or judge but simply observes objectively so as to become conscious of truth. To observe yourself objectively is to activate Sly One.

To enter into self-criticism or self-condemnation is to deepen your own negativity, for it will only produce guilt and bad feelings about yourself. Guilt soon leads to self-pity, which in turn leads you to begin to justify your actions. Every time we criticize ourselves we will, within a short time, need to justify ourselves. Both actions are a waste of time and energy; everything turns sour, because nothing positive can come out of negativity.

Maintaining a nonjudgmental stance is critical to positive self-observation. Life experience is the material for self-observation. Once we begin to notice how we judge and condemn others internally even though we have little if any understanding of them, we can choose to stop our automatic judgments. First, however, we must become conscious of when, why, and how often we are being judgmental.

For example, recently a woman attending a seminar we were giving refused to take notes and frequently interrupted by asking questions in what was obviously a belligerent, argumentative manner. We not only wondered why she had bothered coming to the seminar but secretly wished she hadn't.

Shortly thereafter, we had occasion to learn that the woman suffered from dyslexia. She had great difficulty reading or writing, had been subjected to the most humiliating ridicule all her life, and was now even being threatened with loss of her livelihood because of her disability. In a moment, irritation gave way to compassion. Why? Because now we understood. This experience was definitely material for self-observation. Judgment had been born out of imagined reality, not out of consciousness, truth, or understanding.

Once we understand the limitation caused by our own unconsciousness, pain, and selfishness, we can understand that other people struggle with these same painful realities. When there is no growth or development, people become more selfish, bitter, and narrow-minded. Through positive self-observation we discover our freedom to make new choices and thereby reclaim our God-given right not to be negative.

A word of caution. Practicing self-observation is a lifelong process that requires great effort. We tend to think we know ourselves, but in truth we don't. If we did, there would be no violence in families, neighborhoods, cities, nations, and the world. Violence is impossible where understanding reigns, and understanding begins in self-knowledge. Only through our understanding of ourselves and others will violence decline and societies be healed. Self-observation is the first step in this healing process.

Summary. Objectively recognize the truth of your thoughts, words, actions, feelings, and self-justifying behavior. Then, in identifying the source of pain and in realizing how this behavior feeds egocentricity, you can make a new choice to reclaim the God-given right not to be negative. This attitude nurtures you on the journey home—the journey of the prodigal son or daughter—to reunite with the child, Real Beautiful Self.

Self-remembering

Paradoxically, to remember self is to *forget* who you *think* you are. It means to forget the outer shell definition of your profession, social standing, religious position, or of your relationship to another person, whether or not he or she holds a lofty position. Self-remembering is making a conscious choice to recall that part of yourself that was created to be positive, understanding, loving, and free. It is the choice to remember, awaken, and reunite with the sleeping child, Real Beautiful Self.

As you practice the art and discipline of self-observation you begin to identify and separate from negativity. In these moments of separation from the negative, you can practice self-remembering—contacting and embracing your essence or true self. Through self-remembering you come in contact with internal truth, meaning, and life purpose.

Everyone is created to remember his or her essence and thus to be guided by internal truth and meaning. Yet these valuable parts of self get lost through neglect and abuse because we are born into an egocentric world and must become egocentric and off balance to survive. Until we begin daily to remember and connect with the truth of ourselves, the false personality or outer shell definitions—the compulsive dimension of your Enneagram number—dominate and successfully keep hidden the secret of Real Beautiful Self.

In self-remembering, you develop the courage to empty yourself of deceptive desires that appear to hold the answers to all of life's difficulties. Through remembering the truth of yourself, these deceptive, driving desires are exposed as illusions—empty promises to keep you running after rainbows. Like Jesus of Nazareth, every one of us is tempted to promises of power and wealth. Unconscious, sleeping people continue to succumb to these temptations.

Like self-observation, self-remembering is a long process that requires great effort. Moments of self-awareness, though fleeting to begin with, yield a higher consciousness and understanding of ways to resolve previously insurmountable problems and difficulties in your life. Always, however, each of us must die to the false self in a particular way, die to the ordinary ways of understanding ourselves.

A word of caution. Self-remembering is a frightening experience, like stepping backward off a cliff with no guarantee that there will be a solid ledge below to stand on. Because self-observation and self-remembering require both the effort and the courage to make new choices, many people reject them. Instead, they run from experience to experience, seminar to seminar, and religion to religion in the illusion that transformation will suddenly happen *to* them. There is no such thing as magical, cheap, or easy transformation. There is, however, an exhilarating sense of freedom as one begins to shed the shackles of negativity, self-criticism, and self-justification and embrace light-as-a-feather Real Beautiful Self.

Summary. Acting on the knowledge gained through self-observation, you can separate from negative attitudes and false images by taking time each day to remember the truth of who you are created to be. As you claim the wholeness and freedom of your essence, the unconsciously accepted false outer definitions of self lose the energy and power to control your thoughts, words, feelings, or actions. With new consciousness and awareness of Real Beautiful Self, you need no longer be driven by outside circumstances, expectations, or negative ideas.

Metanoia

The fruit of faithfully practicing the previous two positive attitudes is *metanoia* (Greek *meta,* change; *nous,* mind). *Metanoia* is sparked by a moment of higher consciousness or grace, expanding the horizons of the mind to perceive new possibilities, gain new insights, or broaden understanding of truth and life meaning. Until we begin to think in a new way, transformation is impossible. *Metanoia* initiates a new way of thinking.

Once the light of consciousness reveals new possibilities, we must begin discovering and deciding what we are willing to sacrifice. Sacrifice is always called for, so that there is "room in the inn" for the possible to become real.

Metanoia is both a *specific* and a *practical* application of grace in our lives. First, through experiences of self-observation we recognize specifically how we judge, criticize, or practice destructive behavior toward self and others. Then, in moments of self-remembering we reunite with Real Beautiful Self—with the whole, healthy, creative, and free—while consciously rejecting our false, egocentric selves. These movements create the inner space to *change our minds* about ourselves and others and about situations, thus redirecting our creative energy in a specific and practical way.

If you insist on working in generalities (for example, "I will never be angry again," or, "I will never negate myself again," or, "I will never try to control another person again"), you step right back into the sleeping state, into unconsciousness. This old, habitual way of thinking prevents *metanoia* from taking root in your life.

Summary. *Metanoia* is a moment when the light of consciousness—grace—illuminates the truth of self in relation to self, others, and situations. When truth is revealed, we gain deeper understanding of self, discovering creative new ways to resolve life struggles. Truth also points to those things that must be sacrificed—unhealthy attitudes, relationships, ideas, feelings—so that new life and freedom can emerge. *Metanoia* has a *specific* and *practical* application in our lives. Specific response to *metanoia* has a cumulative effect that eventually leads to God-consciousness or transformation.

Forgiveness

The inability or unwillingness to forgive real or imagined hurts is the single greatest obstacle to human growth, freedom, and potential. Most of us carry around inside ourselves lists of grievances against parents, teachers, institutions, friends, lovers, children, and enemies.

Although these lists of insults and injuries lie primarily beneath the surface of our daily activities, they possess a power to halt our ability to function normally in an instant. Witness the many times someone says or does something thoughtless or intentionally hurtful. The next hour, day, or days are spent internally and perhaps externally examining previous lists of that person's offenses. All the while, the injured one becomes more and more resentful. During this time, occupied with vengeful thinking and self-pity, we lose our energy, creativity, inner peace, and freedom. All these grievances buried in a shallow grave just beneath the conscious mind, not surprisingly, become a compost pile of negativity, eventually providing the prime nutrients feeding the roots of psychological, spiritual, and psychosomatic illnesses.

As we grow in the daily discipline of practicing self-observation, self-remembering, and *metanoia,* consciousness and awareness of self expand, thus deepening our understanding of the whole human condition. We come to *understand,* to know deep in the marrow of our bones, that wounded, sleeping, unconscious people can't help but wound other sleeping, unconscious people.

This inevitable cycle of wounding can only be altered or changed if individuals wake up and become conscious. As we become aware of our own negativity, failures, and narrow-mindedness, we begin to understand the hidden pain and struggle of every other person who has, does, or will walk upon this planet.

Where there is true understanding, violence cannot exist. Thus forgiveness is simply reaping the fruit that nourishes us on the journey home. It is a gift that you consciously give to yourself—a gift so lush that the benefits spill over to enrich the lives of everyone.

This understanding of forgiveness in no way negates the importance of working through the pain and justifiable anger caused by things that happen to you. The all-too-real physical, emotional, spiritual, and psychological effects you suffer with and stagger under because of injustice and evil inflicted by others must be dealt with consciously. Unless you become conscious of your pain and work toward resolving that pain, the burden of suffering continues to grow heavier. It is, in fact, in the working through of your life issues that your wounds are healed and violence is replaced with understanding and compassion.

Summary. Forgiveness is making conscious what *has already taken place within.* Forgiveness is reaching out to accept the fruit of your own hard work and effort to wake up and become conscious, the joyful reunion of self with Real Beautiful Self. Forgiveness, though unnatural to sleeping, unconscious people, becomes as natural as breathing to the person who becomes conscious. For the conscious person, forgiveness becomes a way of life.

Blessing the Past

As you immerse yourself in the transforming, grace-filled light of conscious living, healing happens spontaneously. Healing goes far beyond present reality. Like an eternal echo, it travels through time and space past peaks of triumph and over valleys of darkness and suffering. As you find healing in the present, your past and future are inextricably bound together into an unbroken whole.

Every experience in life—no matter how painful or destructive it appeared to be at the time—becomes a stepping stone up the mountain of transformation and transcendence; finally comprehending this causes us to cry out in gratitude.

Through gratitude we bless and consecrate our pasts. In this prayer of blessing and consecration, the final links of all chains that have held us in bondage to past suffering fall away. When you bless your past, peaks and valleys are made level, becoming a straight road of light into your future. Once you see clearly where you have been, you *know* where your future and your destiny lie. Grateful blessing of the past is the key that unlocks the door to a future of freedom, happiness, and wholeness.

As with forgiveness, blessing the past does not mean whitewashing its painful elements. Rather, it means examining what has happened in your life, admitting the pain, and dealing with it so as to find the gift in the situation for yourself and others. With gifts in hand from each one of life's situations, we have reason to bless all with peace.

Summary. Blessing the past, from the deepest recesses of your being, is the total merging of your spirit with the virtue of humility. Blessing the past is your personal prayer for unity—within yourself and throughout the earth. This prayer joins with and increases the power of the prayer Jesus of Nazareth prayed the night before he died. Blessing the past, he said, "With me in them and you in me, may they be so perfected in unity that the world will recognize that it was you who sent me and that you have loved them as you have loved me" (John 17:23). To bless your past gratefully is to dedicate yourself to life through universal peace and unity.

Transformation: Internal Ecological Balance

Transformation is the process through which we strive to achieve the delicate balance of blending internal idealism with external realism. It is imperative that while we seek to find this delicate balance we practice internal pollution control and energy conservation.

Transformation—far from being a holier-than-thou exercise in self-righteousness, as many would like to believe—is a practical, feet-on-the-ground, heads up, passionate process. A spiritual mentor of ours has been known to caution people in this regard with these words: "Be careful not to become so spiritual that you are no longer of any earthly good."[3]

Internal pollution control is learning to eliminate the negative thoughts and emotions that poison the waters of your spirit and psyche. Once your inner waters have been polluted—and this is true for all humanity—it takes great effort to purify those waters. You must also be vigilant to avoid recurring pollution. It is through self-observation—through activating Sly One—that we control pollution.

Internal energy conservation is strengthening your backbone, conscience, and will by exercising your right to eliminate destructive relationships and unhealthy behavior from your life. As you reclaim your inalienable right to make positive choices, your level of creative energy rises dramatically.

As with all reclamation projects, transformation takes place in several stages. There are times when these stages must be repeated because something went wrong the first time. Simultaneously, various areas will be in different stages of

---

3. David Geraets, O.S.B., abbot of the Benedictine Abbey in Pecos, New Mexico.

the transformation process. Some areas of life may be further along, some just beginning, and other areas not even explored or discovered.

Transformation is an internal reclamation project that naturally progresses through four stages. These stages or movements of transformation are depicted in the diagram "The Process of Transformation."

The Reflective Movement

The Reflective Movement is set in motion by an often veiled action of the Divine—grace. Grace is a gift that creates the courage to question life as you are living it—to question a way of life that has been polluted by your prime addiction as described by the Enneagram.

Very often it is a painful experience that shocks a person into taking a long, honest look at life. When you feel vulnerable or lose control, grace more easily and quickly pierces through your illusionary defenses. Painful experiences in life are inevitable; they are also absolutely necessary if you are to wake up and live life in a meaningful way. When these experiences are of sufficient intensity, a new idea enters your mind and a new vision of your life can emerge.

Unless this experience, painful or otherwise, is intense enough to pierce through our egocentricity, we sink right back into slumber. There we remain, contentedly believing the illusion that our inner waters are uncontaminated.

This movement begins with questions like these: I wonder if thus-and-so could be true about me? Why do I do this or that? What happens when I enter a certain kind of situation or relationship? Could it be that I create this or that reaction by this or that attitude? These kinds of questions are attempts to look squarely at reality and admit your own participation and responsibility for the contamination in your life.

The Reflective Movement is a time of recognition, of clarity of vision. The creative thinking process is awakened when we comprehend the need to initiate a personal clean-up project.

An illustration of the Reflective Movement comes from a man whose father died unexpectedly. Throughout the difficult days that followed, he and his wife commented often on their gratitude that death was swift and painless for him.

The Reflective Movement, he later recounted, began during a restless night shortly after he returned home. Thinking about the previous days, he realized that it wasn't the sadness or loss that stood out to him. Rather, it was a profound awareness of two experiences that seemed as natural as breathing at the time but in retrospect were highly unusual for him. One was remembering that he had prayed often, *very* often, quiet little prayers of thanksgiving for God's mercy in the manner of his father's death. The second was realizing that just a short time after the shock of being informed of his father's death, he began experiencing an all-pervading confidence and peace. He knew—without any doubt—that his father was "home," that his father was in heaven.

Those experiences may not be unusual for some people, but they were for him. Neither he nor his wife had been involved in any religious practice since their college days. The last time he remembered praying was during his childhood and adolescence when he went to church with his dad. His mother had died

THE PROCESS OF TRANSFORMATION

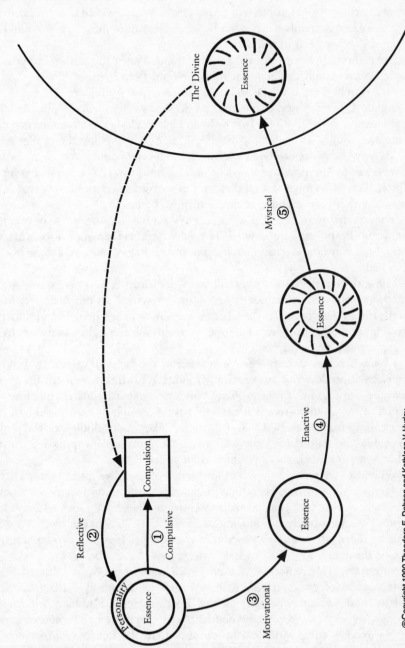

when he was a baby, and his father never remarried. "Funny," he thought, "Dad gave me a gift, and I never had an occasion to use it until after he died."

Then his thoughts turned to his own children, who were nine, eleven, and fifteen. He asked himself if he were to die tonight how they would handle it. Someday they would have to handle his death. Where would they find comfort, peace, solace? Certainly it wouldn't be where he had found it. How could they? They had never been in a church.

Then more questions poured into his mind. Was it too late to bring up the topic? What would the children think? Would they laugh at him for "getting saved"? Surely there must be some way to broach the subject.

As ideas, possibilities, and memories flooded his mind that night, he felt an excitement, a hope about life that he hadn't felt in a long time. Sure, he had made a mistake—but it was never too late. Besides, he'd always loved a challenge!

Tragedy had proven to be a time of grace—an opportunity to explore the new. It was clear to him how this moment of recognition was to be applied in his life. The challenge? To move in that direction in a sensitive, relational way that would include rather than exclude or threaten those he loved.

The internal awareness that some area of your life is crying out to be examined can come home in various ways. It might be a sudden intuition, a nagging thought, a constant irritation, an inexplicable feeling of sadness, a sense of dread or boredom.

Life is the teacher constantly challenging its students to probe, question, and search for solutions to seemingly unsolvable mysteries. In the Reflective Movement, the student perceives that there is a lesson to be learned. Then pondering, probing, and searching one's life, one begins to ask the right questions. In this stage, idealism reigns supreme.

Even when you identify a problem area and ask the right questions, however, transformation does not automatically follow. With this movement the process has only begun, and if it stops here, you are in a worse state than before. The stench of the polluted river has become strong enough to be noticed; the need for clean-up has been raised. Now, if no one takes responsibility for the project, inevitably you will blame others for the pollution problem, pointing out that other rivers are much more polluted than yours.

Whenever we refuse to resolve our own problems, we quickly project those problems out on others, becoming judgmental, critical, and angry with people who have similar unsolved problems. Thus, whenever we judge and condemn another, we are actually announcing to everyone the state of our own unresolved issues. Indeed, there is great wisdom in the saying, "It is better to remain silent and be thought a fool than to speak and remove all doubt."

Summary. The Reflective Movement of transformation is initiated by the divine action of grace. Transformation begins in the mind—with a new idea, insight, and awareness of self. Divine Truth invites the hidden self to grow strong. A voice croons from the depths of our inner water the songs of remembering, reconnecting with Real Beautiful Self. In the Reflective Movement we listen to the wisdom songs of the river and contemplate the embryonic possibilities mysteriously hidden in the desire for new life. If this desire for new life is aborted, the victim will victimize others with the sword of judgmental attitudes and condemnation.

The Motivational Movement

The Motivational Movement begins with catching the vision generated in the Reflective Movement. This stage becomes a time of personal assessment, evaluation, and preparation.

In this stage you assume responsibility for your life with inner statements like, "I could . . ." or "My options are . . ." or "I am capable of . . ." This is a time of gathering and evaluating information from both internal and external sources.

This is the most difficult phase of all. Idealism conveniently vanishes, and realism becomes your constant companion. Alone, realism has a way of magnifying every obstacle and minimizing every prospect for circumventing an obstacle. Realism walks along the riverbank wearing the lead shoes of pessimism and muttering, "You can't!" Idealism laughingly dances on the high winds of optimism, shouting back, "Yes, you can!" It takes the cunning ways of Sly One to convince them that they need each other.

Practically speaking, this is a time of becoming conscious of negative thoughts, words, emotions, and actions—the work of self-observation—and separating yourself from these negative patterns. It is a time of uniting with Real Beautiful Self through self-remembering.

If negativity begins to gather power and steal your energy, croon the river's song, "Litany of the Real Beautiful Self," to recapture and fortify your rightful strength.

Litany of the Real Beautiful Self

Negative feeling is not "I"
Negative thought is not "I"
Negative word is not "I"
Negative action is not "I"
Then who am I?
I am I
I am mystery
I am Real Beautiful Self
I am child of God
I am God-presence living within
I am God-presence manifesting itself from within
I am positive, creative, and free
Created among the stars
Carried into life on the waters of Conscious Love
I remember! I rejoice!

During the Motivational Movement you gather information about the external resources available to help your dream become real. Is education needed? What educational opportunities are available? Is financing an obstacle? What scholarships and grants are available, and how does one apply for them?

Is a support group needed? What support groups exist, and how does one connect with them?

Is a small business on the horizon? How does one do market research? Develop a financial plan? What are the ownership options? Sole proprietorship? Partnership? Corporation?

Is spiritual growth the aim? What does that mean? Would a spiritual director or mentor be helpful? What is the fee? How often would we meet? Are there retreats or workshops that would be helpful?

Search, seek, question, probe. Most of all, stay positive. There are no lasting "quick fix" solutions to any of life's problems. It is an illusion to think there would be.

This is also a time for deciding what you are willing to sacrifice in order to spend time cleaning up the garbage strewn along your riverbank. Reclamation projects require hard work and effort. Is this project worth giving up some precious TV time? How about time spent stopping off for a beer after work? Is it worth a ball game? Is it worth the effort to read a book? Several books? Is it worth keeping a journal, taking time out for meditation, or getting up early to exercise? What is it worth? Anything?

You must desire transformation with all your heart or it won't happen. Transformation isn't free, and healing isn't free; even pain and illusion aren't free. Everything costs something. The cost of transformation and healing is the sacrifice of egocentricity. The cost of pain and illusion is the death of Real Beautiful Self.

You might think that after discovering a new vision, discovering how it can be made real in your life, overcoming negative thinking, and deciding what you are willing to sacrifice for it, you had put so much effort into transformation that nothing else could go wrong. Unfortunately, that is not so. The process can stop at this stage also, and if it does, painful results await.

With the need for a reclamation project readily visible and a plan for the project in hand, if you decide not to go through with the plan, the consequence will be self-criticism and self-blame. "I had my chance and I blew it," will be the theme of your inner talk. "Now I have to live with this mess and pretend it's okay, or pretend it isn't here."

When we refuse, for whatever reason, to do what we know we can and should do, we turn our criticism and judgmental attitudes on ourselves. Thus, whenever you judge and condemn yourself, you are actually witnessing to the fact that the grace of transformation has been aborted at the level of the Motivational Movement.

Summary. In the Motivational Movement of transformation you assess your internal strengths and external resources. Through the hard work of eliminating negative attitudes, your creative energy increases by leaps and bounds. This is a time of self-empowerment and affirmation. When you stop polluting and clean up the garbage along your inner waters, a new, more magnificent vision of the beauty and power of the river emerges. At long last, idealism and realism, naked and vulnerable, unite. New life stirs in the sacred waters of the soul womb. God is good. Life is good. I am good. But new life, if allowed to die and decay in your soul womb, will poison your sacred waters with self-negation, self-criticism, and bitterness.

The Enactive Movement

In the transformation process, the Enactive Movement signals impending birth. A Space Available sign hangs on the entrance to the inn. This is the stage of responsiveness, of actualization. The vision of the first stage and the desire of the second stage are the bones that are now enfleshed. Steadily, you breathe life into a previously lifeless part of yourself, and all creation shouts for joy as the inner and the outer waters of life stream together. In silent power this new river gracefully courses through the parched landscape of life, blessing and revitalizing.

The Enactive Movement is the time for doing, for being. The following excerpt from a poem by an unknown author aptly describes this movement:

> So you learn to plant your own garden
> and water your own soul,
> Instead of waiting for someone
> to bring you flowers.
> And you really are strong
> And you really do have worth
> And you learn and learn ...
> As surely as the dawn comes . . . you learn.

The hard work of this time of life is propelled by the momentum gained in the first two movements and fueled by the exhilaration that is naturally released in creativity. The only blight that can destroy your inner garden and dry up your inner waters at this stage is *pride*. When you admire yourself as a cut above the rest of humanity for making the effort needed to change, you cross the fine line between self-confidence and self-veneration. When pride creeps in, Real Beautiful Self falls back to sleep. Then as the inner ground grows dry and hard, egocentricity gleefully strides out of the shadows to reign once again.

Summary. The Enactive Movement is life, freedom, accomplishment, completion. The possible is becoming actual. Creative power increases as you learn to move to the rhythm of your own life, sway to the rhythm of your own inner river. Life begins to pulsate with the dance of destiny. Only pride can disrupt this natural life rhythm.

The Mystical Movement

The entire process of transformation begins, ends, and is sustained through an action of the Divine. The initial divine action in the Reflective Movement finds its fulfillment in the Mystical Movement.

The more effort you put into allowing the transformation process to permeate every aspect of your being, the more conscious you become of how little you understand and how far you have yet to go. With this consciousness comes also the desire and energy to continue on the journey.

You enter the Mystical Movement by becoming totally committed to the transformation process, by wanting it with all your heart and giving yourself over to it completely. It means allowing grace continually to initiate the Reflective, Motivational, and Enactive Movements in area after area of your life. As you overcome the compulsive dimension of your Enneagram number, the Divine Image at the core of your being is revealed. With great effort, you overcome resistance, and transformation becomes a habit. It is easy to see why many do not reach this goal, for it seems too elusive or unattainable; they lack the inspiration to reach for the stars.

In the first half of life our inner potential lies dormant and passive while our outer lives are active and controlled by illusion and egocentricity. As the process of transformation becomes more and more a way of life, a subtle and all-encompassing shift begins to take place. Consciousness and truth begin to shed light on the richness and expansiveness of the interior world.

We come to understand that reality lies not in what can be seen and touched and possessed, but rather in what is unseen, intangible, and can be possessed by no one. Indeed, reality begins to possess *us*. The interior world becomes the focus of activity, energy, and freedom. The exterior world becomes passive, peaceful, and quiet. Real Beautiful Self is actively planting the garden and watering the soul. The fruit of these labors of love can now freely be given to the world.

The emphasis in life is now on giving rather than taking, on being rather than doing, on listening rather than talking, on loving rather than being loved, on understanding rather than being understood.

Through living the transformation process we are *drawn into* the Mystical Movement. It is not something that we *do*. The paradox of this movement is that you are the only one who remains completely unaware that it is happening in you.

There is no way to be detoured from this movement, for in it the journey home is complete. Without realizing it, one has returned to the Source, to the beginning, and "knows that place for the first time." The union of the self with Real Beautiful Self is consummated, and heaven and earth join in one great cosmic dance of destiny.

CHAPTER EIGHT

Where the River Runs Free

Divine Image and Lifelong Quest

And we, with our unveiled faces reflecting like mirrors the brightness of Christ, all grow brighter as we are turned into the image that we reflect; this is the work of the Spirit.
—SAINT PAUL

T
he last of the missing puzzle pieces are found where the river runs free. Until now, the nine prime addictions have muddied the waters, polluted the shores, and concealed the beauty of the universe.

Long ago, Real Beautiful Self and Sly One were cruelly separated. Sly One refused, however, to forget Real Beautiful Self. With patience, cunning, self-observation, and self-remembering, Sly One's relentless Lifelong Quest to reunite with the lost Real Beautiful Self continued. At long last, where the river runs free, Sly One is crowned with a new name, and the true identity of Real Beautiful Self is unveiled.

Solving the Mystery

The Divine Image, also known as Real Beautiful Self, left near the headwaters of the personality, is different for each pattern described by the Enneagram. Clues to the identity of Real Beautiful Self can be found in the Jewish mystical tradition of the Kabbalah. The Kabbalah teaches the Sefirot, the ten Divine Images of God.

The first is Crown (Keter). It encompasses the wholeness and unity of God, the nothingness or no-thingness of God. Keter is eternal and has no beginning. The nine Divine Images or Faces of God that flow from Crown (Keter) correspond to the nine patterns of the Enneagram.

Thus the Divine Image and Lifelong Quest for each of the patterns of the Enneagram can be named as such:

Achievers' (1) Divine Image is Wisdom (Hokhmah). Through their relentless Lifelong Quest for Real Beautiful Self, Achievers are crowned with the new name of Pathfinder.

Helpers' (2) Divine Image is Understanding (Binah). Through their relentless Lifelong Quest for Real Beautiful Self, Helpers are crowned with the new name of Partner.

Succeeders' (3) Divine Image is Love (Hesed). Through their relentless Lifelong Quest for Real Beautiful Self, Succeeders are crowned with the new name of Motivator.

Individualists' (4) Divine Image is Power (Gevurah). Through their relentless Lifelong Quest for Real Beautiful Self, Individualists are crowned with the new name of Builder.

Observers' (5) Divine Image is Beauty (Tif'eret). Through their relentless Lifelong Quest for Real Beautiful Self, Observers are crowned with the new name of Explorer.

Guardians' (6) Divine Image is Endurance (Nezah). Through their relentless Lifelong Quest for Real Beautiful Self, Guardians are crowned with the new name of Stabilizer.

Dreamers' (7) Divine Image is Majesty (Hod). Through their relentless Lifelong Quest for Real Beautiful Self, Dreamers are crowned with the new name of Illuminator.

Confronters' (8) Divine Image is Foundation (Yesod). Through their relentless Lifelong Quest for Real Beautiful Self, Confronters are crowned with the new name of Philanthropist.

Preservationists' (9) Divine Image is Presence (Shekhinah). Through their relentless Lifelong Quest for Real Beautiful Self, Preservationists are crowned with the new name of Universalist.

A thousand lifetimes would not be enough to comprehend and reveal the glory of the Divine Image that lives within every person. We can, however, discover clues and catch veiled glimpses that will encourage and assist us in understanding the importance of doing the hard work of transformation. These fleeting, numinous clues can expand and clarify the inner vision of our destiny.

We the authors have been privileged to have begun the process of searching for clues and catching glimpses of these nine Divine Images. Led on a winding path through the Kabbalah, the Hebrew Scriptures, the Christian Scriptures, and the Bhagavad Gita, as well as through the writings of many mystics, this investigation has become one of the most profound experiences of our lives. At last we were able to decide on five major descriptors commonly found in all these writings when describing each particular Face of God.

In what follows, we attempt, in three sentences, to begin communicating the wonder and mystery within each Face of God. Of necessity, the three statements that follow each descriptor are as mystical, obscure, and limitless as the Image of God itself.

We hope that our work will stimulate your desire to delve more deeply into this unfolding mystery, not only for your own Enneagram pattern but also for the eight others. Together they create a marvelous mosaic that unveils the beauty at the core of human nature.

Conscious of our own shortcomings in this endeavor, we nonetheless present these statements with the prayer that you, the reader, will continue this work through your own study and reflection as you journey home on the path of transformation.

Following the descriptions of the Divine Image for each pattern is a description of the new name each pattern receives as it travels on its Lifelong Quest to find and integrate the human, the holy, and the hidden. This description is an attempt to portray each pattern free from compulsion, revealing ever more clearly the Image of God at its core. Not surprisingly, we find the golden rule, "Do to others as you would have them do to you," has specific application in this positive description of each pattern. The diagram "Divine Image and Lifelong Quest" summarizes the names for all the patterns of the Enneagram.

One: The Achiever

Divine Image. The Divine Image at the core of the Achievers' pattern is Wisdom (Hokhmah). Wisdom is practical, directive, independent, insightful, and involved.

DIVINE IMAGE AND LIFELONG QUEST

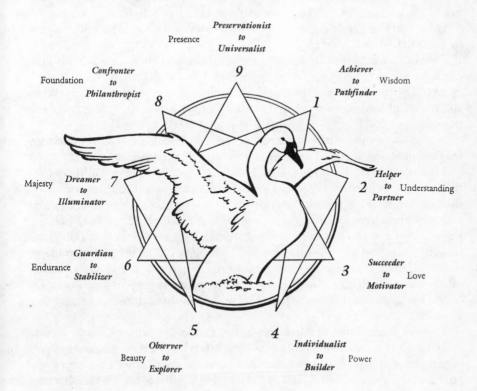

Preservationist
Presence   *to*
Universalist

9

Confronter   Achiever
Foundation   *to*   *to*   Wisdom
Philanthropist   Pathfinder

8   *1*

Majesty   Dreamer   Helper
          to   *7*   *to*   Understanding
          Illuminator   Partner

2

Guardian   Succeeder
Endurance   *to*   *6*   *to*   Love
          Stabilizer   Motivator

3

5   *4*

Observer   Individualist
Beauty   *to*   *to*   Power
Explorer   Builder

Practical. A skill set free in action for the improvement of the world is the directing of divine energy toward its desired goal.

Theories tested in the fire of experience are the bulwark of activities that liberate the human spirit.

It is common to want immediate personal change, but it is unrealistic; divine prudence guides the soul through stages of growth.

Directive. Guiding humanity on the right path lifts the gaze of the human spirit to the divine purpose for humanity, ennobling each task along the way.

An ethical approach to life imbues society with integrity both within and among people, strengthening the fabric of the human community with hope.

A spirit of discovery, exploration, and experimentation produces useful tools that can be shared joyfully with others.

Independent. The desire to dominate personal weaknesses, when balanced with patience, reveals divine goodness to the world.

The ability to struggle and persevere to attain the proper goal is the mark of a magnanimous spirit.

In the crucible of personal achievement is born a wisdom that can unerringly guide others on their individual paths to their divine destinies.

Insightful. Accepting the frailty as well as the potential of humanity opens the mind to wisdom and the heart to love.

Ability to empathize with the struggles in people's lives opens the eyes of the heart; a heart thus formed can then read the hearts of others.

Questions that gently encourage people to evaluate their lives are priceless gifts in the quest for the Divine.

Involved. Spiritual growth develops a quiet confidence, begetting a divine flow of life to others that is unpolluted by any need to control them.

Applying the strength of divine gifts to human tasks expands the heart, liberates the mind, and fortifies the spirit to live joyfully within the principles of the universe.

A glimpse of the fullness of human potential is revealed when new horizons are presented and accepted with an affirming and inspiring intention.

Lifelong Quest: Becoming a Pathfinder. Achievers become Pathfinders as they restrain their intensity for making everything important to them perfect by their own standards. Instead, they open their hearts and minds to a larger, more inclusive, more complex approach to growth and achievement. They become leaders, teachers, and guides for others by developing harmonious working relationships that lead to corporate creativity. Through productive use of available resources, they make vital contributions to the betterment of humanity. In the midst of many projects and activities they accomplish a larger goal—the invention of new value systems that cultivate and encourage positive attitudes and creativity in others.

They are able to listen to others and detect seeds of invention. Then with great imagination they call forth and inspire others to actualize these possibilities and potentialities. They affirm new ideas and forms of expression. They develop a philosophical wisdom that reveals to the world the truths of the cosmos. Because of their practical nature, they can apply their philosophical ideas to the affairs of daily living.

They display their leadership in the personal realm as well. By accepting personal and collective imperfections they establish a firm foundation for community. Their delight in sharing laughter and love with others makes them valuable friends and important family members. They enable and encourage others to be their best selves, opening them to the potential they have for overcoming weaknesses and contributing to the fabric of society.

Thus the key to their transformation is revealed. The Golden Rule in their lives consists in sharing with others the time and effort they formerly reserved for their own pursuit of perfection. When they are caught in dysfunctional motivation, their felt need is for more time and energy. They are zealots determined to make over everything important to them so that it meets their high standards. However, their real need is to defuse their intensity so that the beauty and wonder of life can feed their souls.

Their illusion is that happiness is attained by attacking any reality that does not suit them and making it what they want it to be. In reality, happiness comes to them through acceptance of human nature and the world in general—a mixture of the beautiful and the flawed, of strength and weakness.

Two: The Helper

Divine Image. The Divine Image at the core of the Helpers' pattern is Understanding (Binah). Understanding is sensitive, ingenious, grateful, loyal, and contemplative.

Sensitive. Through the eyes of the heart the hidden sufferings of others become visible to be cradled and nurtured in the arms of divine compassion.

Passion and intelligence converge to create an identification with all that is living and growing.

Warmth and caring are a protective shelter in which the sacredness of personhood is revered and the wounds of life are healed.

Ingenious. An undaunted spirit and internal freedom unearth multifaceted possibilities that overcome any seeming obstacles.

Using a diversity of means to relate with others creates an atmosphere in which the uniqueness of each person is valued and prized.

The hope of humanity lies hidden in each person's ability to respect the unrepeatable giftedness of others with consciousness and humility.

Grateful. Rising like incense from the innermost sanctuary of the Divine, thankfulness becomes a blessing that permeates the universe like the sweet fragrance of a spring rain.

Appreciation opens the heart and mind to new perspectives of life's beauty, intricacy, and wonder.

Freedom to achieve greatness is released in recognizing life's manifold gifts and in consecrating all of life with sincerity and humility.

Loyal. Protecting fragile pieces of broken lives demands a gentle strength that grows into a towering respect for the achievements of the human spirit.

Holding fast the ideals of human liberation gives birth to solidarity with the world's lowly, troubled, sick, and needy in creative fidelity.

In the unity between two persons, an intimacy is born that arrests selfishness and propels humanity toward its Divine destiny.

Contemplative. Through self-consideration and fearless probing of emptiness emerges a strength of spirit that can face and merge with the Divine.

In communion with the Source of all life, faith and mastery of self stand as torches at the portal of freedom to light the Way, reveal the Truth, and ignite the Life in and for others.

Grace springs like a generative stream from a life that is recalled under the guidance of divine light and thus is allowed expression of its true divine calling.

Lifelong Quest: Becoming a Partner. Helpers become Partners as they restrain the prime addiction to serve for the purpose of obtaining others' gratitude. Instead, they develop an appreciation of mutual relationship. Guided by this principle, they call forth their own potential through wholesome self-caring and appreciation. Recognizing the need to develop broader interests, they spend the time and effort needed to expand their personal and intellectual horizons. Having worked at personal development, they enter relationships able to share themselves as well as to draw others out, thus strengthening mutuality.

Helpers who are becoming Partners use their innate gentleness and nonviolent approach to life in new ways. Instead of drawing others to themselves in dependent relationships, they use their insights and gifts to identify and articulate uniquely creative solutions to collective problems. They give others freedom by asking questions and presenting multiple alternatives in a given situation. By using tough love to call forth and affirm the best in others, they show respect for each person whether he or she is frail or strong.

Rather than compulsively focusing on the immediate needs of the person in front of them, they develop a more expansive life perspective. A new sense of vision directs both their short-range and long-range plans. They gain an appropriate sense of priorities by considering experience and goals. Once concerned only with the needs and feelings of people around them, they now gain a deeper sense of responsibility for the outcome of the projects in which they and others are involved.

Thus the key to their transformation is revealed. The Golden Rule in their lives consists in allowing themselves to be served as well as to serve, thereby stepping down from their self-designed pedestal of superiority. When they are dysfunctionally motivated, their felt need is to focus on others' needs and feelings so that they will be thanked and appreciated. However, their real need is to examine themselves and to discover their own weaknesses and needs so that their relationships develop mutuality of sharing and service.

Their illusion is that happiness is attained by serving other people with no regard for themselves. In reality, happiness comes to them through mutual relationships in which they find they have dignity and value as persons apart from what they do for others.

Three: The Succeeder

Divine Image. The Divine Image at the core of the Succeeders' pattern is Love (Hesed). Love is sublime, vulnerable, wholehearted, creative, and encouraging.

Sublime. Surging beyond the barriers of humanly defined limitation, the spirit soars with an irrepressible impulse toward life and growth.

A reckless, wild, and free concern for others marks the life journey of one who is committed to the ways of the Divine.

An expansive capacity for self-sacrifice seeks through Divine dedication the transcendent principles of life.

Vulnerable. Activated by the reasoning of the heart, great depth of feeling is devoted to awakening consciousness regarding the sanctity of human life.

Inviting the Divine to pierce the hidden recesses of the heart as a ray of light penetrates a crystal initiates an open and active relationship with all of life.

Drawn to the Divine center, the soul gains purity and expresses itself in a strength and reality that become the operating forces of the Divine stratagem.

Wholehearted. Enthusiasm for and faithfulness to life release inexhaustible resources that are consecrated to the Divine work of unity.

A glimpse of the diaphanous vision for creation inspires possibilities to explore the mystery that others are, in truth, one's own deepest self.

An irresistible joy and gratitude for the gift of life champions all that lives and moves and has its being in the Divine.

Creative. Recognizing the stroke of the master artist in the human spirit, a passionate desire to know and be known by the Divine Originator of life finds expression through artistic and creative living.

Hope and belief in the essential goodness that permeates the universe gives birth to synthesis and mediation of spiritual philosophies.

Spontaneous joy in the growth and success of all reflects the gifts of Divine encouragement longing to be manifest in the world.

Encouraging. Excitement and imagination fan into a flame the desire of the human spirit to enter the adventuresome journey toward personal growth.

The giftedness of the human spirit is refracted through the prism of accomplishment and lavishes its many hues on humanity, calling all to vitality.

Love freely given in spite of unworthiness speaks to the world of grace, of the possibility of the Divine finding a home amid the human.

Lifelong Quest: Becoming a Motivator. Succeeders become Motivators as they restrain the compulsive need to create a good image for themselves through accomplishment. In its place, they develop healthy relationships that foster unity with and among others. They use their creative energies to form new visions for the future, which now arise not only from their own goals but also from the collective ideas of others. As these visions are translated into attainable reality, they creatively delegate authority and responsibility among all those who are involved. In learning to trust and value others, they also come to trust and value themselves; thus they no longer always need to be at center stage, claiming all credit for success.

By working at relationship, they base their associations on mutual love and respect. They become increasingly comfortable in communicating with others and inspiring them to greater heights of achievement. Able to spot talent and strength, they tap these resources in others by affirming confidence in their abilities.

Achievement for the sake of a successful appearance is replaced by an undying interest in developing their own and others' personhood. Their goal is to become an outstanding member of the human race, striving to rise above pettiness and egocentricity. Their high ideals are balanced by an optimistic acceptance of human limitations. Taking time to reflect upon their lives and upon the divine mysteries yields a healthy love of self and leads them to ponder and understand the true meaning of life. Out of this movement is born a philosophic nature that is expressed through the arts, beauty, romance, and relationship.

Thus the key to their transformation is revealed. The Golden Rule in their lives consists in sharing with others the success that they would grasp for themselves to gain a sense of self-acceptance. When they are caught in dysfunctional motivation, their felt need is striving for competency so that they can create good appearances and be admired by others. However, their real need is to become vulnerable to people by opening their Center of Affect and including others in their lives.

Their illusion is that happiness is attained by working hard to meet their goals. In reality, happiness comes to them through heartfelt relationships. By making others important enough to them to become vulnerable, they find meaning for their projects and hard work.

Four: The Individualist

Divine Image. The Divine Image at the core of the Individualists' pattern is Power (Gevurah). Power is clear-thinking, life-enhancing, steadfast, passionate, and constructive.

Clear-thinking. Penetrating to the core of human experience unearths and unites previously veiled and scattered wisdom.

Perceptive analysis and synthesis become the catalysts for exploring possibilities and initiating the flow of creative thinking.

Resistance to collective thinking yields attitudes and values that transcend mediocrity and continually expand divine consciousness.

Life-enhancing. Respect for truth and wisdom produces the teacher who, with proficient communication skills, leads students to new heights of awareness.

Clear categories of thought expand mental powers to respect all reality and people enthusiastically.

Sensitivity to form yields a sense of harmony, giving birth to artistic expression that feeds the soul with beauty and love.

Steadfast. Dependability in relationships with those in pain and difficulty creates a patient strength that reflects divine commitment in the world.

Having been made cognizant of the multiplicity of motives that underlie the actions of people and institutions, humanity is called to reach for the communion that transcends communication.

Inspiration rising from an inner vision and energy created by the belief that good will triumph over evil unite to effect change in the world.

Passionate. Intensity of thought and expression reveal an enthusiasm for life that unfolds the wings of the human spirit to soar toward the Divine.

The wound of the Divine Healer produces great energy to promote consciousness and unity within and among all creation.

Awakening to the beauty and wonder of the Divine inspires a respectful, creative involvement in the human struggle along with a determination to discover its meaning.

Constructive. Persistent striving of the creative mind to shape the material world develops a quietness of spirit that reveals the Divine.

In entering the furnace of purification and self-discipline the pure gold of originality is shaped into the practical and lasting gifts of service that reflect Divine excellence and achievement.

The idealistic aspirations of the human spirit are the fountainhead of worlds yet to be built and established in love and justice.

Lifelong Quest: Becoming a Builder. Individualists become Builders as they restrain their need to focus all attention on themselves. This effort frees them to redirect their innate creativity in an outwardly constructive way that will change the world. Because of their desire for originality, they challenge outmoded models with ideas born of intuitive perception and conceptual thinking. Thus they are often endless sources of creative response and communicators of new possibilities.

They develop self-discipline and the inner strength that comes with persistence. One of their greatest assets is their ability to synthesize information and refine ideas. By recognizing the futility of self-indulgence, they give birth to the resourcefulness and flexibility needed to actualize ideas in practical ways. In redirecting their energies to improve life for others, they develop an open and positive attitude toward themselves, others, and life.

Because of their deep feeling for others, they become loyal friends who place others' suffering and pain above their own interests. By continually working to become sensitive to others' feelings and letting go of their own need to be understood, they build lasting friendships. Blessed with multiple interests and talents, they learn to use their gifts creatively to contribute to the lives of others. This process gives rise to an ever-growing enthusiasm and optimism regarding life, self, and the world.

Thus the key to their transformation is revealed. The Golden Rule in their lives consists in making others the center of their attention just as they would have others be sensitive to them. When they are caught in dysfunctional motivation, their felt need is to concentrate their energies on understanding their feelings and seeing that their personal needs are met. However, their real need is to use their powers of understanding to accomplish changes that will improve the world.

Their illusion is that happiness is attained by focusing on themselves. In reality, happiness comes to them through focusing on others, resulting in a loss of self-consciousness that allows them to affect the world for the better.

Five: The Observer

Divine Image. The Divine Image at the core of the Observers' pattern is Beauty (Tif'eret). Beauty is merciful, honest, speculative, versatile, and active.

Merciful. Logic unmasks the foibles of humanity, yielding a consistent patience and concern that reflects Divine gentleness.

Knowledge for its own sake is only an ornament, but when put to good use, it uplifts the soul and improves the human condition.

Wisdom that serves itself judges and condemns; wisdom that serves others opens the heart and mind to humanity's Divine destiny.

Honest. Irrepressible curiosity about life and people leads to the discovery of pure truth in service to all.

To be open to all the facts and ideas—whether or not one responds positively to them—is the mark of a great mind.

A wit that casts Divine light upon a situation comes from a soul formed by balance and clear vision.

Speculative. Humanity is not as well served by those who dare to think big new ideas as it is by those who dare to put the smallest new idea into practice.

In touch with the Divine impulse toward progress of the human spirit, the adventuresome mind forges discoveries from possibilities to create a new and better world.

When mind and spirit converge in service to humanity, Divine beauty shimmers and shines as a beacon for growth.

Versatile. Multidimensional achievement is the mark of a spirit sparkling with an omnivorous pursuit of wisdom and a dedicated desire for authenticity.

Divine tenderness makes available the beauty in each piece of creation—no matter how tiny, how plain—to humanity's pursuit of excellence.

Imagination, enlivened through Divine intelligence, becomes a creative voice through which creation's slumbering spirit is awakened and made responsive to the universal call to union in the Divine.

Active. The desire to experience as much of creation as possible firsthand is the result of making friends with divine respect and love.

The wish to improve the world is commonly expressed in criticism, but the ability to improve it is the fruit of a consistent love of life.

The joy of involvement and accomplishment belongs to those who are patient as well as confident of the value of what they have to share.

Lifelong Quest: Becoming an Explorer. Observers become Explorers as they restrain their desire for time alone in reflection. This movement creates the space for them to use their storehouse of knowledge for the welfare of humanity. They have developed agile and flexible thought processes that can deal effectively with complex and ambiguous problems. When no longer afraid to be involved in life, they display a fierce determination to deal with issues before they turn into problems.

They become known for an intellectual openness that allows new ideas to influence them. Their love of new theories makes them natural proponents of change, and they communicate new and exciting ideas with humor, self-confidence, and a broad understanding of the issues. Valuing freedom, especially in the arena of thought, they learn to set others free by respectfully encouraging them to have their own opinions.

In tense situations they exhibit consideration for others, an ability to reserve judgment, and an increased awareness of and empathy with others' feelings and needs. They allow others' issues to become important to them as well. Through exercising compassion, they raise society's consciousness and effect true justice. Often they make their specific contribution through teaching. The result of this transformation is that they become relational. With an increased ease in social situations, they find deep satisfaction in sharing themselves through associations, friendships, and commitment as well as through their minds.

Thus the key to their transformation is revealed. The Golden Rule in their lives consists in a process of sharing with others the knowledge that they wanted to keep for themselves. When they are caught in dysfunctional motivation, their felt need is for time alone to reflect, analyze, abstract, and comprehend. However, their real need is to become involved in the lives of others. This process allows their thinking to be tempered by other viewpoints and expands their ability to affect the world in positive ways.

Their illusion is that happiness is attained by being alone. In reality, happiness comes to them through involvement with others. Private greed is replaced by open generosity.

Six: The Guardian

Divine Image. The Divine Image at the core of Guardians' pattern is Endurance (Nezah). Endurance is persevering, balanced, lively, socially conscious, and devoted.

Persevering. Divine tenacity faces all obstacles with the determined intent to surmount difficulties regardless of personal cost.

Affirmation is born of an unwavering passion to nurture that encourages and sustains others in their daily quest for the Holy Grail of fulfillment and truth.

Purity of heart activates the spirit to conscientiously pursue the personal and spiritual growth necessary for communion with others.

Balanced. Believing in the basic, incorruptible goodness of the human spirit leads to an intense valuing of equanimity and to the moderation of extreme positions.

Logic and levelheadedness transcend egocentric purposes and unite individual gifts and values for the common good.

Divinely enhanced freedom becomes manifest through the creative force of loving discernment that sifts the virtues of openness and self-sacrifice from the chaff of selfishness and prejudice.

Lively. An infectious enthusiasm and delight regarding the gift of life awaken in the hearts of others long-forgotten experiences of joy and wonder.

Reflections of the divine parent are made visible through the love and rejoicing expressed at the good fortune of others.

The glow of physical health yields zest for living; the glow of spiritual health radiates to others and replicates itself in them.

Socially conscious. The irresistible simplicity and impalpable presence of the Divine is a two-edged sword that cuts through the complexities behind which society hides its apathy toward social problems.

From the crucible of divine love flows the nourishment that sustains the impassioned pursuit of justice and fair treatment for all.

The creative tension of balancing meditation and action yields a divine awareness of occasions to teach, heal, and lead humanity to its proper destiny.

Devoted. The kingdom of the heart contains the treasure house of motivation for becoming the hub of community life.

Divine compassion and understanding create deep relationships that can withstand trials, difficulties, and misunderstanding.

Belief in the importance of the individual produces untiring efforts toward encouraging the unique expression and beauty of the Divine.

Lifelong Quest: Becoming a Stabilizer. Guardians become Stabilizers as they restrain their need to create internal security through external laws, norms, and traditions. By reclaiming their own center of authority and peace, they become a powerful still point in an insecure, fearful world. With an almost infinite patience for mediating the differences among human beings, they bring a balance to any society in which they are an invested member. They become expert in creating a comfortable atmosphere in which new ideas are encouraged and possibilities for change are supported. Though they value different ways of thinking and behaving, their natural conservative tendency gives them the ability to smooth rough edges and assist people in the art of fitting together in community.

They are able to apply the right kind of pressure so that people expand their perceptions and use their creative energy to raise the standards of living for all. Naturally gifted in creating and maintaining both balance and harmony among people, they promote, build, and sustain community values on many different levels simultaneously. They come to appreciate the challenge of new ideas, especially when these ideas can improve the lives of the people in their community.

Learning to place the dignity of the individual above their own prejudices, opinions, and rules will prove to be their greatest struggle. Because they must work so hard on this aspect of their personality, acceptance and respect for individual freedom can also become their greatest strength. By learning to let go of real or imagined personal affront, forgiveness becomes their hallmark. As people with value systems different from their own become less threatening, new interests, knowledge, and understanding expand their worlds through life experience.

Thus the key to their transformation is revealed. The Golden Rule in their lives consists in sincerely making others feel as secure as they themselves want to feel. When they are caught in dysfunctional motivation, their felt need is for anything that will mollify their fear—sometimes rules, sometimes defiance of rules, sometimes a flurry of activity. Their real need is for interior quiet that can only come through silent reflection.

Their illusion is that happiness is attained by being subsumed in and feeling a part of a group. In reality, happiness comes to them through discovering and exercising their inner authority and learning to respond with open acceptance to the world around them.

Seven: The Dreamer

Divine Image. The Divine Image at the core of the Dreamers' pattern is Majesty (Hod). Majesty is scintillating, persistent, philosophical, noble, and penetrating.

Scintillating. An effervescent attitude and view of life become the wellspring from which others may drink life-giving waters.

Liveliness creates a magnetic field that draws into its purview the good of the universe.

Optimistic and imaginative thinking unite to form the creative vitality that draws forth and enlivens transcendent characteristics within the human spirit.

Persistent. Consistent application of energy to life creates excitement and vitality, as well as useful tools for the improvement of humanity.

Positive attitudes and unwavering love of life make the earthly journey a series of challenges through which difficulties and problems are overcome.

Tenacious research and analysis clarify and simplify the issues that hold individuals and nations in quagmires of ineffectuality.

Philosophical. Alert observance of human behavior and motivation give birth to an intense sensitivity and response to the human condition.

Mysteries of the universe await revelation through meditation and the resolute development of conceptual systems.

The wisdom and strength that radiate from the contemplative spirit emerge almost magically in the forms of teaching and counseling.

Noble. Graciousness and lofty ideals speak of a glorious love and deep appreciation for life that are expressed in art, music, poetry, and prose.

Consistent respect for individual dignity yields a generous and magnanimous nature.

With regal and heroic charm, charity toward all becomes the crown of honor.

Penetrating. With unrelenting tenderness the human spirit is irresistibly drawn to perceive and merge with the mystery of the Divine.

Futuristic potentials are transformed into constructive solutions in the present if clear intellect, well-honed mental powers, and scientific imagination are used.

When gifts of communication are skillfully and judiciously applied, irreconcilable opposites are led steadily toward a unity of vision.

Lifelong Quest: Becoming an Illuminator. Dreamers become Illuminators as they restrain their desire to avoid discomfort. When free to embrace the total reality of life, they use their mental powers to find solutions to problems the world thought unsolvable. They promote positive thinking and expand the horizons of possibility. Because no problem is insurmountable to them, they can devise concrete and practical solutions by a careful focusing of their constant flow of new and creative ideas.

Because of their innate optimism, they are able to generate enthusiastic support for innovative projects. Often charismatic personalities, they can guide groups to reach decisions in subtle and nonthreatening ways through fluent, versatile communication skills. They are natural philosophers and teachers who, on the more practical side, can be entrepreneurs and make an impossible dream come true.

They exhibit an increased ability to communicate on the emotional level and to persevere through emotionally difficult situations. They learn to take time for contemplation, using these experiences to explore themselves, to seek personal growth, and to face into difficulty and weakness. This movement inward will yield fruit in their relationships. Both friends and family will notice their desire to communicate about personal issues.

Thus the key to their transformation is revealed. The Golden Rule in their lives consists in taking responsibility for the difficult and painful projects in life, just as they have egocentrically expected others to do their work for them. When they are caught in dysfunctional motivation, their felt need is for anything that will circumvent painful and uncomfortable situations. Their real need is for the perseverance to integrate joy and pain so as to become personally involved in improving the conditions around them.

Their illusion is that happiness is attained by an unrelenting optimistic attitude. In reality, happiness comes to them through developing the full spectrum of their emotions and feelings so as to become realistically dedicated to the welfare of humanity.

Eight: The Confronter

Divine Image. The Divine Image at the core of the Confronters' pattern is Foundation (Yesod). Foundation is consecrated, zealous, self-sacrificial, inspirational and realistic.

Consecrated. Bonding with the Divine through covenant love brings dedication to eradicating human suffering and celebrating the gift of life.

In recognizing the sacredness of all creation, the human spirit becomes transparent, thus revealing the Divine Spirit and the Source of life and goodness. Submission to Divine authority creates parameters for the holy use of strength and power.

Zealous. Continual surrender in experiences of the Divine yields a healthy and enthusiastic commitment to justice and mercy.

Assiduous ambition for higher goals opens doors for creative thinking and humanitarian activity.

Honest recognition of human frailty initiates a lifelong passage through the crucible of divine compassion.

Self-sacrificial. Passionate concern expands human consciousness to cooperate in working toward the wholeness and holiness of all humanity.

With the surrender of power and control and consequent death to self rise the privileges of drinking from the common wellsprings of life and carrying the world's wounded to the same restorative waters.

At great personal cost and with superhuman effort, the heart's buried treasures are unearthed to be shared intimately with others.

Inspirational. Through creative living and high ideals, the fires of hope and determination are set ablaze in the hearts of the downtrodden.

Resourceful approaches to difficulties dispel confusion and energize the human spirit with confidence.

Animation and zest for living combine to become a contagious catalyst that empowers the vision, potential, and destiny of others.

Realistic. Common sense and imagination combine to effect progress and improvement in the material world through healthy and wholesome means.

Grounding in the actual and true creates an unfailing sense of direction and purpose.

Authenticity, self-discipline, and strong love are virtues through which heaven and earth unite in natural and substantial harmony.

Lifelong Quest: Becoming a Philanthropist. Confronters become Philanthropists by restraining their need to use power for self-protection. Instead they use their strength, influence, and exuberance for the sake of others and in the cause of universal justice. They are able to lead others in a strong yet compassionate manner. By fearlessly risking their resources and reputations to alleviate the burdens of injustice, they become proficient in causing necessary change. They are practical innovators whose skills at arbitration come to the fore when they are championing individual rights in society.

Keen interpreters of motivation, they temper their political sense with sensitivity and compassion. They convince others of the rightness of a vision by communicating in a way that reaches into the depths of the human soul. They motivate others, creatively enlisting them to enact this vision for the common welfare. By distributing responsibility and coordinating accountability, they bring about a sense of unshakable group unity.

In personal relationships they exhibit an increased awareness of the feelings and needs of others, and their desire to communicate from the heart opens them to new spiritual depths. Mercy and humanitarian goals take over their lives as contact with the Divine frees them from ulterior motives. In sharing their own astute observations and strategies, they evoke the strength from others to face into problems and difficulties.

Thus the key to their transformation is revealed. The Golden Rule in their lives consists in sharing with others the strength that they have used for egocentric motives. They must learn to give to others the just treatment that they have demanded for themselves. When they are caught in dysfunctional motivation, their felt need is for influence in situations so that they can protect themselves and their own interests. Their real need is for heartfelt mercy and compassion and for the unity with others that these qualities create.

Their illusion is that happiness is attained by dominating people and situations so that their own agenda rules. In reality, happiness comes to them through experiencing the pleasure of being part of the human family by including the feelings, needs, and concerns of others in their goals.

Nine: The Preservationist

Divine Image. The Divine Image at the core of the Preservationists' pattern is Presence (Shekhinah). Presence is compassionate, impartial, uncomplicated, resourceful, and mystical.

Compassionate. Patience and generosity are ever-present virtues as people become mutual companions on the journey that breathes life into the human soul.

Tolerance expands the heart and shatters all boundaries, finally encompassing all humanity in love.

Consideration for others merges with selfless understanding to uphold the weak in times of distress.

Impartial. The lack of any trace of prejudice and possession of unqualified moral integrity produces a wisdom through which unity and peace are mediated to the world.

With important values and human needs at stake, the struggle to give fair consideration to all is the narrow road to divine justice.

Sincerity and understanding are the balancing forces that ensure a constant inner harmony in the midst of trials and difficulties.

Uncomplicated. Absence of clutter in the material world leads to a simplicity of life that clearly reveals divine truths and values.

The beauty and peace of nature feed the soul and expand consciousness for the comprehension of divine wisdom.

Simple morality and a forgiving heart breed a clarity of soul through which divine light can shine on humanity.

Resourceful. A creative and capable spirit is activated in selfless service through clever use of the available gifts of the earth.

Using ingenious talent for applying principles to practical problems produces an inventiveness that expands the capacity of the mind.

Continual gratitude for divine love already received equips the spirit for the ascent that lies ahead.

Mystical. Self-awareness and self-knowledge enfold the soul in its own inner conflicts and reveal a longing for union with the Divine.

The revelation of the face of God within inspires the soul to greatness and calls it beyond itself in an unveiling of its cosmic potential.

With spiritual power clarified in the crucible of self-understanding, discernment of the world's values elucidates life's true meaning.

Lifelong Quest: Becoming a Universalist. Preservationists become Universalists as they restrain their desire for peace at any price—including denying the importance of any person or situation that disturbs their tranquillity. Instead, they learn to face into life by taking a stand, accepting responsibility beyond personal gratification, and using their strength to encourage another's passion for life rather than squelching it. Their goal in life becomes promoting selfless service. They accomplish this goal with an active acceptance of and interest in others regardless of their ideas, views, or prejudices. Because of their universal respect for humanity, they develop the ability to resolve conflict and mediate peace in every situation.

Drawing from resources deep within themselves, they move through life with a quiet, interior strength in the midst of often confusing situations. Stress and upheaval do not disturb them. When the situation calls for it, they assume responsibility in a dignified and straightforward manner. Quietly they enact high standards of justice in their personal lives.

They become adept at supporting, affirming, and encouraging creative ideas and potential in others. They share their own ideas in a candid and frank manner. In an unassuming and vulnerable way, they learn to express their values and feelings. Known for their affability, they are warmly hospitable. Their dedication to organizations that exemplify high ideals and leadership through service is inspiring to others.

Thus the key to their transformation is revealed. The Golden Rule in their lives consists in working to ransom their passion for life that has been held hostage by their compulsive desire for peace, thereby calling forth and inspiring a passion for greatness and freedom in others. Their own peace is created through passionate involvement in relationships and bearing their share of responsibility in family and community. When they are caught in dysfunctional motivation, their felt need is for tranquillity that is won by repressing passion, avoiding true relationships, and ignoring important problems as well as the people who cause them. Their real need is to recognize their own importance and intense passion for life and to honor these same values in others.

Their illusion is that happiness is attained by shrugging off responsibility and maintaining a calm, easygoing exterior. In reality, happiness comes to them through exposing the depth and breadth of their feelings and emotions as well as their love of life to others, thus communicating and modeling their universal love and dedication that leads them to work for justice and peace for every individual.

Transcending Illusion

From the beginning to the end of your life, the swan can serve as a guiding symbol. With its long, graceful neck as the phallic symbol and its soft, rounded body as the feminine symbol, the image of the swan ignites visions of wholeness—the integration of power and grace, of the masculine and feminine components in every person. Like the Enneagram wisdom itself, the swan embodies both mystery and the promise of harmony through complexity and diversity.

The phrase "swan song" expresses the mythic belief that the swan sings sweetly at the moment of death. The song would speak to the soul of the listener, revealing the secret desire for illusion to which everyone clings. Yet it is this very illusion that must die before we can rise to the heights of transformation and resurrection.

From time immemorial the appearance of a white swan gracefully gliding across shimmering waters has stirred an unfathomable desire to rededicate ourselves to the continuing journey toward transformation. Inevitably, when rededication is sincere, we begin to dream the tantalizingly possible dream of a world that transcends violence and division, attaining unity through individual transformation.

As we cease to be a puzzle to ourselves and others we can redirect our energies toward revealing our true nature as sacred mysteries. As we attempt to manifest an image of the divine at the core of our being, we make more real the dream of a world of understanding and unity. This is the dream that arises in us when we take into our very being the promise of transformation unveiled by the secret wisdom of the Enneagram.

Plant Your Garden, Water Your Soul

From Compulsion to Freedom

CHAPTER NINE

*After a while you learn the
    subtle difference between
holding a hand and chaining
    a soul.
And you learn that love
    doesn't mean leaning
and company doesn't mean
    security.
And you learn to accept your
    defeats
with your head held high and
    your eyes wide open,
with the grace of a student,
    not the tantrums of a
    child.
And you learn that in the
    darkness of struggle
acceptance and surrender
    mate, impregnating you
    with new life.
And in time you learn that
    even sunshine burns
if you're exposed too long.*

*So you plant your own garden
    and water your own soul,
Instead of waiting for someone
    to bring you flowers.
And you really are strong
And you really do have worth
And you learn and learn . . .
As surely as the dawn
    comes . . . you learn.*
—AUTHOR UNKNOWN

W̲e would be remiss to conclude this book by leaving the empowering message of the Enneagram on the heights of what might be misinterpreted as fantasy. Exploring the Divine Image and Lifelong Quest of each pattern reveals a noble destiny for each person who chooses the hard work of waking up and becoming conscious, but these lofty thoughts and possibilities will quickly revert to daydreams and fantasies, unless we keep our feet firmly planted in the earth of day-to-day living. The Enneagram, although certainly an inspirational inner wisdom, is meant to provide practical knowledge that can enable you to live, work, and relate in a healthy, life-enhancing fashion.

The truth contained in the Enneagram is not truth because someone says it's truth. Wisdom becomes truth as we apply it to life and, over a period of time, the positive effects of transformation, healing, freedom, and peace begin to permeate our lives.

We trust the Enneagram will become truth for you because you internalize and understand its wisdom and move beyond the self-defeating patterns that have prevented you from living in freedom. Like the petals of a flower, the secret promise of your personality will unfold each day as small, often seemingly insignificant weaknesses are transformed into unimaginable strengths. Because you are planting your own garden and watering your own soul, truth will become a vibrant, living, growing reality. You will become truth.

This final chapter, then, is intended for all of us who, tired of being led down the garden path, have decided to do our own gardening and create our own paths. Although planting an inner garden is definitely different than planting a garden in your backyard, there are some basic principles that gardeners of both kinds of plots would be wise to follow.[1]

The first thing serious gardeners do is work at improving their ground rather than attempting to live with problem soil. Something—weeds, at least—will grow in almost any soil. But what gardener would want a garden restricted by natural soil limitations rather than specified by his or her own desires?

Provided the climate is right, any soil can be modified to grow any plant that the gardener decides to grow. The key word here is *modified*. The gardener doesn't discard the soil but instead adds the essential nutrients that will bring it into a rich, fertile balance.

So how do you begin to plan a garden? The first step is to obtain an objective soil analysis, which will answer questions like these: What is your soil composition? What are its natural strengths and limitations? What nutrients are required to grow the type and quality of plant you desire? To get a soil analysis, however, you must send a handful of dirt to a lab to be analyzed.

Yielding a handful of your inner earth for an interior soil analysis may sound, on the surface, similarly simple and basic. Basic, yes. Simple, no. You see, if the purpose of a soil analysis is to modify the soil, this first step confronts us with a prime difficulty of human nature: we're not sure we want modification; we've become attached to keeping things the way they are. We're stubbornly determined to keep throwing good seeds into the ground in the false hope that this year, for some magical reason, we'll have a better crop.

Each year amateur gardeners waste enough acre feet of water to turn an entire desert into an oasis, only to reap a harvest of three or four shriveled—but home-grown—tomatoes. But, the next spring, does embarrassment prevent them from returning to their little plot of ground with a new flatbed of sprouting plants? Absolutely not! Should the garden fail again this year, they can always blame mother nature who didn't provide the right weather or their neighbor who didn't carry out her promise to water the garden while they were on vacation.

Laugh though we may at such transparent excuse-making, we practice the same principle with our inner gardens. We hang on tight to our handful of earth and won't let it go, all the while thinking that life circumstances and other people are the reason for the lack of happiness or growth in our lives.

---

1. Facts about gardening, soil composition, soil analysis, etc. are taken from *Ortho's Complete Guide to Successful Gardening* (San Francisco: Chevron Chemical Company, 1983), esp. pp. 342–75.

Furthermore, we are paralyzed by the prospect of an interior soil analysis. What happens if I send my soil to the lab to be tested, and there's a mix-up? Will I then be expending my energy trying to solve someone else's problem? In fact, is it really worth putting effort and time into creating a garden, especially an inner garden? Wouldn't it make more sense to learn to accept my life—my soil—the way it is, do what I can when I can with it, but not take this inner work so seriously?

These are all valid questions and common fears, and only you can decide on the right response to them. Giving up the familiar for the unknown is always risky business, for there are no guarantees. What we often fail to recognize is that even if we cling to the familiar, the only thing certain is that nothing is certain.

Therefore, the questions you need to answer are: Do I want to give up the familiar and comfortable picture of myself I now have for the precise soul analysis of my personality, with its strengths and weaknesses, that the Enneagram affords? Is it worth the trouble? Is it worth the shock? Do I want the responsibility?

Some years ago we came across the following story, which profoundly illustrates that neither in life nor in death are we made any promises or given any guarantees. If you still fear the risk of forgoing your familiar but faltering garden of compulsion for the unknown, verdant garden of transformation, perhaps this story will assist you in resolving your dilemma.

> Once upon a time there was an old man from the lovely island of Crete. He loved his land with a deep and beautiful intensity, so much so that when he perceived that he was about to die he had his children bring him outside and lay him on his beloved earth. As he was about to expire he reached down by his side and clutched some earth into his hands. He died a happy man.
>
> He now appeared before heaven's gates. God, as an old white-bearded man, came out to greet him. "Welcome," he said. "You've been a good man. Please, come into the joys of heaven." But as the old man started to enter the pearly gates, God said, "Please. You must let the soil go."
>
> "Never!" said the old man, stepping back. "Never!"
>
> And so God departed sadly, leaving the old man outside the gates. A few eons went by. God came out again, this time as a friend, an old drinking crony. They had a few drinks, told some stories, and then God said, "All right, now it's time to enter heaven, friend. Let's go." And they started for the pearly gates. And once more God requested that the old man let go of this soil and once more he refused.
>
> More eons rolled by. God came out once more, this time as a delightful and playful granddaughter. "Oh, granddaddy," she said, "you're so wonderful and we all miss you. Please come inside with me." The old man nodded and she helped him up, for by this time he had grown indeed very old and arthritic. In fact, so arthritic was he that he had to prop up the right hand holding Crete's soil with his left hand. They moved toward the pearly gates and at this point his strength quite gave out. His gnarled fingers would no longer stay clenched in a fist, with the result that the soil sifted out between them until his hand was empty. He then entered heaven. The first thing he saw was his beloved island.[2]

For everyone willing to risk a handful of the familiar for the unguaranteed unknown, the following is an abbreviated soil analysis for the nine hidden gardens in the Enneagram.

2. William J. Bausch, *Storytelling: Imagination and Faith* (Mystic, CT: Twenty-third Publications, 1984), pp. 127–28.

One: Achiever Moving to Pathfinder

Soil limitations. Achievers are intense people whose topsoil is carried away by the four winds as they lose their perspective on life and become bound to earth by details. Their unconscious compulsion to complete the task in front of them demands a determination that leads to resentment and anger. Because they set extremely high standards for themselves, the possibility of actual achievement always tumbles just beyond their reach. These overresponsible people then berate themselves for not having tried harder and reached farther.

Being orderly, hardworking people, they seldom see how they might cause any of the chaos that consistently surrounds them. Rather, they feel that others take advantage of their generous nature and fail to recognize that their exaggerated sense of responsibility and desire to be seen as good are actually the root of the problem. The winds of impatience and criticism toward self and others continue to cause erosion, leaving behind only a poor self-image.

Modifying the soil. Achievers need to release their death grip on responsibility, allowing a cool breeze to lighten them up rather than permitting the wind to carry them away. They must learn to laugh and play, not taking themselves or life so seriously. Much needed are short fallow periods to be spent refocusing their priorities and looking at life in general, thus gaining the broader perspective that will reveal the meaning and purpose of their own lives.

They need to take time to reflect on the true meaning of responsibility—learning how to be responsible for their own lives while allowing others to be responsible for theirs. Two important questions for Achievers are, Where am I going in my life? and How am I going to get there?

Soil strengths. Achievers' Divine Image is Wisdom. They have an innate practical wisdom that they conscientiously and creatively apply in day-to-day living. Because they are ethical, loyal, realistic, and possess a deep respect for the earth and all living things, they are natural leaders. In pursuing their transforming inner work, they will find wisdom expanding to include unseen realities as well as visible ones.

Two: Helper Moving to Partner

Soil limitations. Helpers display a lush, leafy surface growth that quickly becomes entangled with all surrounding life. By avoiding work on their inner lives, they find much of their potential fruit shriveling on the vine—projects that never quite get finished and important personal decisions left drying out in the sun. Impulsiveness and lack of discipline take over their private lives.

Because overinvolvement in the lives of others prevents them from being rooted in their own feelings and needs, they come to believe that their very existence depends on the quality of appreciation and gratitude they receive. Pampering and taking care of others give their lives meaning. Thus although their inner attitude is often possessive and manipulative, people treat them as "saints," which makes it difficult for them to disentangle themselves and tend their own gardens. Conversely, when others initiate disengagement, Helpers easily drift off to greener pastures.

Modifying the soil. Helpers need to send their roots of personal needs and feelings deep into the ground. Learning to communicate directly, setting goals, cultivating self-discipline, and developing assertiveness will allow them to set the healthy boundaries previously lacking in their lives.

When feelings–their own or others'–do not control their lives, they become free to make decisions based on logic rather than appearance. They serve themselves well when they open their minds to ideas that challenge their belief systems through books, courses, and people unlike themselves rather than simply reinforcing already accepted assumptions, ideals, and standards.

Soil strengths. Helpers' Divine Image is Understanding. Their gifts for empowering others and for sorting through the multiplicity of human needs and feelings and their ability to listen without judging can give them countless opportunities in the fields of mediation and diplomacy. Their gentle, nonviolent, caring, and perceptive character unites with self-knowledge and self-awareness through transformation.

Three: Succeeder Moving to Motivator

Soil limitations. Succeeders are showy people who place excessive importance on the flower of appearance–both physically and productively. This is also the trap by which they come to believe in approval only from external sources. Because they undervalue the inner life and the personal dimension, they do not hesitate to use everything–themselves, others, circumstances–to gain recognition.

Disregarding the interior life increases their determination to exercise control over their environment. However, no amount of success in the world can compensate for the inner void created through neglect. In the world of relationship, they primarily develop superficial acquaintances that are self-serving. They are always in danger of becoming aloof, cold, and even cruel because they build impenetrable walls of self-protection against vulnerability, the only agent that can soften their personality.

Modifying the soil. The world of personal relationships and emotions will break up the cementlike hardpan soil that lies hidden beneath Succeeders' seemingly healthy topsoil. Slowing down and setting aside time for friendships and for the interior life will provide the moisture needed for an authentic self to grow.

They need to consolidate the multiple interests that keep them in constant motion. Objective self-observation will be necessary for these strong, stubborn, directional people to recognize that their words and attitudes undermine relationships. A personal journal of feelings, desires, and personal insight–not ideas and plans–is essential.

Soil strengths. Succeeders' Divine Image is Love. Optimistic visionaries, they are gifted with the ability to inspire others to excel in life. Their natural leadership skills, creativity, and dedication apply to both the task at hand and the goal. Their expertise at reading the hidden motivations of others can be used for either good or ill. The deep caring they feel for others is wasted until, through transformation, they learn to give expression to those emotions.

Four: Individualist Moving to Builder

Soil limitations. Individualists' soil have drainage problems, which puts them always in danger of drowning in a stagnant pool of emotional pain. These inwardly strong people outwardly appear fragile, even delicate. Acute focus on the personal realm causes them to take everything personally—comments, ideas, projects, suggestions. Consequently, the person who made the comment or spoke the idea feels confused and frustrated as the Individualist satisfies the inner need to be the center of attention.

Their emotional self-indulgence, lack of discipline in the outer world, and desire to be taken care of makes them master manipulators of people. The combination of well-developed verbal skills, a flair for the dramatic, and pessimism often causes them to appear arrogant when in truth they're feeling insecure and inadequate.

Modifying the soil. Hard work, discipline, and energy spent on doing rather than feeling will solve Individualists' drainage problems and provide a healthy outlet for their creative genius. Interpreting life through personal feelings needs to give way to a more objective, dispassionate, and accurate perception of life.

When overwhelmed with emotions, they become paralyzed and need physical movement to regain balance. Any activity—taking a walk, writing a letter, repotting a plant, or working in the yard—will release the internal pressure and give direction to their energy. Recognizing negative attitudes and consciously choosing positive counterparts will grow easier in time, yielding a healthy, positive self-image.

Soil strengths. Individualists' Divine Image is Power. These perceptive people possess a deep love and admiration for others. Their remarkable sensitivity, which causes so much pain when focused inward, becomes a fountainhead of originality and creativity in the outer world. Naturally gifted with clear thinking and skilled with words and ideas, they discover endless opportunities available to them as they move forward in the process of transformation.

Five: Observer Moving to Explorer

Soil limitations. Observers spend their lives analyzing, reanalyzing, and modifying their soil but never get around to planting anything. They delight in examining and scrutinizing the garden of life from the silent safety of distance. Because they watch and ponder without becoming personally vulnerable, they easily discard as frivolous the feelings, pain, and actual needs of others.

Noninvolvement in daily living, combined with taking excessive amounts of time alone to ponder and reflect, becomes a setup for family members to take care of them by handling all social responsibilities. The mental self-indulgence they enjoy is unconsciously counterbalanced with impulsive bouts of overindulgence to satisfy their physical appetites and/or desire for material possessions. Their cryptic, impersonal communication style creates alienation, which they interpret as solely the problem of others, whom they see as oversensitive and too impulsive, therefore lacking objectivity.

Modifying the soil. The solution for the Observers' garden is simple. Begin planting the seeds of personal involvement in life, start "wasting" time developing intimate relationships, and learn to respect feelings and needs in self and others. Although they've never expected others or life to give them anything they didn't earn, neither do they feel any responsibility to leave the world a better place than they found it.

They correct this attitude by contributing to the world, often by sharing as a gift all the knowledge they have distilled throughout their years of observing and analyzing life, thus expanding the intellectual horizons of others. In giving they overcome their fear of being incapable or unready to give anything to anyone. In this process their lifelong pain of emptiness and loneliness will be healed by feeling and relationships.

Soil strengths. Observers' Divine Image is Beauty. Their adventuresome spirit, love of nature, and appreciation of all things new and different are among their greatest strengths. Versatility, humor, and openness to new ideas, combined with their native intelligence, make them excellent communicators of progress and change. As they move toward transformation, they learn to use their strengths in the personal sphere to find fulfillment.

Six: Guardian Moving to Stabilizer

Soil limitations. Guardians' have their soil analyzed by experts but don't trust the accuracy of the results, so they need to check with everyone else to see what they think. Thus their energies are scattered in a whirlwind of activity. Multiple fears of making independent decisions, of being accepted, of being respected, or simply of being alone—to name a few—along with a need for structure and rules reveal their underlying sense of anxiety. They compensate for these feelings by taking responsibility for everything except themselves.

By talking too much and complaining under the guise of genuine concern, they impose their worrying on others and call it love. Their stubborn independence makes them susceptible to judging others harshly according to impersonal laws rather than personal circumstances. When they do not take charge of their own lives appropriately, others take advantage of them, and they play the martyr.

Modifying the soil. Guardians must finally accept their soil analysis and begin planting. Putting the brakes on activity will help them gain control of their lives and discover the inner authority that produces the peace they long for.

Taking time to reflect is critical, for only then will they dare to answer their essential life questions: Where am I going? What do I really value? What are my actual responsibilities as opposed to those I assume? Apart from what rules, law, or authorities say, what do I think about the important issues of my life? These are only examples of myriad questions they ask others to answer for them. Now they must solve their own riddles. In their search, they will come to trust their own intellectual capabilities, and their lifelong anxiety will be eased.

Soil strengths. Guardians' Divine Image is Endurance. Their high moral standards and willingness to sacrifice for the betterment of others place them in positions of trust and confidence. Their loyalty, hospitality, enthusiasm for life, and genuine concern for others can heal individuals and unite communities. Self-confidence grounded in a solid personal vision will continue to grow as they move toward transformation.

Seven: Dreamer Moving to Illuminator

Soil limitations. Instead of using their gifts of imagination and planning to create a better garden, Dreamers use them to remain in the realm of fantasy. Having a rich and fertile soil, they plant too many seeds—plans and activities—and won't thin them out or water them deeply. Tending toward magical thinking, they treat imaginary solutions and direct action as if they were the same thing. Because they prefer living on the surface, life often passes them by as they sacrifice their native intelligence and caring hearts to the god of good times and fantasy ideas.

Lingering in the realm of ideas is their way of remaining so completely optimistic that they block out any fact or feeling that might make them deal with reality. Their propensity toward overdosing on anything that gives them pleasure prevents them from developing the discipline that will produce anything of lasting value.

Modifying the soil. Dreamers' insatiable desire for everything pleasurable necessitates a good dose of realism and hard work to put the appropriate limits on pleasure seeking. They need to understand the benefits of a carefully completed plan for planting and tending a garden as they grow in self-respect through the hard work that yields accomplishment.

By focusing on and achieving goals, whether in their careers or in the personal realm, they discover new enthusiasm through their ability to overcome obstacles. The reward for this effort will be the reality of the beautiful garden they have always dreamed of, for in following this path they add the missing ingredient of their lives—the creative power that has its origin in discipline and personal involvement.

Soil strengths. Dreamers' Divine Image is Majesty. Their potentially brilliant minds and their deep love of people are a secret serious side of themselves they come to feel comfortable with. They are naturally delightful companions and networkers. Their keen powers of observation and visionary nature will be revealed as they plant and tend their garden of transformation.

Eight: Confronter Moving to Philanthropist

Soil limitations. Because Confronters have little, if any, understanding of sensitivity, either in themselves or in others, they often leave a path of devastation in their wake—like a Rototiller run wild. All too often they talk while others listen then walk away pleased as punch with their communication skills and conversational ability. They want to love and protect those close to them, but their efforts more often resemble the destructive force of a hailstorm than the soothing softness of an earth-soaking rain.

They dispense their personal brand of justice with the harshness of the noonday sun, having little, if any, regard for the twilight shadows of mitigating circumstances. Because they usually get what they want, they tend to be arrogant; once they make a decision, they carve it in stone and become inflexible.

Modifying the soil. The hardness of Confronters' soil is converted into loam by frequent tilling in times of reflection and meditation. Amendment of the soil by the development of their spiritual side brings forth the fertility of compassion and vulnerability. Because they value competence and the exterior world, they are stimulated in their time of reflection by input from experts through books, tapes, seminars, and lectures.

They respond well when exposed to a variety of viewpoints, which they sort out with an innate sense of truth and honesty. By alternating fallow periods of listening and pondering with productive times of working and talking, they come to value relatedness and caring.

Soil strengths. Confronters' Divine Image is Foundation. Their strong love of and commitment to people finds new expression in caring, sensitive ways. They are the kind of people who make a lasting impression on the world, and only compassion will ensure it will be a positive one. Natural leaders, the more they move toward transformation, the more their passion for universal truth and justice will be expressed.

Nine: Preservationist Moving to Universalist

Soil limitations. Preservationists' sandy soil allows them to present contradictory outer and inner lives. In professional and social realms they are warm, friendly, affable, lighthearted, and enthusiastic. However, because their inner life has atrophied through lack of moisture, in the personal realm they are often inattentive, withdrawn, passive-aggressive, and forgetful of those close to them.

Their secretiveness about their thoughts and feelings—a protection against turmoil, tension, or argument—easily becomes deception as they allow personal issues to mount until they become virtually impossible to handle without destroying the relationship. No matter how difficult their personal lives become, they fantasize how life will be different when circumstances change, when others change—but never when they change.

Modifying the soil. Adding the organic matter of emotions and interest in the personal dimension creates the necessary transfer of attention from the public to the private realm. Honest communication with spouse, family, and friends regarding feelings, needs, and responsibilities will require great effort.

Awakening their long-repressed feelings and accepting them as valid will be difficult because, of necessity, painful emotions and buried memories will be uncovered. Both journaling and receiving guidance from a counselor create the accountability that will ensure endurance. Because they are trapped in the past, focusing on the present and the future through goal-setting is essential.

Soil strengths. Preservationists' Divine Image is Presence. They are endowed with a gentle yet powerful interior strength through which they can withstand adversity. This same quality becomes a peaceful haven when expressed in relationships of caring and love. These naturally kind, patient, and resourceful people will discover their generous healing gifts as they move toward transformation.

The secret dream of each of us is to have a place within ourselves where wounds are healed, strength is restored, refreshment abounds, and new dreams are born. That sacred place will have as many shapes and expressions as there are people. Here, however, we could only choose one as an image —the hidden interior garden.

Tending to your hidden garden will be the most meaningful gift you can give yourself. In this sacred place you will touch and be touched by the Divine. Here all little truths that divide and separate gradually fall away—only Truth remains.

We trust that this book has assisted you in discovering the magnificent beauty and strength that lies within you, and that you will continue to nurture the hidden garden of your soul. Happy gardening!

GLOSSARY

Achiever. The name of the Enneagram personality pattern that corresponds to 1 on the Enneagram circle when it is in prime addiction. See also Anger, Dependent Stance, Effective Center, and Way of Reduction.

Affective Center. One of the kinds of intelligence of the human mind. Its purpose is for connectedness and transcendence, but it is commonly used to manipulate a small world of feeling, emotions, and relationships. It is preferred by Helpers (2), Succeeders (3), and Individualists (4). See also Centers, Effective Center, and Theoretical Center.

Aggressive Stance. One of the three approaches to problem solving. This stance is taken by Succeeders (3), Dreamers (7), and Confronters (8). It describes a desire to restructure, mold, form, and shape the world to one's liking. See also Dependent Stance and Withdrawing Stance.

Anger. In the Enneagram, a dissatisfaction with everything for its lack of perfection and a desire to refashion it according to one's preference; the prime addiction of Achievers (1).

Approaches to Problem Solving. In the Enneagram there are three ways that people can attempt to get around life's difficulties: aggression, dependency, or withdrawal. See also Aggressive Stance, Dependent Stance, and Withdrawing Stance.

Balance Points. A name that describes Succeeders (3), Guardians (6), and Preservationists (9) because they repress their Preferred Center so that it will not stand out; in this way they hope to be in balance or harmony with every person and every situation. These numbers are at the midpoints of the centers and so have a unique approach to using the center in which they reside. See also Wings.

Beauty. The fifth *sefirah* (*Tif'eret*), which is the Divine Image for Observers (5) in the Enneagram process of transformation. See also Sefirot.

Bennett, John G. Student of Gurdjieff and one of the primary teachers of the Enneagram in the West, also author of several books about the Enneagram and the process of transformation.

Binah. See Understanding.

Blessing the past. Admitting the facts regarding what took place in a given period of one's life, dealing honestly with the pain it created, and then focusing on all the good that has come from the experience. One of the five attitudes that encourages the process of transformation. See also Forgiveness, *Metanoia,* Self-observation, and Self-remembering.

Builder. The Lifelong Quest of Individualists (4).

Capital sin. A prime spiritually and psychologically dysfunctional behavior, the source from which other dysfunctional behaviors grow. It creates an inappropriate and unhealthy relationship with self and the Self. In the Enneagram, capital sins are spoken of as prime addictions and are understood psychologically, not moralistically. See also Prime addiction.

Centers. Types or kinds of intelligence. The Enneagram posits the existence of three centers in the human mind–the Center of Affect, or the Affective Center, the Center of Theory, or the Theoretical Center, and the Center of Effect, or the Effective Center. A prime addiction is developed by coming to prefer one of these centers, which is called the Preferred Center. Thus another center will be used as an auxiliary center; it is called the Secondary Center. The final center, the Tertiary or Third Center, is ignored and left dormant.

Confronter. The name of the Enneagram personality pattern that corresponds to 8 on the Enneagram circle when it is caught in its prime addiction. See also Aggressive Stance, Effective Center, Lust, and Way of Subjugation.

Covetousness. See Greed.

Deceit. In the Enneagram, a continual disguise of one's own feelings, desires, and opinions so as to gain a political or social advantage; the prime addiction of Succeeders (3).

Dependent Stance. One of the three Approaches to Problem Solving. This stance is taken by Achievers (1), Helpers (2), and Guardians (6), and it describes a desire to know what others are doing so that one can decide what to do next, a desire to be in social relationship with others. See also Aggressive Stance and Withdrawing Stance.

Divine   Attribute. Used   interchangeably with Divine Image.

Divine Image. The presence of the Divine in every human being, although its specific manifestation is different for each of the nine patterns of the Enneagram.

Dreamer. The name of the Enneagram personality pattern that corre-

sponds to 7 on the Enneagram circle when it is caught in its prime addiction. See also Aggressive Stance, Gluttony, Theoretical Center, and Way of Reduction.

Effective Center. One of the kinds of intelligence of the human mind. Its purpose is for movement, the intent and energy needed to complete the work of being a person in the world, but it is commonly used to preserve safety and to focus on one's own instinctual reactions and being. It is preferred by Confronters (8), Preservationists (9), and Achievers (1). See also Affective Center, Centers, and Theoretical Center.

Enactive Movement.   The third movement of the process of transformation. This movement puts into action the new vision gained in the Reflective Movement; thus it is the first movement of the process of transformation in which outward change occurs. See also Motivational Movement, Mystical Movement, and Reflective Movement.

Endurance.   The third sefirah (Nezah), which is the Divine Image for Guardians (6) in the Enneagram process of transformation. See also Sefirot.

Envy.   In the Enneagram, painful awareness of the advantages of others combined with an insatiable desire to possess the same advantage; the prime addiction of Individualists (4).

Essence. All of that with which a human being is created. It is identified with, but not strictly limited to, what in the West is commonly known as the spirit of a human being.

Explorer. The Lifelong Quest of Observers (5).

Fear. In the Enneagram, a sense of

danger from people or situations that profess values different from one's own; the prime addiction of Guardians (6).

Forgiveness. Letting go of offenses perpetrated by people in one's past. One of the five attitudes that encourages the process of transformation. See also Blessing the past, *Metanoia,* Self-observation, and Self-remembering.

Foundation. The eighth *sefirah* (*Yesod*), which is the Divine Image for Confronters (8) in the Enneagram process of transformation. See also Sefirot.

Gevurah. See Power.

Gluttony. In the Enneagram, an excessive capacity for self-indulgence, an insatiable desire to have more of whatever pleases one; the prime addiction of Dreamers (7).

Greed. In the Enneagram, excessive or insatiable desire for knowledge and the time needed to attain it; the prime addiction of Observers (5).

Guardian. The name of the Enneagram personality pattern that corresponds to 6 on the Enneagram circle when it is caught in its prime addiction. See also Balance Points, Dependent Stance, Fear, Theoretical Center, and Way of Mediation.

Gurdjieff, George I. (1869–1949). The man who is credited with discovering the Enneagram in the Monastery of the Sarmoun Brotherhood in the first years of the twentieth century and who then brought this tradition to Europe and the Americas.

Helper. The name of the Enneagram personality pattern that corresponds to 2 on the Enneagram circle when it is caught in its prime addic-

tion. See also Affective Center, Dependent Stance, Pride, and Way of Subjugation.

Hesed. See Love.

Hod. See Majesty.

Hokhmah. See Wisdom.

Illuminator. The Lifelong Quest of Dreamers (7).

Individualist. The name of the Enneagram personality pattern that corresponds to 4 on the Enneagram circle when it is caught in its prime addiction. See also Affective Center, Envy, Way of Reduction, and Withdrawing Stance.

Intensifying. The act of giving in to one's prime addiction. See also Moving against the arrows, Moving with the arrows, and Neutralizing.

Kabbalah. Jewish mystical tradition, part of which reflects contact with the Enneagram through its listing of the ten attributes of God. See also Sefirot.

Keter. Crown, the first *sefirah;* the nothingness or no-thingness of God. It is eternal and has no beginning. See also Sefirot.

Laziness. See Sloth.

Lifelong Quest. The journey of transformation to neutralize the prime addiction and reveal the Divine Image at the core of the Enneagram pattern.

Love. The third *sefirah* (Hesed), which is the Divine Image for Succeeders (3) in the Enneagram process of transformation. See also *Sefirot.*

Lust. In the Enneagram, an intense longing for power, influence, or intensity in living; the prime addiction of Confronters (8).

Magi. Wisdom seekers from ancient Persia who probably were the originators or at least the first organized caretakers of the Enneagram.

Majesty. The seventh *sefirah* (Hod), which is the Divine Image for Dreamers (7) in the Enneagram process of transformation. See also Sefirot.

Metanoia. The product of self-observation and self-remembering. It comes from Greek words meaning to change (*meta*) one's mind (*nous*). In the Enneagram it refers to turning away from prime addiction and toward transformation. See also Blessing the past, Forgiveness, Self-observation, and Self-remembering.

Motivational Movement. The second movement of the process of transformation. Building upon the new vision of the kind of person one could become that is gained in the Reflective Movement, a person questions self to uncover those qualities and resources that are available to put the new vision into practice. Also, in this movement a person determines whether he or she is willing to pay the price exacted for transformation and begins to use emotions as motivators for actually enacting transformation. See also Addictive Movement, Enactive Movement, Mystical Movement, and Reflective Movement.

Motivator. The Lifelong Quest of Succeeders (3).

Moving against the arrows. A phrase referring to the arrows on the Enneagram circle and meaning taking on all the best qualities of the number from which one's arrow originates. It is the most difficult direction one can take with one's life, and it leads to neutralizing one's prime addiction—to transformation. See also Intensify-

ing, Moving with the arrows, and Neutralizing.

Moving with the arrows. A phrase referring to the arrows on the Enneagram circle and meaning taking on all the worst qualities of the number to which one's arrow points. It is the easiest direction one can take with one's life, and it leads to intensifying the prime addiction. See also Intensifying, Moving against the arrows, and Neutralizing.

Mystical Movement. The fourth and final stage of the process of transformation. It is a commitment to the process of transformation—a commitment to self-observation, self-remembering, *metanoia*, forgiveness, and blessing the past; a commitment to pursuing the Reflective, Motivational, and Enactive movements over and over until all the elements of prime addiction are neutralized. See also Addictive Movement, Blessing the Past, Enactive Movement, Forgiveness, *Metanoia*, Reflective Movement, Motivational Movement, Self-observation, and Self-remembering.

Nezah. See Endurance.

Neutralizing. The act of overcoming one's prime addiction. See also Intensifying, Moving against the arrows, and Moving with the arrows.

Observer. The name of the Enneagram personality pattern that corresponds to 5 on the Enneagram circle when it is caught in its prime addiction. See also Greed, Theoretical Center, Way of Subjugation, and Withdrawing Stance.

Partner. The Lifelong Quest of Helpers (2)

Pathfinder. The Lifelong Quest of Achievers (1).

Pattern. In the Enneagram, a formation of personality around one of the Divine Images, which becomes distorted through egocentricity into a prime addiction.

Philanthropist. The Lifelong Quest of Confronters (8).

Power. The fourth *sefirah* (Gevurah), which is the Divine Image for Individualists (4) in the Enneagram process of transformation. See also Sefirot.

Preferred Center. The center or type of intelligence of which a person is most aware. This kind of intelligence is used by the person both appropriately and inappropriately, and because using it is comfortable, it is overused. In the Enneagram, Helpers (2), Succeeders (3), and Individualists (4) prefer the Affective Center; Observers (5), Guardians (6), and Dreamers (7) prefer the Theoretical Center; and Confronters (8), Preservationists (9), and Achievers (1) prefer the Effective Center. See also Centers, Secondary Center, and Tertiary Center.

Presence. The ninth *sefirah* (Shekhinah), which is the Divine Image for Preservationists (9) in the Enneagram process of transformation. See also Sefirot.

Preservationist. The name of the Enneagram personality pattern that corresponds to 9 on the Enneagram circle when it is caught in its prime addiction. See also Balance Points, Effective Center, Sloth, Way of Mediation, and Withdrawing Stance.

Pride. In the Enneagram, seeing oneself as without needs and as being superior to others who have needs; the prime addiction of Helpers (2).

Prime addiction. In the Enneagram, prime addictions are psychological and spiritual addictions—addictions to a point of view. When people are caught in these addictions, they believe there is no other way to see their lives and therefore they have no choice but to act in the way their pattern dictates. Thus, prime addictions are drives within the human personality that cause a distortion that prevents people from seeing or acknowledging the truth about their lives. Each person and each pattern described by the Enneagram has only one prime addiction. The prime addiction of Achievers (1) is anger, of Helpers (2) is pride, of Succeeders (3) is deceit, of Individualists (4) is envy, of Observers (5) is greed, of Guardians (6) is fear, of Dreamers (7) is gluttony, of Confronters (8) is lust for power and for life, and of Preservationists (9) is sloth or laziness.

Pythagoras. Philosopher, mystic, and mathematician of the sixth century B.C.E. who traveled extensively throughout the Near East and learned the Enneagram in Persia before founding his school of esoteric knowledge on the south coast of Italy.

Reflective Movement. The first movement of the process of transformation. It is a questioning of life as it is now being lived, a questioning of prime addiction. In it a new idea enters the mind and a new vision of who one could be is formed. See also Enactive Movement, Motivational Movement, and Mystical Movement.

Relation to Life. See Ways of relating to life.

Samos. A Greek island, the birthplace of Pythagoras.

Sarmoun. A word that comes from Sanskrit and refers to bees who gather nectar to make honey and then preserve it.

Sarmoun Brotherhood. The secret society at whose hidden monastery in the Near East the tradition of the Enneagram has been kept and developed for hundreds and probably thousands of years.

Secondary Center. The center or type of intelligence that a person uses to augment and support the Preferred Center. See also Centers, Preferred Center, and Tertiary Center.

Sefirot (singular, sefirah). The Sefirot is a part of the tradition of the Kabbalah; it is the listing of the ten attributes of God. The first is Keter, or Crown, the nothingness or nothingness of God; as such, it is eternal and has no beginning. Thus, the next is considered the first; it is Hokhmah (Wisdom), followed by Binah (Understanding), Hesed (Love), Gevurah (Power), Tif'eret (Beauty), Nezah (Endurance), Hod (Majesty), Yesod (Foundation), and Shekhinah (Presence).

Literally, in Hebrew, a *sefirot* is a numerical listing. It is a root word for the English word "cipher."

Self-observation. The ability to become objective about one's own thoughts, feelings, reactions, sensations, and actions, as well as the reactions of others to oneself. One of the three attitudes regarding the present that encourages the process of transformation. See also Blessing the Past, Forgiveness, *Metanoia,* and Self-remembering.

Self-remembering. Acting from the awareness brought by self-observation. One of the three attitudes regarding the present that encourages

the process of transformation. See also Blessing the Past, Forgiveness, *Metanoia,* and Self-observation.

Shekhinah. See Presence.

Sloth. In the Enneagram, a disinclination to action or to any exertion by which one would take responsibility in a situation; the prime addiction of Preservationists (9).

Stabilizer. The Lifelong Quest of Guardians (6).

Succeeder. The name of the Enneagram personality pattern that corresponds to 3 on the Enneagram circle when it is caught in its prime addiction. See also Affective Center, Aggressive Stance, Balance Points, Deceit, and Way of Mediation.

Sufis. A sect of Moslem mystics who have had some relationship with the Enneagram.

Tif'eret. See Beauty.

Tertiary Center. The center or type of intelligence of which a person is least aware. It is left dormant and unused and thus is the source of imbalance in a person's life. See also Centers, Preferred Center, and Secondary Center.

Theoretical Center. One of the kinds of intelligence of the human mind. Its purpose is for vision and awareness of the true meaning of all things, but it is commonly used for thinking, calculating, and deciding within one's small world. It is preferred by Observers (5), Guardians (6), and Dreamers (7).

Third Center. Used interchangeably with Tertiary Center.

Transformation. The process by which a prime addiction is neutralized and a person is freed from deception and illusion to act in a truly human manner. Transformation is encouraged by five attitudes: Self-observation, Self-remembering, *Metanoia*, Forgiveness, and Blessing the Past. Transformation happens in four stages or movements: the Reflective Movement, the Motivational Movement, the Enactive Movement, and the Mystical Movement.

Understanding. The second *sefirah*, (Binah), which is the Divine Image for Helpers (2) in the Enneagram process of transformation. See also Sefirot.

Universalist. The Lifelong Quest of Preservationists (9).

Way of Mediation. One of the three ways to Relate to Life described by the Enneagram. This view is held by Succeeders (3), Guardians (6), and Preservationists (9), who look out at the world and, seeing themselves on an equal footing with it, are confident that they can make whatever adjustments are necessary to produce the proper response. They can act in this manner because they are repressing their Preferred Center and thus are called the Balance Points of the Enneagram. See also Balance Points, Preferred Center, Way of Reduction, and Way of Subjugation.

Way of Reduction. One of the three Ways of Relating to Life described by the Enneagram. This view is held by Individualists (4), Dreamers (7), and Achievers (1), who look out at the world and see a big and overwhelming reality that will probably threaten their ego interests. Thus they focus the interests of their Preferred Center within themselves. See also Idealizations, Preferred Center, Way of Mediation, and Way of Subjugation.

Way of Subjugation. One of the three Ways to Relate to Life described by the Enneagram. This view is held by Helpers (2), Observers (5), and Confronters (8), who look out at the world and see little that is unmanageable because they sense within their Preferred Center the capacity to deal with whatever the world presents to them. See also Preferred Center, Way of Mediation, and Way of Reduction.

Ways of relating to life. In the Enneagram there are three different ways people can relate to life: the Way of Subjugation, the Way of Reduction, or the Way of Mediation. See also Way of Mediation, Way of Reduction, and Way of Subjugation.

Wing Numbers. These are the numbers in the Enneagram that are on the edges or "wings" of each center—2 and 4 in the Affective Center, 5 and 7 in the Theoretical Center, and 8 and 1 in the Effective Center. These patterns expand or round out their personalities by taking on qualities of one or both of the other two numbers in their own center and qualities of any or all of the numbers in their Secondary Center. This way of understanding wings encompasses the more commonly held understanding of the term (explained in the Glossary entry Wings), while allowing for greater variety in expression of one's Enneagram pattern. See also Balance Points, Centers, Preferred Center, Secondary Center, Tertiary Center, and Wings.

Wings. This term refers to the numbers on either side of a given number on the Enneagram circle. One is said to take on some of the qualities of one or both of these "wings," which expand or round out one's personality. See also Wing Numbers.

Wisdom. The first sefirah (Hokhmah), which is the Divine Image for Achievers (1) in the Enneagram process of transformation. See also Sefirot.

Withdrawing Stance. One of the three approaches to problem solving. This stance is taken by Individualists (4), Observers (5), and Preservationists (9), and it describes a self-protective approach to life in which one retreats deep within oneself to discover all one's needs for life's journey. See also Aggressive Stance and Dependent Stance.

Yesod. See Foundation.

Zoroaster. Persian religious reformer and wise man of the sixth century B.C.E.